Moshe Feiglin
WHERE THERE ARE NO MEN

The Struggle of the 'Zo Artzeinu' Movement
Against the Post-Zionist Collapse

Published by Jewish Leadership
Jerusalem 1999

PUBLISHED BY
JEWISH LEADERSHIP

Copyright © 1999 by Moshe Feiglin

ISBN 965-222-984-9

Translation: Menachem Bloch, Jay Shapiro, Yitzchak Sapir
Translation Editor: Menachem Bloch
Cover design: Ephrat Susswein
Project Director: David Diamant

Printed in Israel

Hebrew and Russian editions also available
To order additional books or copies of the Zu Artzeinu video tape (available in English
and Hebrew) please contact us:
In Israel:
        Phone: 972-9-7929318
        Fax: 972-9-7920172
In the U.S.A:
        THE JEWISH LEADERSHIP MOVEMENT
        MANHIGUT YEHUDIT USA
        Phone: (973) 736-6656
        Fax: (973) 736-6654

Email: david@pocket-ce.com

"What I have achieved and what you have achieved – all thanks to her."

(Tractate Nedarim 50.)

To my wife Tzippy
and my children: Na'amah, Ayelet, Aryeh , David and Abraham

"…And where there are no men, try to be a man."
(Sayings of the Fathers, 2.6)

TABLE OF CONTENTS

By Way of Introduction
Cheshvan 5758 (October, 1997)

... **In my summation, which was relatively short,** I reminded the judges of the government's imperviousness to what half of the nation was saying, the many lies exposed in the testimony of the police officers, and, once again, the principles of nonviolent civil disobedience which were our guidelines. In conclusion, I argued that, in light of the government's violence, it was fitting for the court to rebuff the prosecution's claims, thus sending an unambiguous message to any future government that might be tempted to exercise similar brutality against its own citizens.

Ending my words, I asked the judges for permission to read aloud a short passage from *The Little Prince,* one of the world's humanist classics. I presume that *The Little Prince* had never before been quoted in an Israeli courtroom. The trial that had begun as an indictment of an extremist, violent group would now come to a close on a completely different note. When I picked up the thin book to read, those present, amused by the scene, could not refrain from smiling.

"Sire – over what do you rule?"

"Over everything," said the king, with magnificent simplicity.

"Over everything?"

The king made a gesture, which took in his planet, the other planets, and all the stars.

"Over all that?" asked the little prince.

"Over all that," the king answered. For his rule was not only absolute: it was also universal.

"And the stars obey you?"

"Certainly they do," the king said. "They obey instantly. I do not permit insubordination."

"I should like to see a sunset...Do me that kindness...Order the sun to set..."

"If I ordered a general to fly from one flower to another like a butterfly, or to write a tragic drama, or to change himself into a sea bird, and if the general did not carry out the order that he had received, which one of us would be in the wrong?" the king demanded. "The general, or myself?"

"You," said the prince firmly.

"Exactly. One must require from each one the duty which each one can perform," the king went on.

"Accepted authority rests first of all on reason.

"If you ordered your people to go and throw themselves into the sea, they would rise up in revolution.

"I have the right to require obedience because my orders are reasonable."

From the verdict in criminal case No. 3996/95
(The State of Israel v. Feiglin and others):

...They gave expression to the opinion of tens of thousands of people who felt that the government was indifferent to them, not only in rejecting their opinions, but also in not paying any attention at all to their opinions. It may well be that, as a result of the error of the heads of the government, the defendants and others were driven into the path, which they followed and which has led to this indictment. It is incontrovertible that those wielding the reins of power as a result of their having been elected in a democratic electoral process must lend an attentive ear to conflicting viewpoints and the feelings of the public.

...but when the court has to decide on the sentence of the defendants for having broken the law, it cannot ignore the harsh example provided by the behavior of the police and the disregard of this behavior by the authorities responsible for law enforcement, until the issues were brought to the attention of the court. Just as the demand for obedience to the law falls on everyone, so are all violators subject to the enforcement of its provisions...

...The violent conduct of the policemen vis-a-vis the defendants' proclaimed and evident desire for nonviolent confrontation with the police emphasized the message and the call of the defendants to refrain from violence...

Tubas

In the blistering heat of summer, the company of soldiers trudged heavily uphill through the main street of Tubas.

Tubas, a well-established Arab village situated northeast of Shechem (Nablus) and populated by prosperous, property-owning families, many of whom divide their time equally between Jordan and Samaria, is considered the capital of northern Samaria. As the young commander of a company of reserve soldiers, I tried to abide by all the rules concerning the curfew in which the village was to be held. But the soldiers of my unit, many of whom were old enough to be my father, were suffering from the heat as they proceeded up the main street carrying their heavy packs and weapons. One could almost get the impression that the Arabs who threw furtive glances at us from behind their windows sympathized with the sweating soldiers. We were all wearing helmets with a transparent visor in front to protect our faces. These appurtenances were soon covered with a mist of perspiration and it was difficult to see through them. In addition, we were wearing heavy gear and carrying all kinds of equipment for the dispersal of demonstrations. We had become a ridiculous body of law-enforcers whose function was to patrol and maintain order in an occupied country.

Reserve duty in Israel has always been a fertile opportunity for discussions and debates among the enlisted. My company was a typical, faithful mirror of the full gamut of opinions prevalent in Israeli society. Eli Rodrigez, my company sergeant, was an articulate and enthusiastic representative of the Left. He had come to Israel as a child from South America, had been educated for a while in a kibbutz, and absorbed their politics and values. He frankly admitted that his position was not based on any moral grounds. "If I could, I would drive all the Arabs out of here... but that is impossible. You settlers, with your stubborn and foolish beliefs, are complicating things for all of us and you will get us involved in a terrible war..."

The lengthy arguments with Rodrigez were never bitter and were always conducted in good humor, interspersed with what were apparently juicy Spanish curses which I never understood. "Ah! If I could only bring General Pinochet here," he would conclude with a grin, "he would put you settlers in your place."

At times, the discussions that went on late into the night were calmer and more thoughtful. I remember how, several years later, after the Oslo Agreement had been signed, I patiently described the dangers inherent in its execution. Eli confidently declared: "Don't worry. After we give them Gaza, we will build a good, strong fence, and if the Arabs there make trouble, we'll close them in before you can say 'Jack Robinson', and throw them peanuts..."

This kind of thinking was dreadfully naive, typical of the inherent contradiction which was characteristic of the average Israeli in those days. People like Eli wanted, at all costs, to achieve a degree of peace, while maintaining the macho Israeli attitude that would, in their opinion, make the agreements work.

When it was shown to them logically that the agreements could not possibly work, they always fell back on the standard argument, the default position: "It is not conceivable that Yitzchak Rabin, Chief of Staff of the Six Day War, is not familiar with the arguments that you are now advancing. Do you imagine that he is prepared to commit suicide?"

No, I did not believe that those who had foisted on us the Oslo Accords wanted "to commit suicide". However, from every conceivable logical angle, it was clear to me that this was the undeniable national significance of these accords.

I did not know what to reply.

★ ★

In Tubas, I encountered the *intifada* face-to-face for the first time. It had begun a year before, but during that year I was busy with personal matters. At the time I was living in Rehovot. The younger of our two daughters had just celebrated her second birthday and my thoughts were occupied with supporting my family and running my business. My confrontation with the *intifada* brought an unpleasant reality to all the words that I had heard that year: Israelis are occupiers, and occupation corrupts the soul of the occupier. To inspect civilian automobiles, to physically examine individuals for weapons, to break into houses in the middle of the night – all these aroused in me deep revulsion.

One of my fellow officers told me that every time he was called upon to perform these police actions he felt "as if he was in enemy land". Was he right? Had we indeed become a conquering nation policing a land that was not ours, an enemy country?

It seemed to me that in such circumstances, the Left was indeed in the right. As long as we relate to the Land as belonging to an enemy, as long as we refrain from internalizing our natural ownership of the Land and seeing ourselves as the proper, true claimant, we will be merely occupiers and thus, by definition, immoral. If we wish to consider ourselves a moral nation and not as colonists in a strange land, it is imperative that we acknowledge our legitimate ownership of the entire Land of Israel, that we feel the same warm attachment to the hills of Samaria that we feel to the hills of the Galilee, that we feel in Judea as we feel in the coastal plain. If we do not feel that this is indeed our land, then the best thing would be for us to clear out of here, and the sooner the better.

If this is our land, then it is both moral and just to do all we can to defend and protect it from those who covet it. If this is not our land, then the most trivial act of occupation, such as searching the trunk of an Arab-owned vehicle, constitutes an immoral action.

The *intifada* is simply a direct result of our lack of a national sense of possessiveness over all these areas. Had we only internalized the nation's legitimate stand and viewed any threatened area as if it were Kfar Sava or Petach Tikvah, we would have felt sufficiently justified in crushing the *intifada* when it first reared its head, instead of allowing the IDF to become embroiled in the ostensibly immoral situation in which I now found myself.

Such were the thoughts that occupied me as I led my company up the main street of Tubas.

We marched in two columns toward the top of the hill. Rodrigez was at the head of the right-hand column and one of the squad leaders led the left-hand column. The village was quiet. The Arabs knew the rules of the curfew and obeyed orders. It was like walking through a ghost town.

The road leading to the top of the rise prevented us from seeing who was on the opposite side of the hill as we approached it. Two people could approach it from opposite sides without seeing each other until they met. And that is exactly what happened. Our ridiculous helmets rose slowly over the top of the rise just as the figures of two little girls appeared opposite us – one about five years old and the other about two. It was obvious that they were sisters. Apparently, because of the curfew, their parents had sent them on an errand, assuming that the soldiers would not harm little girls. The lead soldiers and the little girls surprised each other. Although we were accustomed to our own appearance, the little girls were shocked by the frightening apparitions that had suddenly come into view. The younger one broke into a cry of fear and dropped a small package that she was carrying. The older one grabbed her arm and pulled her in the direction of home, abandoning the package. At that moment, in my mind's eye I saw my own Na'amah and Ayelet, who were approximately the same age as these little girls.

I felt dizzy. Unable to keep my balance, I quickly sat down on a rock at the side of the road in order to regain my composure.

My reflections were interrupted by a loud guffaw which brought me back to reality. It was Rodrigez.

"So everything you said until now was hogwash," laughed Rodrigez. "I knew all along that you didn't believe what you were saying. Here we finally face reality, and you melt like butter!"

I had neither the strength nor the will to argue with him.

"You simply don't understand," I murmured. "You simply don't understand."

I got up, resumed command and completed the patrol.

The 'Gan Vradim' Crossroads

After all the preparations were completed for the 'big party' scheduled to take place that afternoon, I was left with only one small, unresolved problem. As one of the planners of the first attempt at organized civil disobedience in the short and turbulent history of Israel, it was obvious to me that I had to participate personally in the anticipated events. The problem was to choose the intersection for my direct involvement, out of the many where demonstrations were expected to occur. I decided that the best location would be the 'Gan Vradim' crossroads between Rehovot and Rishon-le-Zion. I am not sure whether I chose this particular place because I knew many of the people I expected to come from Rehovot, the town of my birth, to join the demonstration, or because I was aware that the local organizer was Susie. I feared that the whole plan might end in failure and the fact that Susie was known to be a tireless and capable organizer gave me some measure of confidence and comfort. Or perhaps I made this choice because I was conscious of the fact that the media would attempt to depict the demonstrators as wild-eyed and violent radicals, and I wanted to counteract this by getting the television cameras to concentrate on an intersection where I was sure there would be professors and academicians from the Weizmann Institute and the Hebrew University Agriculture School, unquestionably solid and upstanding citizens who could not easily be dismissed or maligned. I assumed that the reporters and cameramen would be looking for me and I wanted to be sure that professors surrounded me rather than thick-bearded men who could easily be branded as religious extremists.

All that day, the radio and television programs had competed with each other in deriding and mocking what they considered would be a short-lived, Lilliputian organization which had the audacity to claim that it would tie up the country with a demonstration on the highways. As late as 5:15 in the afternoon, fifteen minutes before the scheduled operation, the popular TV program 'New Evening' carried disparaging references to us and our plans. I found myself caught in the tension created by the gloomy pictures painted by the media on the one hand and the optimistic information that was available to me on the other.

I asked myself whether something big was really going to happen or whether it was all just a childish fantasy.

The bus carrying the demonstrators from Rehovot, sparsely filled with apprehensive children and older women, gave the impression of a children's outing. I sat in one of the front seats and prayed for a miracle. All the demonstrations to date that had been sponsored by the *Yesha* Council [the Council of the Communities of Judea, Samaria and Gaza] had been ridiculed by the government and had proven to be quite ineffective. The Prime Minister had disdainfully declared that "they don't impress me" and "they can spin like propellers", and other choice epithets. These responses, meant to delegitimize those who disagreed with the government, were certain to have some degree of negative impact on the people who supported our movement. During the time that our demonstrations were being planned, I made an effort to create an atmosphere of confidence and optimism. Now, at this last moment before the critical event, the moment of truth, I was not really sure whether we would succeed. I was almost overwhelmed with mixed and conflicting emotions. I had the satisfaction and calmness that comes of knowing that I had done everything possible to ensure success. And yet I was nervously uncertain of what would actually take place. I did my best to hide these feelings. Susie, who was better informed about who was expected to arrive from Rehovot and the other nearby areas, was cool and composed, and, heavy with child, relaxed on two available seats. During the few minutes that the bus drove from Rehovot to the selected intersection, I had the opportunity for some personal thoughts and recollections.

The familiar scenes of my childhood flitted before my eyes. I tried to savor the feeling of anonymity that surrounds the rank and file, yet I was aware of the fact that in a few moments this privilege would soon be a thing of the past. From now on, I would probably be recognized everywhere and would be greeted with friendship or hostility by all who met or even simply saw me. I would no longer be another private individual.

The bus stopped near our destination and the waiting police cars lined up at the corner interrupted my reveries. The passengers clambered out. Nearby was a broadcasting van from the Israel Television Authority, its crew idly awaiting the events that were to unfold shortly.

The disdain, which Rabin had shown for the 'settlers' and the 'two percent of the population' for whose security the government did not consider itself responsible, had its effect on the police, the army and the government-controlled television authority. To them, it was ludicrous that we had the audacity to think that we could interfere with traffic and bring the country to a halt. In their eyes, we had been barking in vain for three years, and all that they had to do was to continue to treat us with utter contempt. Despite our public announcements, including a press release with details of our plans, the national police chief, Asaf Hefetz, had announced on the previous day that "there would be no change in the normal flow of traffic and there was no reason for drivers to be apprehensive about being on the road during the time of the planned demonstrations". He apparently assumed that this would be another demonstration in the format of the previous ones held by the Right wing (that is, the Zionist and nationalistic sector of the political spectrum). He did not take seriously the plans of 'Zo Artzeinu' or the willingness of a large segment of the public to follow the well-publicized instructions. To tell the truth, I had hoped that this arrogance would mean that no police would be at hand at the junction, but my hopes were shattered, as a small police detachment did show up. The blow that the police were about to suffer to their prestige would be the cause of a shift in their perceptions and increasing police brutality during the coming days, when the demonstrations would increase in intensity and size.

Since I feared that our relatively small group would be frightened by the presence of the police, I suggested to Susie that we begin the demonstration a short distance away from the intersection. Susie preferred – correctly as it turned out – to wait a few minutes. Within a short time, more buses arrived bringing hundreds of people from Rehovot and Rishon. And the crowd included a real cross-section of Israel: professors from the Weizmann Institute, yeshiva students, working men and women, college students, religious and secular, young and old. Many were carrying homemade posters and others toted placards displaying slogans that we had popularized.

At this point, the policemen organized themselves and approached the crowd, obviously assuming that this would turn out to be like all the previous demonstrations which they had dispersed with little effort. The crowd also acted as they did in the past, that is, they stood on the sidelines, obviously enjoying the horn blasts of encouragement from the passing cars. But this was not what we wanted! This was what we had had for the past three years! I could not contain myself and, almost without thinking, I ran into the center of the intersection, hoping that others would follow suit. For a few moments I found myself alone, one person stopping the traffic. Then, as though a dam had suddenly burst, the crowd joined me. The restraint of meek public compliance had been breached.

Now, in the center of the intersection, bringing all traffic to a halt, there sat dozens of people, including Dr. Moshe Peretz of the Weizmann Institute, Professors Eli Pollack and Israel Honokuglu, and many others whom I recognized, as well as others who were unknown to me.

One of the things which had considerably worried me during the planning stage more than anticipated police action was the possible reaction of drivers finding themselves in the midst of a traffic jam. Although I intuitively felt that a sizable proportion, perhaps the majority of the population, supported our actions, I could not be sure. This was primarily due to the incessant propaganda being spouted forth by the media, which were trying to give the impression that we were just a marginal bunch of cranks. The last thing we needed was for the television to film a fistfight between demonstrators and drivers. I had no doubt that the media would make sure that all the attention would be drawn to such an incident and the entire effect of the demonstration would be lost. I knew I could depend on our TV crews to see to that...

Anticipating such a likelihood, we had prepared tens of thousands of notices which were distributed to drivers at all the blocked intersections. But, fortunately, there was no need to worry.

EXPLANATORY LEAFLET for DRIVERS

We regret your being stuck in traffic

THIS IS A STRUGGLE
against a mad government
which is handing our land over to an alien people
splitting our nation into two camps
making a pact with a terror organization
bringing into our land an army of saboteurs
and arming them with 20,000 automatic rifles
ENDANGERING THE LIFE OF EVERY JEW EVERYWHERE

We will rise up and prevent the destruction of our state, land and people
We will obstruct the attempt, in the name of so-called 'peace',
to send us back to the diaspora, to the unfulfilled dream

Remember!
This Is Our Land!! -- And it is yours....

Explanatory leaflet for motorists

The demonstrations turned into a huge countrywide 'happening'. The newsmen and women reporters reporting from all over the country could not conceal the good spirits of all those at the intersections, drivers as well as protesters. The television anchorperson admonished the reporter who was reporting live from the field for what he denounced as 'sympathetic' reports, to which the reporter replied that "I am sorry.... we can only report what we see..."

The news media found themselves in a predicament from the very beginning of 'Zo Artzeinu's' activities. On the one hand, the struggle of a popular, extra-parliamentary body of ordinary citizens to protect its rights and ideals against a political system that used the established agencies of government to repress and subdue its opponents was a topic that generally draws sympathetic reportage. The tendency of the media is to be supportive, particularly when the methods employed are nonviolent and passive, like those employed by protest movements in other democracies. Indeed, the reporters in the field, by and large, were sympathetic. The problems began when the reports reached the anchorpersons and editors. There, professionalism was thrust aside and replaced by the political preferences and biases of the personalities involved. The popular news program *Mabat* was opened by anchorman Chaim Yavin that evening with the words, " 'This is our land' [*zo artzeinu*] shouted *the settlers* as they blocked intersections all over the country." The fact of the matter was that, at the intersection where I was positioned, among the hundreds who crowded the streets and sidewalks, I was the only one who lived on the other side of the Green Line separating Israel proper from the land that came under Israeli control in the Six Day War. And this was true at all the other intersections. Nonetheless, Yavin continued to refer to 'the settlers' who were causing the blockages. The 'settlers' had been the target of the media for years. They were invariably spoken of in derogatory terms and now, according to Yavin, they had come down from their mountain tops with their large families, having taken a break from their usual activity of vexing our peaceful Arab neighbors, to disturb the peace and keep the real Israelis from getting home after a hard day's work.

Meanwhile, at junctions all over the country, drivers were joining the demonstrators or were honking their horns in agreement and encouragement. There was an air of excitement, exhilaration, and camaraderie – a real 'popular happening'.

At our intersection, the police had brought in a fire engine which began spraying the crowd with water hoses. Dr. Moshe Peretz and I remained seated in the middle of the street with our backs toward the hoses. We locked arms and found, to our surprise and pleasure (it was a warm evening), that this was an excellent way to resist the force of the water. Other than the momentary psychological shock, there was no other effect.

The ringing of the mobile phone that I carried in my backpack took my thoughts off the local happenings. I picked up the receiver to hear the excited voice of my wife, Tzippy, who had remained home with the children. Tzippy had shared with me the burdens and tension of the last few months. She excitedly and happily related to me what the TV stations were reporting. The scene at Gan Vradim was being repeated all over the country, north and south, in cities and villages, everywhere. The whole country was in ferment.

I was content. It was not the gratification of successfully exerting power, which would be expected of a dissident who had locked horns with the establishment and had proved his strength. No, it was no such feeling. I was a mere individual, without connections. The established state apparatus was beyond me; I had never been close to the makers of policy and the dispensers of patronage benefits. In a few moments I would be arrested, and my fate would be in the hands of others. – So what precisely did I feel?

I think that I felt like an inventor who had created a preposterous machine, which earned the scorn and ridicule of the entire world, when, lo and behold, he presses the button – and, it works!

But it was not only the pleasing report that made me happy. It was the tone of Tzippy's voice that thrilled me. She had allowed me to engage freely in every activity that I saw fit, even when she knew it would be at the expense of family income, her privacy and that of our children. I did not know what delighted me more: the report from the field, or my wife's happy voice as she relayed the reports. For a moment I was overjoyed.

I went back to the junction, to make sure that the demonstration would end on an appropriate and successful note. For months we had tried to impress our supporters with the importance of getting themselves arrested, as an integral part of the theory of civil disobedience that we were trying to implement for the first time in Israel. If we could eliminate the fear of arrest, we would nullify the primary weapon that could be used to muzzle us. Consequently, strange as it may sound to those not familiar with the various theories of civil disobedience, it was important for me, because I was perceived as the leader, to set the example and serve as the model by being arrested. I had prepared an 'arrest kit' containing *tefillin* (phylacteries), a toothbrush, and some cookies.

The few policemen at the intersection were incapable of dealing with the large crowd of demonstrators, nor did the arrival of reinforcements change the situation perceptibly. They began to push and drag people in the direction of the waiting vans and the demonstrators were careful not to oppose their arrest in any way. At this stage, the policemen behaved most properly. When I was finally approached and seized by the officers, who directed me to follow them to a van, I refused, but offered no resistance as they pulled me toward the waiting vehicle. At last, I thought, the long-awaited arrest was in sight. Unfortunately, the overworked policemen had their hands full with other demonstrators, so they instructed me to wait while they made further arrests. They did not use handcuffs or any other means of restraint and it was difficult for them to guard those already arrested. This was not leading toward the mass arrests that were vital to our movement and for which we had planned. So I made my way back into the intersection. I was rearrested and dragged away several times with the same disappointing result – that is, I was left to my own devices. Finally, I heard one of the policemen shout, "Arrest him, he's the leader!"

At later demonstrations all that I had to do to get arrested was to show up. But this first time, it took an almost superhuman effort!

I entered the police van jubilantly, and was taken to the station in Rishon-le-Zion where I joined dozens of others who had been arrested in demonstrations all over the area. Somewhat later, most of the detainees were released, but I was secretly taken to the jail in Rehovot. There was apparently a fear that if my place of detention was known, there would be further demonstrations to obtain my release. Late at night I was issued a mattress and, for lack of space, I placed it in the small exercise yard in the center of the compound and lay down.

THE JERUSALEM POST

WEDNESDAY, AUGUST 9, 1995 ● AV 13, 5755 ● I RABIAS 13, 1416

Police and border policemen try to clear the Ayalon highway of right-wing protesters yesterday. Demonstrators caused major traffic jams on this and many other roads throughout the country. (Reuter)

I now had the first opportunity that tumultuous day to reflect on the activities of the previous twenty-four hours. It seemed as if a year had passed since the morning, and I was totally exhausted. Lack of sleep, the nightly travels to outlying settlements, and the tremendous effort exerted in the last few months all now left their mark. The change-over from managing great numbers of demonstrators and taking responsibility for an extreme step on a nationwide level, to a situation in which one is not free even to attend to his pressing bodily needs naturally led to a degree of disorientation. I mused upon the ramifications of all that had happened, trying to analyze what could now be expected, but the reality was somehow too large for me to grasp. I took out a small book of Psalms that I carried and I prayed that what had been accomplished today would have meaning, that I and others like me would have the strength to continue. Fate had ordained that many people, including hundreds that I had never met, now looked to me for leadership. I was moved to tears as the realization hit me that I had entered upon a road from which there was no turning back. I prayed for the strength to do whatever was necessary to justify the trust and responsibility that had suddenly become mine. I lay quietly on my back looking up at the stars. I was so wound up that I thought sleep would never come. At least in that I was mistaken.

Flags in the Shomron

The overloaded old Citroen groaned its way uphill through the Arab village of Azzun in a valiant effort to gobble up the last few kilometers to our new home in Samaria. I warily surveyed the alleyways and side streets that emptied into the main thoroughfare in order to be prepared to avoid the stones that could suddenly be thrown at us. At the same time, I also kept an eye on the road ahead in order to avoid the *ninjas*, those bent nails that always landed with the point upward and punctured tires. An eventful week had passed since we rented a house in the Neveh Aliza neighborhood of Karnei Shomron, and we already felt like old-timers. Our memories of Rehovot were already fading into the past.

It was 1988, and the Arab uprising, which they called the *intifada*, was in full swing. The road to our new home passed through the Arab towns of Kalkilya and Azzun, and anyone passing through these places without being the target of a barrage of stones could consider himself fortunate. At that time there were no protective shatterproof windows for automobiles, and the army was incapacitated by conflicting orders and the desire of the officer class to protect itself from blame in the event of serious incidents. The area had become a 'Wild West'. This lack of direction was the policy of the then-Minister of Defense Yitzchak Rabin. Rabin was a Labor Party minister in the National Unity government, and was fully supported by the Likud Prime Minister Yitzchak Shamir. Rabin did not fathom the depth and breadth of the conflict and thought that it could be quelled by beatings. His response was summed up in his inelegant statement, which was to become notorious, that the proper way to stop the uprising was to 'break their arms and legs'. But when soldiers were put on trial and jailed for actually carrying out these verbal orders, Rabin denied having given them. The army was left without direction. The Arab rioters who threw stones and an occasional Molotov cocktail were generally youngsters who could easily escape from the armed and heavily equipped troopers. In addition, there was no effective way of dealing with those who were caught. Imposition of curfews was not sufficient and, of course, collective punishment was not an acceptable alternative. The legal authorities of the military refused to look upon the situation as an armed conflict. The only course was to treat the troublemakers as criminal offenders. The fact that the political echelons viewed the outbreak as an ordinary political demonstration by members of a minority, and not as the nationalistic war that it really was (even though 'hot' weapons had not yet been employed) completely tied the hands of the military, preventing them from adequately defending themselves and those dependent on their protection.

The Arabs who, as a result of the Six Day War, respected the IDF and never dared a head-on confrontation with the army quickly grasped the significance of the Israeli restraint. Aware of the Israeli army's constraints, the Arabs took every opportunity to embarrass and degrade the soldiers. Arab children urinated on them from the rooftops, women screamed and cursed them to their faces – and the soldiers were unable to respond. With the loss of their ability to retaliate properly, more soldiers had to be called in simply to keep order. Before the uprising, it required no more than a company of Border Patrol policemen to keep order in all of Samaria. Now it required many times that number, and the IDF was forced to use reserve duty soldiers with no training in crowd control. In addition, the reserve units were composed of older men who had neither the capability nor the desire to chase after children. They were aware that they could be tried for the simplest act that could be misinterpreted, and they were further aware that even if a youth was apprehended, he would be tried and then would quickly return to the street. The PLO paid the fines imposed on the parents of the children, so that this punishment did not serve as a deterrent at all. As a result, the reservist preferred not to get involved, to get through his tour of duty as uneventfully as possible and return to his civilian life. The army thus served as a fig leaf to cover up the nakedness of the government, which was unable or unwilling to make decisions. Although the problem was an ideological issue, the government acted as if it were a military matter. The army, on the other hand, in the absence of clear direction from the government, approached the dilemma in the only manner that an army could – awkwardly and without creative thinking. It simply kept increasing the forces in the field, and replaced the reserve units with regular army troops. The latter were not trained riot policemen but were from the rear units, often with nothing other than administrative experience. When these proved inefficient, they were replaced by artillery men, armored division troopers, combat engineers, paratroopers and, eventually, even frogmen and elite combat troops. These soldiers found themselves chasing children in the back streets of Shechem instead of undergoing the special training required to prepare themselves for the next war.

But this lack of real training was not the worst blow that the army suffered. The fighting spirit and sense of mission required for any kind of military success were drained away. Draftees who spent their first army years in the *intifada* absorbed the anti-military thinking that was seeping down from the Chief of Staff to the lowest ranks and that affected the army's functioning in other areas as well. An entire generation of officers and soldiers grew up in this atmosphere of defeatism that was symbolized by the comment of then-Chief-of-Staff Dan Shomron that "there is no military solution to this conflict".[1] Officers in the field shirked responsibility and tried to shift blame for inappropriate actions to the lower rank officers and soldiers, since advancement in rank and even the possibility of good positions after retirement from the army were dependent upon a clean record and successful cover-up of the

---

[1] The Chief of Staff claimed that there was no military solution, but continued to take responsibility for what was taking place.

politicians.[1] All that was left to the rank-and-file soldiers was to brave the stone-throwers, curse their lot and wait impatiently for their discharge.

★ ★

The residents of Samaria generally, and the residents of my new neighborhood in particular, were unable to do anything about the situation, which was rapidly deteriorating. Neveh Aliza was a new neighborhood founded by a group of *Olim* (immigrants), most of whom had arrived in Israel from the United States and the United Kingdom in the early eighties. Their dream was to create a settlement in the Shomron with the blessings of the government. Neveh Aliza was named after the recently deceased wife of Prime Minister Menachem Begin. This very name was symbolic of the relationship between the newcomers and the government, and the faithfulness of the former to the goal of Jewish settlement in the heartland. These *Olim* never dreamed that the road to their new homes would be strewn with danger and deathtraps, besieged with stone-throwings, Molotov 'cocktails', ninjas and the like. These *Olim*, who came from a culture characterized by respect for, and obedience to, law, found it difficult to acclimate themselves to a situation of lawlessness and disorder. The rapid deterioration from calm to violence, together with the obvious inability of the government to take the steps required to handle the situation, was extremely disquieting. Left to their own devices, the inhabitants of the area were often pressed to the point of protecting themselves by the use of firearms which they owned legally. But such actions generally meant unpleasant and unjustified entanglement with the authorities, including the prospect of incarceration for long periods if they had succeeded in retaliating against the troublemakers. The mood in the settlement was quite gloomy, and the arrival of newcomers at the height of the troubles was met with two emotions – pleasant surprise and a feeling of encouragement.

My wife, Tzippy, had emigrated from the United States with her parents in the seventies and it was her acquaintance with many of the residents of Neveh Aliza that brought us to this spot. The neighborhood was an unusual one for Yesha. Most of the people were professionals: doctors, lawyers, computer specialists, engineers and the like. Most of them worked in the Tel Aviv area and made the long hazardous commuter trip every day. Most were university graduates who had finished their education in the late sixties; they were all religiously observant and were characterized by personalities and norms that reflected western, particularly American, culture of that period. Being educated, both religiously and secularly, they were community oriented, well aware of current events, open-minded, and outspoken. Most of them were still in the process of overcoming the difficulties of a new society, language,

---

[1] Thus the higher army ranks became politicians in military uniform. Shomron distributed among his staff commanders copies of the book *The Mad War for Peace*, which deals with the French withdrawal from Algeria. This was the message that the Chief of Staff wanted to pass on. Biblical areas, the heartland of our country, the cradle of the Hebrew nation, all these are no more than a colony beyond the seas, like French Algeria.

culture, etc., and now they found themselves with the additional burden of a dangerous and unpredictable situation. The old-timer, Israeli-born settlers around them had no solution to offer for coping with these conditions, so it was obvious that these 'Americans' felt quite lost.

Neveh Aliza was an ideal place for my family and me. The American temperament and the non-homogeneous social fabric suited me to a tee. I was not acquainted with any of our new neighbors and I did not make much of an effort to adapt. I am, by nature, a private person, an individualist, not particularly gregarious, and I preferred keeping to myself and concentrating on my work. Tzippy, on the other hand, is completely different in personality and in a short time became well-known and involved in community affairs. Tzippy and I had never been actively involved in settlement activities and demonstrations, but we deeply believed in our right to the Land and our obligation to settle in it, and it would only be only a matter of time until we became an integral part of the nationwide settlement effort. However, we were never part of the 'hard core' of the settlement movement. During the seventies we were too young to take an active part in the settlement movement and, after four years in the army, I had turned my attention to establishing and developing my career. I was demonstrably not part of any public movement or cause. The Ministry of Housing was handling the settlements in Yesha on a regular basis, as elsewhere in Israel, and it seemed that the 'heroic' period of confrontation and settlement was over. I remembered with admiration the efforts of Gush Emunim and its projects, but although I had heard of an entity called 'theYesha Council', I did not know any of the personalities involved, and I assumed that they performed their functions, whatever they were, properly. I did not know the leaders of the settlement movement but I liked the sound of their names – Harel, Etzion, Elitzur, Ariel, and 'Zambish'... They had a Palmach-like ring, which called up images of biblical-style sandals, loosely fitting shirts, open collars, unkempt hair blowing in the wind, suntans – in short, the salt of the earth, a modern mutation of 'a Palmachnik named Dudu'. I was not one of this 'clique', nor did I intend to be. They radiated an aura that was a positive mixture of responsibility, dependability, reliability and credibility. It could well be that this was the subjective feeling of someone like me, a typical rank-and-file individual with a psychological need for some form of credible leadership.

As the ancient Citroen continued its slow climb up the narrow road, we passed a car that apparently came from one of the Jewish communities in the area. I was shocked to see that the windows were covered with metal protective screens. The occupants, a family with children, looked like mice in a moving trap. I was sure that the local Arabs enjoyed this depressing spectacle. I was shocked. Deep in thought, I got home and related this experience to Tzippy. To my utter surprise, Tzippy took this quite calmly and remarked that many families traveled in this fashion. And despite the discomfort, there seemed to be no alternative. I could not stop thinking about this.

One Saturday evening, my wife told me that there was a regularly scheduled sport competition held in the summer evenings and she insisted that I participate. "You will finally meet the neighbors and get some exercise at the same time," was her convincing argument.

I dutifully left the house and went to join a volley ball game. After my team was defeated, I stood on the sidelines listening to the conversation among my neighbors. They were talking about one of the local residents, a middle-aged woman, who had been hit by a rock on her way home through Kalkilya, and was now hospitalized in Tel HaShomer. My neighbors vented their frustration and anger in animated conversation, including various suggestions as to how to get even with the Arabs. "Let's go down to Kalkilya and stone Arab cars!" and "Let's go block the main road so that the Arabs cannot pass!" were among the frivolous proposals that were apparently part of the customary ritual after a stoning incident. A group of neighbors would finally go down to Kalkilya or Azzun, not knowing precisely what to do, would create quite a rumpus, as if to say "hold me back before I do who-knows-what", hoping in their hearts that the army would intervene and 'force' us to vacate the area. This ritual was repeated every time there was an occurrence of violence on the part of the Arabs. Eventually, the settlers would despair of venting their frustration in this manner, and the stonings were left without response.

I did not think that our problem lay with Arab conduct. The essence of the problem, in my view, was to be found in our own behavior, and I did not see any benefit to be derived from this type of response.

That evening, after all the usual suggestions had again been raised, I realized that they were waiting to hear what I had to say, perhaps hoping I would propose a novel approach. I quietly suggested that "we should display Israeli flags prominently on our cars". They all looked at me in astonishment. At first they thought that they did not understand my native Israeli Hebrew, but I continued. "I see cars traveling with screened windows. We act like trapped rats. This is the Arabs' greatest achievement. We are reacting like the army, and if this keeps up, we will soon be traveling in armored cars. We have to turn the tables on them. They want to see us squeezed into cages, so we must open the windows, drive slowly and confidently, and most importantly – with an Israeli flag flying on top. If we feel at home even in the heart of Kalkilya, they will respect that and leave us alone."

My suggestion was received with hedged approval. The obvious question was, if we are already attacked now, what would happen when we present ourselves as more obvious targets? Clearly, the Arabs would target those cars identified by the flag. "The Arab mind works quite differently from what you imagine," I explained. "They are not attacking us because they lack something. On the contrary, they are better off here than in any Arab country. But they recognize weakness..., are attracted by it, and attack. Their nationalism is no more than a counteraction to Zionism, only an excuse to cloak their anti-Semitism and their propensity for violence, a means of turning their leaders into wealthy despots, and only finally a need for an undefined national identity to find expression. The Israeli flag will not irritate them. On the contrary, it will gain their respect and calm them down. In fact, the whole concept of nationalism is new to them, something that was forced upon them at the end of the First World War. By nature, they are tribesmen and clansmen, and you are assessing them by Western, Judeo-Christian criteria. In the culture of Islam, if you run away and show weakness, then you must be in the wrong, that is, you must be bad. If, on the other hand, you show strength and win, you have proved that you are right and good. Israelis do not realize why the Arabs anticipate constant conciliatory gestures, always raising even higher demands. The concept 'I owe you one' is simply foreign to their culture. If you have given in, it is a sign that you had no choice and that you are weak, in which case they are strong and right, and therefore are entitled to more. They will not hate you if you demonstrate conviction and strength; they will rather respect you."

My surprising comments were favorably received, although with a degree of disbelief. They had had a totally different view of the other camp. My theory struck them as interesting. Some of the listeners agreed with me, but none was willing to volunteer to be the first to face the *intifada* with flag unfurled on his automobile. The matter continued to occupy my thoughts and I discussed it with my wife. At the first opportunity, I bought a large flag in Tel Aviv and spent quite a bit of time preparing an appropriate attachment that would enable me to fly it above the center of the roof of our car. I had decided not to leave any room for doubt. The flag would definitely be visible, displayed in the most prominent place, in order to test my theory.

Few believed that I was serious and many thought that I was just bragging childishly. No one believed that I would drive in that manner through the 'wilds of Kalkilya' and they thought that I would remove this large 'sail' as soon as I drove out of the settlement. But I was dead serious and drove out with the flag unfurled. A neighbor, a lawyer named Reuven Friedman, saw the flag and assumed that I was on a suicide mission. Without telling me, he followed behind at a respectable distance in order to be able to help me or call for help as soon as I was attacked. My theory did not seem realistic to anyone since, after a year of *intifada*, the Arabs were feeling quite confident. They had the occupying army on the run and were even willing to suffer the financial losses resulting from their attacks on the Jews. To tell the truth, the thought that my theory might be incorrect made me somewhat uneasy, and I resigned myself to the worst. If I am wrong, I thought to myself, it would not take long for my car to disappear under a shower of rocks as soon as I entered Azzun.

I drove into the village at a normal morning hour just as the villagers were leaving for work or school. The Arabs opened their eyes in wonder when they caught sight of the large flag on my automobile. I neither accelerated nor decelerated, but kept going at the usual clip. I may even have slowed a little. The wondering looks followed me until I left the other end of the village. No one attempted to disturb my ride. "Well," I thought, "either it really worked or they were too shocked to respond." Now, I prepared for the real trial. In a few minutes I would enter Kalkilya. This would not be a short passage like the one through Azzun but rather a long ride, and the inhabitants of Azzun had plenty of time in which to alert the Arabs of Kalkilya. There was also the possibility that I would be caught in the heavy traffic and get stuck in the main thoroughfare. Now my mad theory would get its real test.

There was an army barrier at the entrance to Kalkilya and the soldiers caught sight of the approaching flag before they could clearly identify the vehicle under it. They were unaccustomed to such a sight during their service in the 'territories'. On the contrary, their orders were to prevent anything that could 'heat up' the situation. As a matter of fact, the Israeli flag had been removed from atop most army positions, and was certainly not to be seen on military transport. The sight of a vehicle with an Israeli flag surprised and pleased the soldiers, who snapped to attention. As I drove past them, I returned the salute, forgetting for the moment that I was a simple civilian in need of protection and not an officer returning the salute. I was pleased that I could restore to these soldiers at least a bit of their self respect. But I also knew that within the next few moments I might be unable to depend on them as I snaked through Kalkilya and traded glances with the local Arabs, who would certainly check out this new phenomenon.

I reached the center of town and had to stop, as expected, at the main intersection. I felt as if every eye in town was on me. Those sitting in front of cafes playing backgammon put down their morning coffee and rose from their stools, trying to figure out what this was all about. Most of the cars behind me kept a safe distance from me – there was no telling what this freak was up to. As we wound our way past the carts delivering goods to the various markets, I opened my window and rested my elbow on the door in an affected casualness. I tried to look as calm as possible considering that I might shortly be the target of a barrage of rocks – or worse. I did not avoid the stares and glances of the crowd, and displayed no outward sign of dread.

After a short while the traffic jam unclogged and I slowly drove through the town. I saw the military barricade ahead, and my foot was impatient to press the accelerator, to quit the last houses in the town and find release from the tension. But no – if so, it would arouse doubts regarding the results of the experiment...

The soldiers at the barricade at the western entrance to Kalkilya were expecting me. They had received a radio report from the barricade at the eastern side (through which I had entered) that a 'suicidal settler' had entered Kalkilya. They signaled me to halt and one of the soldiers, with a huge grin, looked me over, and examined my car. "Terrific, *Kol HaKavod,*" came the shouts from the rest of the soldiers. I continued on my way to work. It was just a slightly extraordinary beginning of an ordinary workday.

★★

My retiring personal nature did not fit the 'pose' of a vehicle with a large Israeli flag fluttering over it making its way through the streets of Tel Aviv. Many times afterwards, when the phenomenon of car flags had become fairly well established, I often found myself lowering the flag as I left the Kalkilya barrier.

★ ★

Now, another struggle was to begin, an internal struggle in full view of the people of Israel, whether in Kfar Sava or Tel Aviv.

That evening, upon my return home, I began a campaign to coax my neighbors to do likewise and attach flags to their cars. I spent almost all of my spare time on this effort. After I had gone through the experience again and again, I felt that I could convince them, since indeed I was never attacked. Tzippy also began driving with the flag and actually reached the point where, when the flag had worn out and I did not replace it immediately, she confessed to being frightened to drive *without* the flag. Although she would not admit it, Tzippy showed tremendous courage. When I did reserve duty near Shechem, she did not hesitate to drive through this Arab city to visit our camp and bring freshly baked goodies for all my soldiers – with the flag flying on the roof of the car.

Our efforts now turned to financial and technical matters. There was a need to devise a light, easily attachable flagpole that would be adaptable to all types of cars. And it was necessary to make them available to all who wished to acquire them. Together with one of my neighbors, David Romanoff, I located a manufacturer who was able to make the flags and the proper poles for attachment to cars. We ordered a large quantity at our own expense. At that time it was not customary to show the colors on cars daily, as is usual on Independence Day, so the concept was quite novel. I spent quite a bit of time visiting the various settlements and selling the flags. I am sure that there were a lot of people who thought that this was the way I made my livelihood and that I was 'making a fortune', while, as a matter of fact, I quietly shouldered the enormous deficit with my personal financial resources.

Slowly but surely the number of Jewish vehicles traveling in the Shomron with flags increased. Although no one has made a scientific survey, I am sure that, even if flag-bearing cars were the victims of stone throwers, they were stoned less frequently than the 'unmarked' cars. In any case, the overall atmosphere took a turn for the better and the Jews stood a little taller. No more ostrich-like avoidance of reality and no more hiding in mobile cages. On the contrary, there were more open windows in cars and more self-assurance. A driver displaying the flag would meet a comrade on the highway and blink his lights in recognition. A feeling of camaraderie and shared feelings, even between strangers, was created.

In my travels, I occasionally met some of the recognized leaders of the Yesha Council while distributing my flags among the settlements. Needless to say, I was surprised that the vehicles of these 'leaders' were never adorned with a flag. It was only later, when I tried to expand my activities and found myself hampered by these 'leaders', that I began to understand the behavior pattern which I had first noted in the matter of the flags. In any case, the number of cars bedecked with flags continued to grow and succeeded in catching the attention of the local media, even earning a scathing article by Yehonatan Gefen. (symbol of young Israeli bohemians) In short, we scored a bull's-eye.

Interestingly, the Arabs did not seem to look upon the settlers' new behavior as a provocation. If anything, things were calmer than before. Obviously the appearance of the flags was not the only reason for the calm. The Arabs were worn down by the extended closures of the entrances to Israel, where they earned their daily bread, and the government learned to live with the situation, despite its basic weakness. By-pass roads were paved[1] enabling the maintenance of more-or-less normal existence for the settlements. At the same time, the Arabs began using more lethal weapons, but on a much less frequent basis. The popular uprising began to peter out, and what remained of the intifada was only its name and a number of professional killers who moved about the territories armed. It appeared that the fortitude of the settlers, together with the overwhelming economic strength of Israel, would be decisive in this confrontation. The intifada was on the wane; our flag campaign had played a role in this development and perhaps contributed to hastening it.

The Arabs learned to accept the flags and even respected the drivers who flaunted them. Opposition to the flags came from an entirely unexpected source – the Israel Defense Forces.

The Commander of the Central Region at that time was Amram Mitzna. Mitzna was an indubitable left-winger (as was proved after he shed his uniform[2]) who never understood why the IDF was in Samaria to begin with. He had no use for these territories containing a hostile population that was a burden on the military. Mitzna's single goal was to complete his tour of duty as the local commander with minimal

---

[1] The by-pass roads, like the increase in the IDF forces, did not solve problems but merely ameliorated the immediate suffering of the travelers, allowing the politicians to continue to play for time. Eventually, Prime Minister Shamir went to the Madrid Conference, which became the link between 'Camp David' and 'Oslo'.

[2] This allegiance was of course denied while he was still in service, but, like so many other senior commanders before him, his connection with the Labor Party became clear to all as soon as he retired from the army and became the party's candidate for the mayoralty of Haifa.

problems from the Arabs. Zionism, national pride, respect for the flag – all of these were pushed aside and sacrificed on the altar of pragmatism, a pragmatism which, in the long run, was paid for in blood. There was no point in expecting any appreciation from Mitzna of the whole settlement movement and anything related to Israel's right to the homeland. Much later, when Mitzna was mayor of Haifa and Netanyahu had been elected Prime Minister, Mitzna attacked him for referring to the Temple Mount as one of the foundations of our existence in Israel[1]. With such an attitude towards the Temple Mount, Mitzna certainly could not be expected to be more enthusiastic about Judea and Samaria, whose defense was entrusted to him.

The news about cars with flags wandering about his area of responsibility apparently disturbed Mitzna. This behavior was contrary to what he wanted and he decided to put a stop to it. But the flags created a new kind of problem for him. He could not simply declare a 'closed military area' and kick the settlers out. There was no physical confrontation between settlers and soldiers. On the contrary, most of the soldiers probably identified with the actions of the settlers and even encouraged them. But Mitzna would not be stopped. He issued orders prohibiting the flying of flags on cars. Cars were stopped by soldiers who, embarrassed by the presence of Arab onlookers, ordered the removal of the flags. On many occasions, the drivers refused and told the soldiers to take them down themselves. Often this was met by the soldiers casting furtive glances in all directions and telling the drivers to move on quickly – with the flags still flying.

This was a no-win situation for Mitzna. Women drivers refused to stop at army checkpoints and the soldiers were not enthusiastic, to put it mildly, about carrying out their orders. One interesting incident occurred when Dubi, a neighbor of mine, a truck driver, who had flags of all sizes painted on just about every part of his commercial vehicle, asked the soldiers "How am I to remove them?" The war against the flags did not add to the army's glory, and eventually the ridiculous order was rescinded. Then, suddenly, Israeli flags began appearing on all IDF outposts. Perhaps it was belatedly realized that national pride does not cause provocation, but precisely the opposite reaction. Perhaps, recognizing the futility of the struggle, it was decided to change the approach to 'if you can't beat them, join them'. Military vehicles began to display the flag prominently attached to their antennas. Thus Mitzna's order became nothing more than an embarrassing anecdote in the history of Jewish settlement in Samaria.

The intifada continued to wane and the PLO leadership in Tunis was falling apart. Yassar Arafat had backed the wrong horse, Saddam Hussein, in the Gulf War. As a result, Saudi Arabia ceased supporting the PLO. The loss of the economic base, which Arafat needed to buy and pay off his thousands of dependents and supporters, as well

---

[1] In a radio interview after the Arab rioting on Succot 5757.

as the splintering of his organization into many small factions, proved to be almost fatal blows. As for Israeli life in Yesha, no longer was there a feeling of tension in the daily existence of the settlers. What really mattered to them was continued building, while security concerns gradually faded.

The Arabs tired of their intifada and the Jews no longer felt that the display of the flag was necessary. The point had been made.

The idea of displaying the flag was adopted by private entrepreneurs, and in the ensuing years, unfurling flags on vehicles became an integral part of our Independence Day celebrations.

And the PLO?

Its savior appeared from an unexpected direction.

"Israel is waiting for Rabin"

Chapter 4

One summer morning in 1992, shortly before the elections, I drove from my home in Karnei Shomron to my work in Tel Aviv. At that time I had a firm that specialized in cleaning and maintaining the exteriors of high-rise buildings, most of which were in the downtown Tel Aviv area. At that time, like most of those who had settled across the Green Line in Yesha, in what the media called 'the territories', I was quite sanguine about the upcoming elections. Obviously, we preferred the continued control of the government by the Likud, rather than by the Labor Party, but no one was really a very partisan devotee of the Likud. We assumed that Jewish settlement in Yesha was an established fact and had passed the point of no return. We thought that the public debate concerning whether or not to 'return territories' to our Arab neighbors was no longer relevant.

As I slowly inched through the congested Morasha junction, I noticed a small demonstration by the Meretz youth group. They carried signs with an ingenious slogan, which is engraved in my memory:

"YOU are in traffic jams, while the settlers are in scams."
(That is: money is being spent wastefully in the territories.)

I knew that this slogan was a malicious lie and was no more than a cynical but clever attempt to create a false propaganda picture for the consumption of frustrated drivers stuck in traffic. I knew that there was no direct budgetary relationship between the conditions in Tel Aviv and the settlements. As an ordinary citizen of Israel, that is, one who struggles to support his family, pays a hefty proportion of his salary in taxes, and serves forty-five days in annual reserve duty, I was annoyed by this fabrication. There were times when the thought even crossed my mind that it might be nice if Labor won the elections, if only to leave us in peace. Let them enjoy the levers and perks of power, I said to myself, and go about cleaning up the ugly atmosphere they have been creating. I did not imagine that they could really do any more serious damage to the settlement movement. After all, Rabin, the candidate, had declared that there would be no negotiations whatsoever with the PLO; that, in his very words, "anyone who withdrew from the Golan Heights would endanger Israel's security", and that the Jordan Valley was Israel's natural defense border in the east. We assumed that, if elected, he would increase investments in the Golan and Jordan Valley and stop the incessant attacks upon the 'settlers'. I knew from personal experience that my neighbors and I had received no special benefits when we built our homes in Samaria. As a matter of fact, we even had additional expenses resulting from the repairs that were required every time stone-throwing Arabs damaged our cars.

Even the most elementary analysis shows that every sector of society has special needs that are funded from the national treasury. And the sectors that exploit the annual budget, that is to say, public funds, to the greatest extent are the bloated so-called socialist institutions such as the Histadrut Kupat Holim (Sick Fund), the kibbutz movement, and the Histadrut's failing industrial enterprises. However, the fact that a lie underlay the slogan in the signs held by the Meretz youth didn't keep them from holding the placards up for all to see, and I knew that the suffering drivers would be aroused.

At that time, the unity government, in which Labor's Shimon Peres and the Likud's Yitzchak Shamir shared power, had ended. The inability of the Likud to govern properly, combined with the well-publicized personal animosity between members of the ruling party, had caused a large part of the population to turn away from the Likud in disgust. Shamir, pressured by the political Left, had agreed to participate in the Madrid Conference in November 1991. He assumed that he would thus reduce both the domestic and international pressure. However, as usually happens in this kind of situation, the moment a crack appears in the dam, the pressure mounts. The large aliyah that was occurring at that time, particularly from Eastern Europe, required huge resources. Israel was seeking American guarantees so that foreign loans could be obtained to cover these expenditures. The United States took advantage of this situation and conditioned the furnishing of these guarantees upon cessation of all Israeli settlement in Yesha. Israel succumbed to this blackmail, but the Americans were not forthcoming. On the contrary, they made it clear that the Shamir government was not to their liking and that Israel would only get the loan guarantees if it was voted out of office. In other words, if we want the loan guarantees we should vote as we were told. (And, indeed, when Rabin was subsequently elected, the guarantees were provided. The irony was that by the time the loans were available, the aliyah had shrunk and the funds were no longer needed as desperately as before.)[1]

The opposing camp, the Labor Party, meanwhile had taken steps to distance itself from its former image as a politically corrupt body, and placed at its head Yitzchak Rabin, who had always won the admiration of many members of the Israeli Right, including myself. I followed with great interest the earlier struggles between Rabin and Peres and always rooted for Rabin, unable, as I was, to anticipate the depths of the disaster

---

[1] The myth of Israeli dependence on American largesse is deeply rooted in Israeli consciousness. This is not the place to refute it, so I refer the reader to Prof. Ezra Zohar's book, *The Concubine in the Middle East*, which deals with the issue. It seems to me that the Israeli reliance on American 'aid' is actually not economic but psychological, the need to feel that we are not alone, that we have a 'daddy'. A Prime Minister who severs the people that dwell in Zion from American 'aid' will in effect be compelling them to come to terms with the ancient maxim, "It is a people that shall dwell alone, and shall not be reckoned among the nations," while the whole essence of Zionism was to ensure the normalization of the Jewish nation. In the elections of '92, it was this 'normalization' that won, as a result of which the dam of American funding was opened.

that he was to bequeath us. Yitzchak Rabin, commander of the Harel Brigade of the Palmach in the War of Independence, Chief of Staff in the Six Day War, the prototypical tough sabra, 'Mr Security', charmed us all. The photograph of Rabin together with Yigal Alon in the War of Independence, his shy smile, his typically Palmach shock of hair, and his personal record of positions of highest importance in the defense establishment – all this captivated the imagination. No one actually delved into his personal record with a critical, objective eye. Rabin astutely promised the Israeli voter the best of all worlds, both security and peace with the Palestinians, which he would achieve within three months. No one at that time realized how completely he would withdraw from Zionist and Jewish values, and he himself probably did not anticipate the extent to which he would descend into post-Zionist doctrines.[1] No one took the trouble to question how indeed he contemplated fulfilling all his patently contradictory obligations as voting day approached.

On the morning of Election Day we were at the home of a friend who had invited a few guests to a garden party. The probable outcome of the election was, of course, on everyone's mind, and each guest wrote his predictions on a note, which was given to the hostess.

There was no particular feeling of anxiety, as no one expected anything remarkable to happen.

The hostess read the notes and turned to me in surprise. "You know," she said, quite astounded, "according to you, the Likud is going to lose."

I was somewhat taken aback when it turned out that I was the only one who predicted a Likud loss.

"Yes," I said, "I am sure of it." And a short time later my prediction was confirmed when Chaim Yavin announced the results on television. He referred to it as an 'upheaval', although I am not sure whether such exaggerated wording reflected the usual news hype or whether it reflected the happiness felt by the left-leaning media. The remainder of the television coverage that evening was devoted primarily to the victory celebration at Labor headquarters. Rabin's oft-quoted words that evening,

---

[1] After the elections, Rabin went ahead and realized the most extreme post-Zionist ideology espoused by the Meretz party, and formulated by such leftists as Uri Avneiri, Yossi Sarid and Shulamit Aloni. The Hebrew word *meretz* means: energy, drive, vigor, force, vitality. When Sarid, speaking of Rabin, said that Rabin "*yumratz*", it was a brilliant Hebrew play on words, expressing on the one hand the thought that Rabin would be *driven* to take (unimagined) steps, and on the other hand, the fact that such steps would identify him with the extreme leftist *Meretz* Party...

which were declared so ecstatically and theatrically, "I will decide...I will lead...I will navigate", were to follow him until his tragic death.

However, the real surprise was not the electoral victory of the Labor Party. The real surprise was carefully swept under the mat, and, as is typical in this age of the mass media, did not get the attention it certainly warranted.

For, despite the collapse of the Likud and the parties of the Right, despite the American support for Labor, despite the fact that Labor had a charismatic candidate, despite the support provided by all the agencies which Labor controlled, such as the Histadrut, and, most significantly of all, despite the undisguised support of the left-leaning media, Rabin and the Labor list did not capture a majority of the votes. Rabin was the beneficiary of several independent factors that made his victory possible. These included the diffusion of votes for the Right among a number of splinter parties, including several that had no chance of passing the minimum percentage required for representation in the Knesset, and successful inter-party agreements affecting surplus but insufficient votes (which is unique to the Israeli parliamentary system). Rabin subsequently set up a minority Jewish government with the support of the Arab parties that did not formally join the coalition. This government, which did not represent the majority of the Jews of Israel, then proceeded to lead the nation to the brink of disaster.

The process euphemistically called the 'Peace Process' included recognition of a terrorist organization whose declared goal is the destruction of the Jewish State. This organization, which had been boycotted by the United States and other so-called 'enlightened nations', was on the threshold of complete bankruptcy and disappearance from the stage of history when Israel recognized it, assisted in arming it and began a campaign to raise funds to maintain it. The agreement with the PLO included transferring to its control all the areas liberated by Israel in the Six Day War. These areas contain almost all the historic and religious sites, including Jewish archaeological finds thousands of years old, upon which the Jewish claim to this land is based. All this was to be accomplished prior to final negotiations on the status of Jerusalem, the right of return of Arab refugees who had fled as the result of wars initiated and lost by their leaders, and the fate of the Jewish settlements. The agreement, for all practical purposes, would result in the establishment of a terrorist state from Kfar Sava to the Jordan River, from Afula to Arad, connected to Gaza by a strip five kilometers in width that would cut through the Negev. The agreement would leave the strategic highland overlooking the coastal plain in the hands of the Arabs; Arafat's PLO terrorists would be located on the western summits of Samaria, sixteen kilometers from the sea.

Concurrently, Syria's Assad would be rewarded for his aggression by the return of the Golan Heights up to the shores of Lake Kinneret. The Syrians would sit comfortably on the Golan Heights overlooking the Galilee, and be able to observe the soup served up in the mess hall of Kibbutz Gadot. The major part of Israel's water sources would be in hostile hands. Israel's water commissioner declared[1] that the Oslo Agreement is "a death blow to Israel".

The most idiotic, misbegotten, ill-conceived process in modern political history, a process compared to which the appeasement policy of Chamberlain and Daladier on the eve of the Second World War was the epitome of foresight and vision, this process was marketed to the public in a grating public relations campaign as the height of political wisdom.

The public did not grasp the ramifications of this agreement and assumed that the elected leadership knew what it was doing. "They must certainly know things that we don't," was the general feeling of the man-in-the-street. "After all, it is unthinkable that Rabin would knowingly lead us to national suicide... And let's bear in mind that at last we are heading toward the peace that we all want."

The hardest thing to accept was the handshake between Yassar Arafat and Yitzchak Rabin. From the very first, all of Israel's leaders, from the Left and the Right, understood that recognition of someone who denied our right to exist, who actually advocated driving us from our homeland and taking over, would be tantamount to resigning ourselves to extinction.

And now a representative of Zionism, none other than 'Mr. Security' himself, had violated this general understanding!

From that point on, after the reptile had been "declared kosher", leftists and fellow travelers beat a path to his door to be photographed shaking hands, hugging and kissing.

★

Ivan Michai Pachefa was the head of the Romanian Secret Service under the former president, Ceucesco. After defecting to the West, he wrote his memoirs and included, among other things, his relations with Arafat. In his book *Red Horizons* (page 45 of the Hebrew translation, published by Ma'ariv), he describes how he provided Arafat with young men as bodyguards, who were then filmed in the act of having homosexual activity with him. "After reading the report on Arafat's behavior," says Pachefa, "I felt the urgent need to take a shower every time Arafat kissed me or even when he just shook my hand." This testimony was supplied by the head of a brutal communist

---

[1] On February 18, 1996, at a forum with international water experts.

intelligence service who certainly was not overly sensitive and had seen many a terrible and disgusting thing in his life. How starkly this compares with the behavior of Israel's left wing politicians who rushed ecstatically to experience the dubious pleasure of a bristly kiss by the arch-terrorist of our time.

★

A clearheaded analysis of that infamous agreement to which Rabin was a party leads to the conclusion that he had simply lost his faith in Israel's independent ability to ensure its existence. He had apparently reached the conclusion that Israel was no longer capable of maintaining its independence and he was now willing to make our survival totally dependent upon the goodwill of the United States and those nations with which we were now in confrontation. A dismembered state, shoved into a narrow coastal strip while all the strategic highlands and water sources are in the hands of its sworn enemies; a state whose leadership believes that its very existence was a crime against the rightful owners of the land; a state hungry for international approval and peace, even if temporary; a state willing to waive its rights to historical sites which justified its very existence; a state willing to give up or at least share its historic capital, Jerusalem; a state willing to depend for its existence upon the caprices of terrorists like Arafat and Assad – such a state has begun a countdown to elimination as an independent entity.

However, Rabin was motivated by something much deeper than his belief that Israel could not defend and maintain itself in this difficult part of the world. Israel is unique among the nations of the world for several reasons. It is the only nation in the world whose right to exist is considered a major concession by its enemies. Its enemies are not only among neighboring states but also in other parts of the world that have almost no relation and certainly no borders with it. The world, including the United States, has not recognized Israel's right to proclaim Jerusalem as its capital, something that no other nation is denied. This conflict has impressed upon the Israelis that they are indeed different than others. But many Israelis, rootless and alienated from the sources of their history and authentic culture, want desperately to be normal, to be like everyone else. They don't want to be involved in a conflict, the causes of which they either deny or which they don't even begin to understand. These Israelis want to be free, at almost any cost, of the burden of Jewish identity and culture which makes them different. The question of how ostensibly intelligent people like Yossi Beilin, Uri Savir, and the like, could conceive of patently lunatic ideas such as the unbelievable agreement to provide arms to terrorists masquerading as policemen, how apparently normal Israelis could trip over each other in the rush to be embraced by the worst Jew killer since WWII – this question can only be answered by the following analysis.

The agreement signed between the representatives of Israel's left wing and Arafat was not intended to bring peace. It was essentially a deal in which Arafat was hired as a contractor to enable Israel to rid itself of the 'cursed territories' that came under Israeli control in the Six Day War. ('Cursed territories' was the precise expression used by Yossi Sarid to describe the heartland of Eretz Yisrael, the cradle of our faith and nationhood.) The connection between the Jewish people and these sites has been the source of inspiration and strength for thousands of years. This connection, expressed particularly by certain sites such as the Machpela Cave in Hebron, was a burden too heavy for Sarid and his ilk to bear. The agreement was intended to uncouple this intimate relationship and allow the Jews to be like all other peoples. No longer a chosen people, nor a people who, despite insuperable odds and against the wishes of other nations, had returned after thousands of years of exile to its natural and yearned-for homeland – no, just another 'normal' nation, the 'Singapore of the Middle East' as defined by Shimon Peres, or, even more, according to Mr. Peres (in his fantasy-inspired book *The New Middle East*, page 78), part of the newly created 'Middle East People'. In other words, the purpose of the agreement was to bring about the deliberate self-destruction of the Jewish People and its replacement by some other still-to-be-formed entity.

Thus, our connection to places like Mount Moriah, site of the Holy Temples, Rachel's Tomb, the Machpela Cave, where our forefathers are buried, the Dotan Valley where Joseph's brothers tossed him into a ditch, and all the rest of the Biblical landscape – this connection would be broken by this agreement. And the breaking of this holy link and its replacement by 'a New Middle East' was to be accompanied by celebrations, colorful convocations attended by heads of state, and the awarding of international honors.

One of the least publicized but most significant articles in the agreement deals with archeological sites. In accordance with this article, all the archeological sites in Yesha were to be turned over to Arafat and, furthermore, he would be given all the artifacts that had been discovered and unearthed during the period that Israel controlled these areas. It is shocking that this article was agreed to by Israel without reservation. The Israeli government thus admitted that all the Jewish historical relics – Herod's fortresses, the remains of the Hasmonean period, the graves of Biblical personalities, ossuaries, lamps with designs of the Temple, and everything else – were really Palestinian! With a stroke of the pen, thousands of years of Jewish history and culture were erased and the 'New Middle East'[1] opened for business.

This shedding of every national value was marketed to the masses as the modern fulfillment of the vision of the 'End of Days', the age-old hope for a better world. Peres, Sarid, Beilin and their cohorts wrapped their activities in a thick mantle of morality, concern for the welfare of man, equality between all races; in brief, as the realization of enlightened democratic liberalism. However, the voices of these staunch defenders of the rights of man died away when the atrocities carried out by Arafat's terrorist regime in the cities transferred to his control became known. Close to 1500 of

---

[1] I am indebted to Elyakim HaEtzni for having called this issue to my attention.

those misguided Arab residents who had cast their lot with the treacherous (pragmatic...) Jews have already been liquidated in a hundred varieties of horrible death. There is no way of ascertaining exactly how many Arabs suspected of collaboration with Israel are at this very moment hanging on the hooks used for torture in the interrogation chambers, and by what methods they will be tortured to death. Yet, no matter how hard you strain yourself, you will never hear the voices of these chivalrous knights of morality raised in protest. After all, the end, apparently, justifies the means, and of what significance are the lives of a few thousand 'ay-rabs' who, to their misfortune, had cooperated with the Jews, when 'peace' is at our doorsteps?...

So complete was the calamity that at first no one could really grasp what was taking place. However, it soon became apparent that not only was this nightmare a living reality but worse, it had been part of a carefully planned deception devised well ahead of the Israeli elections in illegal meetings between representatives of Israel's Left and the PLO terrorist organization. In dozens of gatherings, most of which took place in Cairo, the following plan was conceived: in exchange for PLO assistance to the Labor Party in the elections by influencing Arab voters, the Labor Party agreed to three conditions, which eventually were to comprise the basis of the Oslo Agreement: freezing of Israeli settlement, repeal of the law prohibiting meetings with the PLO and other terrorist organizations, and agreement to negotiate with the PLO on a compromise to be based on United Nations resolutions 242 and 338.

One of the witnesses who appeared in the trial of the leaders of 'Zo Artzeinu' on charges of sedition was the journalist Yehoshua HaMe'iri. Yehoshua was stationed in Cairo for four years, including the period in which the secret meetings took place.

After reminding the witness that he was under oath to tell the truth, the judge continued, "Please answer Mr. Feiglin's questions."

Since I was representing myself at the trial without the aid of a lawyer, I was allowed to interrogate the witnesses.

Q. "Mr. HaMe'iri, please tell us about yourself, including the time you were stationed in Cairo."

A. "In 1990, I was posted to Cairo as the correspondent for the daily *Ha'aretz*, and I remained there until 1994."

Q. "And what did you do there?"

A. "I covered Cairo for Ha'aretz, as well as for Israel Broadcasting, Ma'ariv and Hadashot."

Q. "Please tell the court what level of connections you reached there, and with whom you were in contact. In what offices were you made to feel at home?"
A. "I was close with the Israeli Embassy and also with the ruling élite of Egypt. I could make an appointment with Mubarak at a half-hour's notice."

Q. "Did you know anything of contacts and meetings between representatives of the opposition parties in Israel and the PLO?"

At this point, the presiding judge interrupted. " I don't understand the relevance of this line of questioning to this case."
I addressed the presiding judge. "This is highly relevant because in the investigative file that was furnished to the court, I was quoted as having claimed that the government, the Rabin government, was established on an illegal and criminal basis, upon illegal meetings. I want to prove this by the evidence of this witness."

I returned to my questions. "What did you publicize on this subject?"
"On January 19, 1992, a meeting was held in the conference room on the thirty-second floor of the Ramses Hilton Hotel in Cairo. The participants included Yossi Beilin and Nabil Sha'ath, the assistant to Arafat. This meeting was held at a time when there was still an Israeli law prohibiting such meetings. Also, El'azar Granot and Yair Tzaban frequently met with Sha'ath during that period.

"Prior to the Israeli elections in May, 1992, eight members of the Labor Party led by Yossi Beilin met with Abu Mazan and Mahmoud Abas in the office of Asma Albaz in Cairo. At that time, Abas was the head of the political arm of the PLO."

Judge Dotan interjected a question. "Was the nature of these meetings revealed to the public?"

"Yes, this too was published. *What was discussed was an attempt to ensure a Labor Party victory in the elections.*[1] Beilin gave Amri Musa, the Egyptian Foreign Minister, a letter of commitment from Shimon Peres. A copy of the letter was provided to Robert Flattero, the American Ambassador to Egypt, who forwarded a copy to PLO headquarters in Tunis. Peres made three commitments. In exchange for PLO efforts to influence Israeli Arabs to vote for Labor, if Labor formed the government, three promises were made:

First, to repeal the law prohibiting contacts with the PLO; **second**, immediate autonomy for the Palestinians; **third**, granting the right of return to Arabs who left Israel since 1948."

★ ★

---

[1] Emphasis mine (the writer's).

It is thus evident that all the promises made to the voters before the election, i.e. that the detested PLO would not be recognized, that there would be no Palestinian state west of the Jordan River, that the Golan Heights would remain in Israeli hands, and that Jerusalem would always be the capital solely of Israel, all these promises were made after an agreement had already been reached between the representatives of the Labor Party and the terrorist organization committed to Israel's destruction, an agreement that meant that not one of these promises to the Israeli voter would be honored.

In other words, the Labor Party did not come to power and then suddenly realize that the situation called for a change in the policies that had guided all governments since the founding of Israel. On the contrary, the whole scheme had been carefully arranged ahead of time with the concurrence and assistance of a terrorist organization dedicated to the destruction of the state. This ignominious behavior was compounded by the fact that a complete change in policy would require the government, on moral grounds, to call for elections and seek a mandate based on its real platform and not on the empty promises that it had used to achieve power – a call which was never made.

Upon announcement of the election results, the President called upon Rabin to form a new government. Rabin, without hesitation, formed a government with the radical left-wing Meretz Party. This minority government was supported by the Arab parties, which were not part of the coalition, but whose votes were used to prevent the fall of the government. The ideological basis of this new government was the newly defined 'post-Zionism'. The Israeli voters had chosen Rabin without really knowing what he stood for. He was essentially a Trojan horse who surreptitiously brought anti-Zionist radicals Yossi Sarid and Shulamit Aloni, and pro-PLO Arabs Me'iri and Darawshe, into positions of power.

The results of the election were beyond belief. The Deputy Minister of Education, Micha Goldman, made it clear that even the national anthem, *Hatikva,* was no longer sacred to the secular, when he proposed that it be changed so that it would reflect the hopes and dreams of the Arabs. That is, the words *nefesh Yehudi homia,* "the Jewish soul stirs", were not appropriate for the new post-Zionist Israel, the one which would be a state of all its citizens and not merely of the Jewish people.

Much valuable time was lost before those Jews who remained loyal to Eretz Yisrael and the ideals upon which the state was founded began to realize the magnitude of the change that had occurred and tried to react.

★ ★

On the day after the elections, I went south for extended reserve duty. I was thus cut off from the daily news. When I returned home to Samaria at the end of the month, I discovered that the new government had wasted no time in executing its dismemberment policy. The opening shot was a decision to freeze all construction in Yesha. No one could have imagined that we were witnessing the fulfillment of promises made to the PLO and the American government, this latter promise in exchange for an American commitment to guarantee loans for Israel. The repayment of these loans, together with the high interest, would be left to later generations...

The process of freezing construction activities was extremely costly. A very large number of people had signed valid agreements to purchase housing, some of which was already completed, and the government was forced to disburse large funds in order to break these contracts. Whole neighborhoods that were only partially constructed became ghost towns. The contractors took the compensation from the government and removed their equipment to other areas. The deserted houses became targets for thieves and vandals from the neighboring villages. Worse, criminal elements from other parts of the country broke into many of the homes and became squatters. The half-built homes and neighborhoods became silent monuments to the post-Zionist revolution perpetrated by the new government.

At the same time, the government was unable to cope with the housing shortage in the coastal plain and prices of homes began to equal those in Manhattan and Tokyo. Thus, the government paid twice: once for breaching the contracts in Yesha and a second time for the astronomical costs of building in the center of the country. The American loan guarantees enabled the government to hide this economic folly and to give the impression of economic growth. The loans, originally for absorption, were used to artificially overheat the economy and stimulate the growth of consumerism, as well as to cover the costs of the new 'peace', which were the result of freezing construction and the need to redeploy the army to its new, absurd positions.

Those opposed to the government's policies were at a loss as to what to do and naturally turned to the parties of the Right and the settlers for hope and solutions. The political Right was composed of factious opposition parties (Likud, NRP, Tsomet, and Moledet) engaged in interparty battles, and of the Yesha Council. The Yesha Council was seen as an extraparliamentary body capable of taking action but, in truth, it was completely dependent upon the government establishment. In any case, whether within the Knesset or without, the opposition demonstrated by the Right was pathetic and unable to provide direction or leadership. Slowly, and under grass roots pressure, quiet and moderate public demonstrations began to take place. When the Oslo Agreement was announced and the depth of the deception became known, the demonstrations increased in both size and scope. Many organizations were formed whose sole purpose was to protest. Interestingly, the tone was set by those living within the bounds of the Green Line, who planned and systematically carried out protest gatherings in their local areas and at major intersections. The Yesha Council brought these groups under its auspices by the creation of *Mateh Arim*, which, roughly translated, means the 'cities' committee'. The volunteers and activists eagerly accepted this affiliation with the Yesha Council, because they were looking for leadership and anticipated getting practical instructions for extending the struggle. But this never came. No one realized that by virtue of its dependence upon the government for funding and legitimacy, the Yesha Council was essentially impotent and could do no more than pay lip service to the struggle against government policies.

To fill the void, all kinds of groups came into being. Some joined up with the *Mateh Arim,* while others acted independently. These included individual communities from the other side of the so-called 'green line', which made their way to government offices in Jerusalem to give voice to their protest, huge demonstrations organized by the *Habad* movement, and groups of citizens formed on an ad hoc basis who staged some form of protest and then disappeared from view. Tent camps opposite government offices, hunger strikes, marches, sit-ins and just about every conceivable type of protest became daily fare in Israel.

In the meantime, as the Oslo process continued, terrorism spread. The availability of asylum for terrorists in the cities handed over to them, the tens of thousands of automatic weapons placed in their hands, and the growing self-confidence felt by the Arab militants, all combined to increase terrorist activity to new levels. Terrorism after the signing of the Oslo Agreement was greater than in any period since the founding of the state, including the period of *fedayin* (infiltrators) in the early years of the state. Terrorism took every conceivable form – individual stabbing, drive-by shooting, bombs, and ultimately the use of suicide bombers on busses and busy intersections.

The waves of murderous acts led to increasing public demonstrations against the government. Like many others, I found myself, often with my family, in symbolic protest tents across the street from the Prime Minister's office, huddling in the cold and wet Jerusalem evening with a poster in hand, and sweating like thousands of others in Tel Aviv's Malchei Yisrael Square. The most common slogan in those dozens of gatherings was *'Don't Give Them Rifles!'*, a reference to the weapons furnished by our government, which the terrorists then used for the murder of Jews. But the voices of protest and the hunger strikes by bereaved parents were of no avail. All the tragedies were discounted as the unavoidable price to be paid for the 'peace process'.

It slowly began to dawn on me that legally acceptable protests were leading nowhere, that they would not bring about any shift in government policy. No one was paying attention, no one was making any effort to respond to the public's distress. The government was not only inured to it, but even worse, as the protests grew, embracing ever-greater sectors of the public, the government became harsher, more antagonistic and more violent in its response. Instead of trying to understand the exasperation and anger of the protesters and form some kind of bridge over the growing chasm within the public, the government policy was to delegitimize the opposition. Those who disagreed with government policy were labeled 'enemies of peace'. Shimon Peres noted brilliantly that "there are no longer Jews and Arabs, there are only seekers of peace and enemies of peace in both camps". Rabin did even better. 'Collaborators with Hamas' was the name he applied contemptuously to those who disagreed with him. Thus the majority of the Jewish public, and in particular the residents of the Yesha settlements, worried, troubled and disturbed as they all were, were dismissed as being outside the alleged 'national consensus'.

The political Left, assisted by the mobilized, supportive media, completely controlled the shaping of public opinion, with total disregard of, and contempt for, the opposition. In a normal society, the opposition expects to be assisted by a fair-minded media, even when unsympathetic, since it should act as a watchdog over the activities of those who wield power. But here, the media followed a line perfectly synchronized with the government, denying coverage to those expressing dissenting views. The settlers and the Religious Zionists were demonized by the media and were consistently referred to as 'the Radical Right'.

RABIN: THE LIKUD -- COLLABORATORS with HAMAS

Rabin: About the settlers in Pesagot: "Who the h-- needs them?"

Ha'aretz, March 26, 1995

Most of their demonstrations and protest activities were ignored by the media, and their serious arguments totally rejecting the flawed Oslo process, no matter how logical and legitimate, could not find their way into public consciousness. On the other hand, any time that the media could find some fringe character who made wild and absurd statements and declarations, he was given maximum coverage. In fact, it was later shown that many of these 'characters' were the brainchildren of the media.

How the media tried to silence the protests is described in the testimony given by Michael Fou'ah:

"Your name, please," said the presiding judge to Michael Fou'ah, a 'Zo Artzeinu' activist who had occupied himself with the subject of the media's attitude to the burning questions of the day.

"My name is Michael Fou'ah and I live in Mitzpe Netufa in the Galilee."

"Please answer Mr. Feiglin's questions."

I asked: "Please tell the court who you are and what you do for a living."

A. "By profession I am a teacher and educator. I have eight children. I serve in the reserves as a major. I fulfill my military responsibilities even though I became legally exempt from reserve duty after our sixth child was born."

Q. "When did you first join in protest activities?"

A. "In the beginning of 5754 (1994). We set up a committee in the Lower Galilee comprising secular and religious citizens to protest the government's policies. Even in those early days we encountered hostility by the media and I would like to relate to this court a certain conversation.

"We wanted to protest legitimately and democratically. All we had in mind was to stand in protest.

"Of course we wanted our demonstration to get public exposure and coverage, so we notified the media in ample time before it was to take place. But nothing at all about our demonstration was reported.

"When I spoke with the correspondent, Shula Shmerling, after the demonstration and asked why they had ignored our demonstration, she asked me: 'Are you planning to block an intersection? Will anyone be arrested?' I asked her if it was necessary for us to break the law in order for our protest to be made known.

"I thus learned at this early stage that the only way that a protest by the Right can hope to get attention is if the law is broken.

"Three months later we were in the protest tent at the Golani junction. Members of the political opposition met with us and the media were notified in time to provide coverage, but not a word appeared in any of the news programs.

"To make this point perfectly clear, I would like to note that after our protest tent was taken down and replaced by one manned by the leftist Meretz – which was not even a demonstration, and was not visited by any known political personalities – it was immediately given coverage by the media..."

Michael went on to describe how he had left his family and spent three months opposite the Prime Minister's office holding a toy gun pointed at his chest, to bring attention to the dangers we all face as a result of government policies. Despite his basic right as a citizen to protest, he was continually harassed by the police, including false arrests and beatings, and at every step and move he took he was hemmed in.

"EVEN A SETTLER HAS THE RIGHT TO LIVE!"

What irked him most of all was the way that his protest was completely ignored by the media.

One day, he finally heard a broadcast description of his protest, which portrayed him as someone who had attacked somebody else.

"I spoke with Nikolai Rosenbaum, editor of the news, and asked him to correct the false report. 'Your mobile news unit was less than twenty five meters from where I stood, so they could clearly see that nothing of the sort took place.' But he made no effort to amend the distortion."

Michael continued to describe many other examples of media distortion and indifference, before he went on to describe what he had done within the framework of 'Zo Artzeinu'.

★★

Michael was not the only one. He was one of many thousands who independently went out on demonstrations throughout the country. The Israeli media totally ignored this spontaneous phenomenon, thus creating a sense of distress and frustration among the demonstrators. The Left, which completely dominated the media, did not allow the general public to become conscious of the protests of the supporters of Eretz Israel.

The only way open to the demonstrators in their vain attempts to get media attention was by way of violent action in one form or another. "Otherwise, it's not newsworthy." Thus did the Israeli media provoke individuals, who had became weary of fruitless campaigning, into extreme declarations and provocative actions. These did earn wide reportage, and contributed to the process of demonization. The vast majority, who had invested so much energy in quiet, orderly demonstrations, not only were not accorded the expected coverage, but were even tainted with charges of hooliganism and violent behavior. The media thus betrayed its natural function and played its part in raising the level of violence. The average citizen began to refrain from taking an active role in protests (after all, who wishes to see himself photographed in the next day's newspaper in the worst possible stance caught by chance by a diligent photographer, above the caption "Violent Confrontation at the Demonstration of the Extreme Right"...?). The public pressure cooker threatened to explode, and extreme and wild individuals began to think up simple, direct remedies.

The media, by their nature, normally serve as a vent allowing the release of stresses and bringing to public notice various points of view. They are a balancing factor enabling the expression of all opinions, in a degree proportionate more or less to the weight of the various constituencies, and generally favoring the 'underdog', those who are not part of the establishment and who try to give voice to their protest. By doing so, the media foster free and open debate, reduce the strains and pressures, and lessen outbursts of frustration and violence. The Israeli media functioned (and still function) in a distinctly contrary fashion. Despite their being in the main a governmental service which, according to the law, should be a vehicle for the expression of all shades of opinion, our media transformed themselves into a tool at the service of only the Left. The supporters of Eretz Israel – the majority of the citizenry – found their voice effectively muzzled.

The general demonization served as the background for an incredible development, a measure that no one would have believed possible in Israel of the '90s.

The IDF established a volunteer military unit for the forcible evacuation of the Yesha settlements!

The unit practiced their training not far from the settlement of Kedumim, and these exercises included simulating the cries of women being dragged off. The sound of the drills could be distinctly heard throughout the settlement. Anyone who could still recall the horrible period during the pre-state, British-mandate years in which the Left recruited volunteers for action (known as 'The Season') against the Right, who were fighting the anti-Jewish British regime, was shocked to realize that such trends against political dissidents had not faded from our landscape. Those volunteers probably did not include members of the Right... and thus the IDF, the present-day shield of the country, returned to the days of the pre-state political militias, with the reins of government firmly in the hands of the Left.

My interest and involvement in what was happening politically grew as I became more concerned with the processes that were occurring. I gave more and more thought to the sources of the conflict, the histories of the various political parties in Israel and their ideological development. In particular, I eagerly swallowed every word written about the heads of the Labor movement – the leaders of the Oslo 'peace process' – and how they had gone about executing their plans.

At that very time, the eminent military historian and researcher Dr. Uri Milstein published his book *The Rabin File*.[1] To my surprise and dismay, I discovered that the myth used by Labor to achieve power, namely, the myth of Rabin as 'Mr. Security', had no basis in fact.

It became clear to me, on reviewing his personal history, that despite his continued failures he was always pushed upward in the nation's hierarchy because of personal connections with the élite who actually ruled the state. His reputation was built solely on the positions he had held, but no one seemed to be troubled by how well or how poorly he had fulfilled the responsibilities of those posts. He met the national need for a myth and, as such, no stigma could attach itself to him.[2]

Some astounding facts about Rabin's background never entered the public's consciousness.

I became aware that he had never been in active command in an actual battle and that he had always found a way to evade combat. In the only battle in which he was forced to participate, as commander of the Palmach's Harel Brigade (the battle of the convoys to Jerusalem in April 1948),[3] he fled from the scene on the only available jeep, leaving

---

[1] Uri Milstein, *The Rabin File*, published by the Survival Institute, 1995 (the facts recorded here are taken from his book and from conversations with the author).

[2] Anyone seeking an example of humble submission to a myth need only read the description of Rabin provided by Prof. Anita Shapira in the introduction to her book *The New Israelis*. One need not be a historian in order to comprehend that this phenomenon has to do with mysticism rather than history.

[3] From December 1947 until April 1948, Rabin served as commander of the front covering the road to Jerusalem. He was assigned that theater of operations because it was assumed that this area, which according to the United Nations decision was to remain internationalized, would not become the target of enemy activity, which would most probably be directed elsewhere. It turned out that this particular front became a major one, and that an incapable commander was in charge. His failure in discharging this weighty responsibility led to the US government's retraction from its earlier assessment regarding the relative strength of the two sides to the conflict. They now believed that the Yishuv [the Jewish community in Palestine] would be

his soldiers behind to the Arab crossfire and their decimation by Arab marauders.[1] His absurd excuse was that he had gone to muster assistance. He did not return to his troops, who were under withering fire of the enemy, but, instead, went to take a nap in Kiryat Anavim. In any normal army, a commander who acted that way would have found himself court-martialed and facing a long prison sentence. Or he would have found himself in front of a firing squad, after conviction of desertion under fire. However, in the nascent Israeli army, decisions were made based on party affiliation rather than upon the merits of the case.

Notwithstanding his cowardice in real action, Rabin responded with alacrity when called upon that same year, when he was actually on leave, to participate in the firing upon the 'Altelena'. In that one-sided battle, he was in charge of the troops shooting at the helpless survivors of the exploding arms ship who were trying to swim to safety to the shore of Tel Aviv. Years afterwards, Rabin bragged, in inner circles, [2] how he had "bumped them off on the deck of the burning ship and while they were trying to swim to safety".

At no time in his military career was Rabin actually in the line of fire, yet he somehow achieved the reputation of a fearless leader and illustrious commander. As chief of staff, two weeks before the Six Day War, at the height of the tension, he had a nervous breakdown[3] and was removed temporarily from all decision-making responsibilities.

---

vanquished by the Arabs. As a result, the US withdrew its previous support for the 'partition plan', which meant that the chances for the establishment of the Jewish state were almost completely nullified. (The second time that Rabin endangered the actual existence of the State of Israel took place when he signed the Oslo Accords.) Rabin was dismissed from command by Ben-Gurion and Yigal Yadin, and was assigned the insignificant position of communications officer. However, shortly after, Yigal Yadin changed his mind and appointed him the Harel Brigade Commander, so that he again found himself in charge of the same front. When Ben-Gurion realized that the British were evacuating Jerusalem, he decided the time had come to break through to Jerusalem in a large convoy in order to seize control of abandoned British outposts. Rabin opposed this plan (19.4.48), and Ben Gurion, who had already had enough of Rabin's schemes, did the only thing he could to impose his will. He himself appeared the following day at the head of the convoy and literally compelled Rabin to execute his wishes. The head of the convoy reached their destination, while Rabin found himself in a battle with a third of the rear party, which was still at Sha'ar HaGai.

[1] The Arab force consisted of 30 men, under the command of the lawyer Amil Guri. Under Rabin's command at that front were 1500 armed fighters, but what was missing was proper command and control.

[2] At an Independence Day celebration, in the Israeli Embassy in Washington, while on service there as Ambassador

[3] "From the day that the tension forced its way into our lives... I felt that Chief-of-Staff Yitzchak Rabin's condition and stability were deteriorating...We therefore decided to spread the rumor that he was suffering from nicotine poisoning... I issued commands to the Southern Command to move brigades and divisions... I issued orders to the Commander of the Air

This was fortunate since it allowed the General Staff to carry out an offensive which was in complete contrast to the defensive plans made by Rabin. This did not prevent Rabin from boasting about his service as a commander in the Palmach and as the victorious Chief of Staff of the Six Day War.

When Milstein published the results of his research, he was savagely attacked by the establishment, and besmirched, of course, by the Israeli media. The most prominent critic was the partly official historian Me'ir Pa'il, who had himself participated in some of the serious events which Milstein had revealed.

I recall how, at the height of the arguments over Milstein's publications, I arrived at one of the high-rise office buildings in Tel Aviv to collect payment due me for work done. The manager of the building, an elderly, incisive gentleman, a Palmach veteran, was incensed over the disclosures.

"Who is this Milstein who dares impugn Rabin's character?" he turned to me, knowing my political convictions.

"Do you have any idea at all as to what it meant in those days to be a Palmach fighter? I was in a breaching unit! All the time, fighters fell around us – and Milstein dares talk? Do you know what Rabin was for us? When he arrived at our unit, it was as if God had arrived."

I saw that the man was very agitated. I also felt uncomfortable arguing with a person who had endangered his life for the sake of the country, and had lost many of his close friends.

"All right," I said. "Forget about Milstein. Milstein lied all along the way... But just answer one single question: How long did you serve in the Palmach?"

"Almost from the start," he answered.

"And always in the front line of battle?"

"Always!" he replied, without a trace of boastfulness.

"Did you ever, even once," I queried, "ever see Rabin at your side while the bullets were shrieking by?"

The man stood there, tongue-tied, speechless.

Force... Not one of the officers inquired as to the whereabouts of the Chief of Staff, and no one questioned my authority." – Ezer Weizman, *Yours is the Sky and the Earth*, pages 258-259.

I felt ill at ease in the presence of this honest, dignified man.

I took the cheque and parted from him with a heavy heart.

A year and a half had elapsed since Rabin's government had taken over. A year and a half of destruction, of stark impotence amongst the leadership of the Right – which led me to the inescapable conclusion that the typical tactics of protest were a total flop. One day, I found myself seated in front of a word processor, writing out the details of a plan of action to be used in the struggle against the Rabin government.

"...And where there are no men, try to be a man."

Chapter 5

At the very end of a street with almost no houses on it, at the edge of Karnei Shomron, we built our home. The windows of our home overlooked Nachal Kana, the small wadi that was the historical border between the ancient tribes of Ephraim and Menasseh. This enchanting, ancient panorama charmed us and inspired us into settling down precisely at this spot. Many of our new neighbors were surprised that, particularly at this 'dangerous and unsettled' time, we chose to build in this somewhat isolated location. However, it appears that the 'psychological' consideration that was so effective in the case of the flags was also applicable here.

I particularly enjoyed the view of the Shomron (Samaria) hills in the evening when the bare hills changed hues with the setting sun. There is no fence around our community and in those early days there was also no road or lighting to discourage infiltration. At night, our isolated house at the end of a lonely street was completely enveloped in darkness, and the myriad stars twinkling overhead were not blurred by any artificial lighting from below. Our kitchen door opened upon a fallow field. Today, to my regret, there is a security road, with ample lighting to compete with the heavens, and an electric cable connecting the projectors cuts across the landscape. On the positive side of the ledger, I note with satisfaction that all the building plots on our street have filled up, leaving not a single empty lot.

One evening I sat facing the hills, engaged in reflection, allowing my thoughts to wander. A neighborhood couple were walking by, enjoying the few moments of twilight before returning home to put their children to bed.

At my invitation, they joined me.

"Nu, what's to be done?" asked the man in the way that Jews have, assuming that the subject of the question is understood.

"Settlements," I answered.

"What do you mean?" asked my neighbor, somewhat confused.

"Settlers. Building new settlements."

"But the army will immediately evict us!"

"Look at those bare hills. See how close they are. How easy it would be to walk a distance of, say, ten minutes from here and establish a new settlement. You and I and a few other families from here could easily do it."

"And what will you do about the army?"

"I will let them evict us."

"So what do you gain?"

"If the same thing is done simultaneously by a hundred already-existing settlements, or by fifty, or even by only fifteen, the army will not be able to handle it."

"I get the idea but ... so what? It will take the army two weeks instead of two hours to kick them all out – then what?"

"Then every group has two weeks to reorganize and do it again!"

"Wait a minute. Do you really mean that we should start a new settlement – or that we should merely play cops and robbers with the army?"

My neighbor had inadvertently touched upon one of the most basic questions concerning settlement in Yesha. The term consistently used by Prime Minister Rabin was 'political settlements'. This slogan was particularly disliked by the settlers, but as for me, I totally agreed with his terminology. Certainly the settlements were political, in the sense that their establishment served a political purpose – to establish facts on the ground. And I saw no contradiction between the settlements being normal places for people to live in while serving a political purpose. The fact is that the original borders of the state were determined by Jewish settlements which, in that sense, were thus all political. There was no economic justification for establishing Tel-Hai, nor any of the eleven settlements that were set up overnight in the Negev, all of which served clearly political purposes. Even the settlements that were established in the south in the '50s for new immigrants were created in order to ensure a Jewish presence. Economically, it certainly would have made more sense to settle new immigrants in the larger urban areas, which had adequate infrastructure to provide opportunities for employment, which is precisely what was done with succeeding waves of immigrants in the seventies and eighties. The difference is that, in the early years of the state, national interests (disparagingly referred to by Rabin as 'political interests') were taken into account in determining where settlement should be carried out. What Rabin was actually saying by his reference to settlements as 'political' is that in his eyes they were not legitimate. Since they had not been inspired and established by the Zionist Labor movement, their existence had no justification. Starting with this slogan, whose aim was to delegitimize the settlements, it was not a far stretch to statements such as "They are only 2% of the population and don't deserve the same security protection as the others." Needless to say, a statement like that from a prime minister has terrible implications.

From the early days of the settlement attempts in Sebastia and the Park Hotel in Hebron, the leadership of the settlement movement made a tremendous effort to convince public opinion of their legitimacy. In the face of the attacks by the Left, in which the settlements were described as 'bedroom communities' and 'dummy neighborhoods', the settlement leaders attempted to convince the public that there was no essential difference between a resident of Kedumim who travels every day to work in Tel Aviv and a resident of Rehovot who travels for a similar purpose to Petach Tikvah. This is the nature of modern economies and Israel is the same as other countries. Interestingly, they found that the percentage of residents who live and work in their own community is higher in the settlements than the national average. In response to the argument that the settlements are a burden on the army, it was retorted that the communities in the north of the country require much more manpower and resources for security, and yet no one would think of questioning the legitimacy of Galilee towns like Kiryat Shmoneh and Misgav Am because of the casualties and costs incurred in maintaining their security. But all these arguments were, and would always be, inconsequential. The settlement of Yesha was in opposition to all that the Left stood for. Since the Left in Israel determines what is and what is not legitimate, there was no way that the settlements could become part of the national consensus. The idea that it was possible to convince public opinion by rational arguments and facts was not effective against the leftist propaganda, which was ready to go to any lengths to simply delegitimize the settlements.

Without meaning to, the settlers themselves contributed to this sad state of affairs. The Religious Zionist movement, which had created the Mafdal Party and generated what has become known as the 'crocheted-kippa generation', had never contested the authority and leadership of the Zionist labor movement, the 'sole representative' of Zionism. 'The historical covenant', the name given to the cooperation between the Religious Zionists and the Labor Zionists, was based on the following division of functions: Mapai (the main party of the Left) would set the national secular and Zionist goals, while the Religious Zionists (the Mizrachi Party) would simply add an ingredient of *Yiddishkeit* to Labor's efforts. The Mizrachi Party supported (in the Zionist Congress of 1907) the establishment of a Jewish State in Uganda, a historical fact that its present leaders would probably prefer to efface from memory. Minister Shapira, the Mafdal representative in the national unity government formed before the outbreak of the Six Day War, expressed his concern over the possible conquest of all of Jerusalem: "We will never be able to quit that area afterwards." The Mizrachi considered Zionism a practical movement whose purpose was to solve 'the Jewish Problem', but not a movement with its own redemptive goals for the Jewish people. There has been no real change in their approach since the founding days. The rush to settlement which followed the Six Day War was in stark contrast (and did indeed find its inspiration in the Merkaz Harav Yeshiva headed by HaRav Kook, and not in Mafdal), but it too came about only after it was granted grudging approval by historical Zionism, that is, the Labor Party, and came to a halt as soon as this stamp of approval was removed.

The settlers who made their stand on the rocky hills of Samaria were of the same mold. For them, perhaps subconsciously, as for their predecessors, Zionism meant Labor. They tried to be 'more royal than the king', with the Labor Zionists as their role model. Neither the ideals of Jabotinsky (espousal of *hadar*: nobility of conduct) nor the image of a strictly observant farmer in the fields of Kfar Hassidim could compare with the studied slovenliness of the Palmachnik. The new generation of religious settlers imitated the appearance of the Palmachniks (the wind-blown shock of unkempt hair, the shorts and sandals, the shirt always protruding over the pants), and adopted similar family names and nicknames – in short, a religious 'Dudu'.

But the hoped-for legitimacy in the eyes of 'legitimate' Zionism was not achieved, and the only harvest they reaped was the contempt and ridicule of the Left and its adherents in newspapers such as *Ha'aretz*.

It seems to the writer of these lines that the early settlers would not have dared to initiate settlements (certainly not when the Labor Party was in control) were it not for their conviction that within the Labor camp there existed a great measure of support for this ideal. Alon, Galili, and even Peres still savored and acted in accordance with the activist-Zionist dream which had inspired them at the beginning of the road, when the influence of post-Zionism had not yet infiltrated into the ranks of the upper echelons of the party. In those days, the settlements represented the true desire of the Labor Party, which was still Zionist, and therefore the settlers dared to proceed, and thus they were able to hang on.

This does not detract in any way from the intensity of the dedication of the settlers. This in no way minimizes their genuine love of the land, their fundamental faith, and the great difficulties they had to overcome. It is obvious that in the absence of such qualities not one house would have been erected in Samaria and Judea. The settlers wanted this, and the Labor government wanted this, and all that was left was to play the game of 'cops and robbers' on the hilltops in order to solve certain internal and external political problems. And so Kedumim and Kiryat Arba became a reality.

That was the situation in the seventies.

In Israel of the nineties, the game became drastically different.

The government no longer favored it.

Rabin and Peres of the nineties were not the Rabin and Peres of the seventies. No longer were their heartstrings moved by the classic Zionist values; in their place came the ideology of Yossi Sarid. The classic Zionist teachings of the Katzenelson and Tabenkin school of thought were replaced by post-Zionism, which was the realization of everything that Uri Avineri had preached for, decades earlier.

Rabin, the indomitable myth of the Israeli public, actually served in the hands of the Israeli Left as a Trojan horse. Yossi Sarid did not even attempt to disguise it. Expressions such as 'the body is of the Labor Party, but the head belongs to Meretz', or 'Rabin *yumratz*' [see footnote on page 34] were routine, and succinctly expressed the development that had evolved. It may be that Rabin was not cognizant of what had transpired. Dazzled by the power vested in him, he did not try to explain (to himself) the radical change in his perceptions.

On the other hand, Peres perfectly comprehended what was going on, but rather than ignoring the change in direction and disregarding the contradiction between his earlier Zionist preaching and the new post-Zionist ideology which he had subsequently adopted, he reformulated his world outlook, and in his book *The New Middle East* he erased at one fell swoop all the truths he had once believed in, and which he had detailed in his earlier books, and in their place substituted a new 'ideology' consistent with new political alignments.

In place of Zionism – a new Middle East, integration into the region.

The Labor Party was no longer interested in settlement in Yesha – quite the contrary, it began an all-out assault on the entire effort. And when the Laborites became opposed – the wearers of crocheted skullcaps no longer dared.

After all, they were Zionists, and Zionism was to be equated with the Labor Party.

Against this background, there appeared a young fellow with pretensions of being free of such complexes, who was making an effort to get the settlement machinery back into working order. At the time, I really had not properly sized up the situation. Now I realize that the inevitable confrontation had to take place with crocheted-cap key men, much before setting out to contend with the major forces – and in this I failed.

"I explicitly intend to struggle against the politicians by creating a most problematic situation, possibly even an impossible one, for their forces of law and order," I told my neighbor.[1] "The direct goal is not the houses, the yards, and the parks, but the actual struggle itself," I added. "A psychological upheaval, from being squeezed in behind

---

[1] This assertion, which was later openly declared and recorded, became the main, official basis for our being charged with sedition, when the program was actually carried out.

fences to breaking out into the open, will lead to the renewal of settlement activity, of that I am sure, but that is not the real goal at present! I explicitly wish to exploit the settlement issue as a political weapon. Today there isn't much significance to the actual number of settlements on the ground. Whether their number be a hundred and thirty or a hundred and forty doesn't really matter. The Oslo Accords threaten everything! But as a spoke in the wheels of the train heading toward the abyss – that's how every single tent erected can be extremely meaningful!"

My neighbor reflected on what I had said. He had never heard such talk before.

"O.K. But what will you actually achieve? Rabin will hand you over to Arafat, you and your ridiculous settlements. In the end, he will forsake you on the land and laugh all the way to Oslo."

"Do you believe that Rabin is capable of negotiating the future of the land at a time when it is functioning independently and he is no longer in complete control?" was my rhetorical question. "Can you imagine that Arafat will speak with him at all? Why, all of the world media will be daily documenting the sprouting of new settlements, and Rabin will be hard-pressed to supply excuses to the entire world. Let's not forget that for CNN there is no difference at all between a miserable tent on a barren hilltop and the city of Ariel – both are illegal constructions. Rabin is not a subtle thinker. He is nervous and jumpy, and therefore won't leave anyone to himself for more than five minutes.

"He will send a regiment even after a pup tent and two girls.

"Don't worry – the army will arrive at the scene.

"You can bet on it..."

The conversation came to an end. The couple returned home and I went back to my daily routine. But, as in the story of the flags, that annoying 'mosquito' continued to buzz in my ear, giving me no peace. By nature, I cannot let a good idea stagnate.

I wrote out the thoughts I had expressed to my neighbor in an orderly, reasoned document.

Upon finishing, I thought about what steps should follow. This time it would not be a simple, private, individual matter of flying flags on vehicles, but a concerted drive by dozens of settlements in Yesha. And I had no pretension or desire to carry this out on my own. I assumed that there existed some sort of leadership framework that would be prepared to adopt the scheme, and I tried to find my way to it. I was quite unfamiliar with the intricacies of the internal politics of the settlement leadership, and did not know the opinions and outlook of their prominent figures. I photocopied my plan and sent off copies to all the names I knew, from the leaders of the settlers and the Yesha Council to the columnists and writers for *Nekuda,* the organ of Yesha. From Benny Katzover of Elon Moreh to Rabbi Yoel Ben-Nun of Ofra, from Uri Ariel, Chairman of the Yesha Council, to the heads of the various local councils. Dozens of letters. Even the Chairman of the Likud Party, Benjamin Netanyahu, received a copy.

I checked by phone to make sure that the letters had all been received, yet not one addressee responded.

One evening Rabbi Yoel Ben-Nun, a member of the Yesha Council, and Uri Ariel, its Executive Secretary, arrived at our Karnei Shomron settlement to talk to our residents about the burning issues on the national agenda. Yoel Ben-Nun described the severity of the situation, and, raising a clenched fist upward, declared: " Although I generally believe in compromise and moderation, it is clear to me that in order to have them relate to us at all, we will have to display a clenched fist."[1] When questioning by the audience began, the participants asked to hear details of any specific plan of action, not merely a meaningless review of the facts. No such plan was presented. All that was asked of those present was to sign up for future calls, if and when they should be made. I finally raised my hand, briefly explained my proposal, and inquired as to why Rabbi Ben-Nun had not replied to my letter. He did not reject my ideas, but claimed that he had not received my mail. I approached and again clarified his exact address, and he promised to react upon getting my letter.

Upon returning home, I again mailed off my proposal to Rabbi Ben-Nun. No reply was received. Ben-Nun also evaded my telephone calls. Thus a few months flew by, while I interpreted the silence to mean that those in charge were doing their utmost to move things ahead, and, apparently, were 'awfully' busy.

---

[1] This is the same Yoel Ben-Nun who knew exactly which side of his bread was buttered. Upon Rabin's assassination, he loudly expressed his denunciation of his maligned associates. His anemic buddies crawled into their burrows when he went forth looking for easy prey. One can well picture what would have happened to a kibbutz member who had besmirched his fellow-kibbutzniks in all the media upon his entering their mess-hall accompanied by two personal bodyguards, as Ben-Nun did when he entered the synagogue of Ofra for services. Ben-Nun did well in both worlds: On the one hand, he earned the affection of the media and the Left as someone who 'endangers himself' in confrontation with his own 'violence-prone and decadent' social surroundings, while, on the other hand, continuing to live most comfortably in that very hothouse of settlers who never even entertained the thought of ejecting him from their midst (certainly not harming him physically in the least). Ben-Nun knew that he would enjoy such a non-malevolent attitude when he assumed the mantle of 'prophet of wrath' against his former associates, nor was he the only one to improve his standing on the backs of his suffering friends. In this connection, it is interesting to compare the demand made by Chief Rabbi Low of Bibi Netanyahu, that he apologize for having made his uncalled-for remark about the non-Jewishness of the Left, with Rabbi Low's protracted silence when Prime Minister Rabin hurled his defamatory accusations against the supporters of the Land of Israel.

On the eve of Rosh Hashanah 5754 (1994), I reworded my letter as a plan for action, and posted it up on the neighborhood bulletin board, although I did not really believe that the English-speaking community of my neighborhood would take the trouble to peruse a multiple-page document written in Hebrew. I went to the Rosh Hashanah services and gave the matter no further thought. On the second Holy Day, shortly after the mid-day meal, there was a knock at the door. The neighborhood rabbi, Rabbi Me'ir Berglas, and a follower wished to speak with me. I was pleased to see them and asked them in. They wanted to clarify the particulars of my scheme, and posed a number of questions. Eventually the Rabbi suggested that he raise the subject in the context of his afternoon lecture, and invite anyone interested to a meeting in my home that night.

Naturally I agreed. I had no idea how matters would turn out, but I was gratified that the proposal would finally be aired. Shortly after the close of the holiday, residents began streaming into our home. The word had spread throughout the settlement, so that not only members of Neveh Aliza appeared but also residents from all quarters. My house could not accommodate the large gathering, so it took place outside. I spoke about the proposal. One of the rabbis present, who had arrived from the Yeshivat Hesdar of Karnei Shomron, expressed opposition, but did not provide any rationale for his stand, nor did he propose an alternative course of action, a fact that was surprising, but, as with the case of Ben-Nun and the others of the top echelon with whom I had come in contact, these portents passed by without my grasping their significance.

The meeting came to a close with the decision to set up a team that would go up to Jerusalem, to the offices of the Yesha Council, in order to have a talk with its Executive Secretary. Four representatives were chosen, Rabbi Berglas, an academician (to make an impression), Dr. Danny Felsenstein, Shmuel Sackett, who had made *aliyah* [had emigrated] from the USA three years earlier, and myself. The meeting with Uri Ariel took place on the Fast of Gedalyahu (third day of *Tishrei*). We were received most politely. Uri apologized for being unable to offer any refreshment, due to the fast, and listened attentively to our explanations. As for his failure to acknowledge receipt of my proposal in the past, he pointed out that hundreds of ideas reach his desk all the time and he simply cannot cope with the flood of proposals. Finally, although he did not disapprove of the operation, he claimed that it was not feasible. "We have an acute problem regarding financial resources and manpower. We have no men! We have no men!" he repeated.

"Where there are no men, try to be a man..." I reflected, recalling the saying of our rabbis in Tractate Avot (*Sayings of the Fathers*). I almost quoted that statement to Uri, but since the overall atmosphere was so positive, I refrained. I did point out that the entire project required the active help of just a few people, and an extremely limited list of supplies. Uri wriggled about in his seat, and then uttered a few words, which ever since reverberate in my ears: "Draw up the file," which meant: "Go ahead and get down to the nitty-gritty, work out all the details, and ... then, we'll see."

That was a sophisticated way of getting rid of us with a friendly smile. Uri apparently thought that once the matter passed from the stage of discussion to the stage of implementation, once the ball was returned to the court of these pests, the members of the team would back out, "and the redeemer will come to Israel..."

We were not overly perturbed by the fact that Uri Ariel was the executive of an organization which was meant to represent us, which allocates public funds, employs a staff and pays them wages, among other things, to 'draw up files' of this nature according to need. The fact that when the Yesha Council finally has to justify its functioning in confronting the imminent danger to the settlement movement and the land in general, it prefers to hand over such a file to a bothersome group of volunteers, seemed a bit odd – but we were imbued with a sense of purpose and an excess of energy and drive, and did not occupy ourselves with such trivialities. The veteran leadership has been worn down by daily concerns and no longer believes in the potential for struggle prevalent in the land – so I meditated; we will prove to them that there is willingness to act, and then they will surely assume leadership of the struggle.

We agreed among ourselves that we would finalize all the details of the undertaking, and maintain close contact with the Yesha Council.

We returned to Neveh Aliza, and began 'drawing up the file'.

★ ★

Of the group that had met with Uri Ariel in the Yesha Council, Shmuel Sackett was the only one who truly assisted in 'drawing up the file'. Shmuel, who was a relatively new immigrant, was working at that time as sales manager of one of the departments of the Postal Authority. The contrasts between the two of us in both background and temperament could provide material for separate sociological research.

Shmuel, newly arrived from the USA, speaks an inarticulate Hebrew with an 'Anglo-Saxon' accent, is very gregarious, always in a good mood, with a juicy bit of Jewish humor always rolling off his tongue. He grew up and lived all his life in New York, a New-Yorker in the fullest sense of the word. Always ready to do an improvised successful imitation of a black man, Italian, Puerto-Rican, or Jewish grandmother.

A fellow of large build is Shmuel, seemingly ungainly, clumsy, sloppy, but his stride is purposeful, and the fringes of his inner garment blow in all directions. Videocassettes of American soap operas cover the shelves of his bookcases alongside sacred Jewish volumes of all kinds. Shmuel cannot forgo small delights, cannot refuse a slice of good cake, and is quite capable of stopping in mid-action, while blocking the various roads of the country, to listen avidly to a good joke. Generally speaking, an appreciation of humor, which normally is a very healthy attribute, becomes an absolutely necessary condition for those engaged in the type of activity which we were about to carry out. And Shmuel certainly was blessed with an ample degree of this quality.

Shmuel arrived in Israel as a veteran of public struggles. Throughout his youth he was actively involved in the struggle for the release of the Jews of the Soviet Union. He was thoroughly familiar with all the techniques of civil campaigning in a democratic country, and we benefited greatly from his experience. Despite his slovenly appearance, Shmuel was remarkably diligent and capable. He always remembered the names of the activists, knew when to differentiate between the main things and the trivial, and could organize events down to the smallest details. Any time I became overly tense before a specific undertaking and pestered him with technical questions, he always maintained his serenity, made sure all the technical arrangements had been properly taken care of, and managed to joke at my expense.

Shmuel Sackett in action

As for me, precisely the opposite is true. Thin and tidy in appearance, while in reality a hopeless slob, a person who flees from dealing with details, sees the forest – but bumps into the trees. A native-born Israeli, combat officer in the reserves, fluent in Hebrew, and totally at home in the typical Israeli culture and milieu. While I was sweating away in boot camp, Shmuel was battling black toughs in the New York subway, or throwing eggs at the offices of the Russian Airline Company. And while I was accompanying buddies and subordinates on their last journey during the war in Lebanon, Shmuel was squatting on the roads in Washington, taking part in the demonstrations opposite the Soviet Embassy on behalf of the Jews of the Soviet Union.

Shmuel chose to begin his testimony, at his trial for sedition, with the following tale:

"At the age of 14, I had already begun joining the demonstrations in the USA against the confinement of the Jews of the Soviet Union. One day I was arrested while participating in such a demonstration, and my father came down to the police station to arrange for my release, with a big grin on his face. The New York policeman filled out all the necessary forms meticulously, and when he had finished, he could no longer contain himself and turned to my father with a question: "Dozens of parents come here every day to have their sons released from custody, but this is the first time that I have met a father coming in here looking so pleased. Could you explain yourself?"

"My father," continued Shmuel in his testimony, "looked at the cop and said: 'I can never erase the pangs of guilt that I and my friends have suffered for not having demonstrated against our government here in the USA, during the Second World War. We knew what was taking place in Europe, we knew – but we kept silent! My son does not remain silent when Jews are mistreated in another spot in the world – that's why I am happy.' "

It appears that Shmuel and I were a rare union of two lunatics. The division of labor between us was never clearly defined, but it became apparent from the very start. I was to be responsible for the ideological content and for conveying the pertinent messages to the Israeli public, Shmuel – for the practical execution. I – the face of the struggle and its leadership; Shmuel – its hands and legs.

This is not to say that Shmuel did not help me shape the ideology, or that I shied away from all technical matters, but these were the areas of responsibility, more or less.

Our basic assumption was that if we mobilized the settlement movement for the realization of our program of action, the Yesha Council would consent to take hold of the reins. In our naiveté we believed that 'the horses were lazy' and required just a bit of prodding to get them out of the stables, but we didn't know where to begin. Neither of us was associated with the hard core of the settlement enterprise. We belonged to the outer circles of settlers who joined up after the initial founding of settlements, and thus did not know the key figures. Consequently, we decided on the following step: From the Yellow Pages directory covering Judea and Samaria, we copied out the names of all the hundred and thirty settlements. We listed them alphabetically, and next to each, left blank spaces in which we hoped to jot down the names of likely contacts. One night we gathered 20 neighbors in the community shelter and hung the list up on one of the walls. Our goal was to identify the members of the various settlements who could be relied upon to pass on directions and messages to the others in their respective communities.

★ ★

Actually, the residents of Neveh Aliza were the least suitable people of all those living in Yesha to undertake this initial push, since they were all new immigrants who could barely communicate in Hebrew and whose circle of acquaintances in the country was quite limited. But these disadvantages were counter-balanced by their zeal and enthusiasm. The American mentality, which rejects all violation of basic civil rights and espouses the right to protest infractions and, if necessary, torment the makers of governmental policy – all this was ingrained in their personalities. The great majority had acquired their academic education in American universities during the heyday of the anti-Vietnam War riots on the campuses. Opposition to a corrupt political establishment and recognition of their right to protest and affect the decision-making process, not just once every four years, flowed in their veins. What they did not have was the docile acceptance of the authority of the establishment which was innate in the Israeli soul.

This assertion will be rejected by anyone who is not accustomed to life in a country that is fully democratic. The fact of the matter is that the perception of democracy among Israel's citizenry is very shallow, bordering on primitiveness, far behind that of developed countries. The Israeli voter takes the view that his responsibility is to appoint a dictator over himself for the next four years, and as long as he does not violate any law, that democratic dictator is free to employ his power as he sees fit.[1] The important thing is not to be sensitive to the wishes of the public, but rather to ensure full insurance against any possible judicial investigation. Granted that most of our prime ministers in the past behaved properly and did not make excessive use of the power vested in them as a result of this defective attitude; however, that was not the case with Yitzchak Rabin and his government, who adopted a behavior quite at odds with their predecessors' (except for Ben-Gurion; but the conditions under which he functioned were totally different).

Long after the activities of 'Zo Artzeinu' had come to a close, people still accused us of having followed an anti-democratic path by our violations of the law. In a public debate with the spokesman of Meretz (Yossi Gazit), in the presence of hundreds of pupils of the HaShomer Hatza'ir 'Kinarot' Institute, my opponent argued that the blocking of road traffic by 'Zo Artzeinu' was an anti-democratic step. I failed to grasp how any thinking person could make such a ridiculous assertion.

---

[1] With the élite sectors of society on his side, the dictator will not hesitate to break the law – which is precisely what happened.

"It is precisely in democracies that the blocking of roads takes place!" I responded. I do not know which of us was more taken aback: Gazit, who suddenly realized he had erred, or I, who had anticipated a more thoughtful discussion.

It became apparent to me that the Israeli Left, which is in control of all the media, had developed its own theories regarding the essence of democracy, created a demonic image of its antagonists, and made successful use of the subservient media for its own perpetuation. Thus the Left enclosed itself in a frame of 'orthodox' patterns of thought, a kind of impenetrable bubble, in which it both produced and consumed its own views, completely secluded from opposing opinions. Public radio, television, the daily press, the large publishing firms,[1] the academic elite, the financial elite – all are high-handedly controlled by leftists. Admission into these élites is barred to rightist authors and academicians, so that their impact is negligible. Anyone who aspires to a career in journalism will quite naturally develop a leftist orientation. Why begin the struggle for a career on the left foot (that is, the right foot)? The same holds true in all other areas; one must display 'politically correct' views for acceptance, and anyone thinking differently must generally conceal his convictions, gaining entrance into that bubble without any chance of influencing it.[2]

The absurd perception of the nature of democracy by intelligent people who were suddenly confronted with contrary views illuminates this reality. I doubt whether the Meretz spokesman would have come up with such a ludicrous claim had he not been compelled to reply to my simple arguments in that confrontation. On the other hand, those loyal to the Land of Israel are constantly exposed to sharp criticism from every side, and are repeatedly called on to defend their ideology against the leftist arrows of disparagement. In truth, the Israeli Right did not pass the test, and with the exception of isolated islands of ideology rooted in authentic Jewish identity, the Right proved itself inadequate to the post-Zionist attack which rained down on them upon the accession to power of the Rabin government.

Voicing the claim that 'passive civilian opposition' (or, as the public knows it, 'civil disobedience') runs contrary to democracy, and this from the mouths of those who see themselves as 'guardians of democracy' in the nation, highlights the degree of primitiveness of Israeli society's concept of democracy. What the Israeli Left is asserting is that a law (or a legal decision) which has been promulgated by the majority in accordance with legal procedures is *ipso facto* right and proper, and must not be breached. Thus an apparatus that was designed to facilitate decent human living

---

[1] All the large publishing firms that received a copy of the manuscript of this book noted that it was indeed a riveting and important report, while presenting various excuses for rejecting it for publication.

[2] Again an example that is related to this very book (in the Hebrew original) which you are now reading. The writer who edited the Hebrew manuscript, a very distinguished member of the literary community, exacted from me an oath not to disclose his identity, for then "I will never again find work...".

conditions has become a religion in itself. The truth is that there is no connection at all between law and morality. A decision accepted by the majority is not necessarily just and there is no more foolish assertion than the banal assumption which says: "The majority is always right." In my opinion, not only is this incorrect, but at times what is correct is precisely the opposite, namely, "The majority often errs."

In any case, despite democracy's serious flaws, there is no other political system that is preferable, as Winston Churchill declared. But from grudging acceptance of this reality to converting it into a religion in itself, the way is long indeed, and anyone attempting to do so will find himself in danger of moral perversion, exactly similar to that characterizing any totalitarian regime.

Countries with a democratic tradition have coped with this problem and provided for avenues of struggle in situations in which governmental bodies attempt to unjustly exploit the authority invested in them by law. Various criteria and models have been developed in order to define controversy and dissension as democratic, even when legal limits have been formally violated. But such a tradition was non-existent in Israel when we set out on the path of struggle, at a time when the conceptual world of western universities was quite at variance with that of the Israeli democracy which we faced.

The neighbors called to the gathering began to trickle into the small public shelter. They had just finished their evening meal, and instead of dropping into a soft armchair to view the evening's TV programs, arrived exhausted for a meeting. We had few expectations from this group, but could think of no other way of forging contacts with the various settlements. We read off the list of the Yesha settlements which we had compiled from the telephone directory, and asked those present to raise their hands if they knew any person living in any of them. To our surprise and joy, we learned that there was hardly a single settlement in which at least one resident was not known. Each of the participants accepted the responsibility for contacting the persons whom he had mentioned; they were to describe the essentials of the campaign, and issue an invitation to an assembly to take place in Ariel, at which proper 'activity files' would be distributed. These go-betweens were to gather their neighbors, explain what was afoot, and set up a nucleus for action. Thus was set in motion, in effect, a framework for a completely extra-establishment movement, which circumvented all the existing organizations and by its very creation threatened the authority of the existing Yesha establishment. At that stage, we were still oblivious to the fact that we were treading on sensitive toes.

★ ★

The neighbors who had assumed the responsibility for developing our contacts fulfilled their tasks with utmost fidelity. It was no simple matter. In order to communicate with five individuals, one has to carry out three calls on average to each destination – in the evenings, of course.

Most of the public were happy to learn of the planned campaign of the Yesha Council, and evinced willingness to take part. The date for the distribution of the activity files was set for Friday, 19th of Kislev, 5754 (December 3, 1993), and we went full speed ahead with our preparations to ensure the success of the assembly. Up to now, that is, until the conventions of 'Zo Artzeinu', the settler movement had been accustomed to haphazard, undirected gatherings. Residents gather from all over the country, the designated hour is not adhered to, confusion reigns, and at the close – no one really knows just what he expected to get out of the meeting. For us it was vital that the whole business should be different – and so it was.

Representatives from nearly all the Yesha settlements arrived at the convention, which was to take place in the "Eshel HaShomron" Hotel in Ariel. Each delegate received a clear, detailed file covering all aspects of the campaign. One after the other, members of the Yesha Council ascended the podium: Nissan Slomiansky, head of the Elkanah council, Moshe Peled, MK of the Tzomet political party, rabbis, and various representatives of the Right and of Religious Zionism. The speeches dragged on and on, and I was left little time to elaborate on the project, but I resigned myself to this reality, and was content that we had succeeded in creating a united front.

Among those who came to the convention was a young fellow, bareheaded, immaculately dressed, who looked and acted like a bodyguard. From the very start, he tried to take the whole event under his wing. He gave out instructions to the ushers, took the activity files, which were meant for distribution to the activists, and handed them out to the journalists, without even knowing the contents, creating the impression of being the organizer of the whole proceedings. He did not know me at all or I him. When I explained to him that the files were not meant for the journalists, he looked at me disdainfully and carried on. The convention was in progress, and I could not afford to get into a tiff with this chap. I was calmed by the soothing words of my neighbors of Neveh Aliza, who stood bewildered by the objectionable behavior of the young careerist. His name was Shai Bazak[1], and at that time he was serving as deputy spokesman of the Yesha Council. (There is such a thing there).

In the few remaining minutes allotted to me, I finished explaining the campaign. I fielded questions from the audience, and with the singing of *Ani Ma'ameen* and *Hatikvah* we dispersed, all of us feeling that the campaign was off to a good start.

---

[1] Shai Bazak later served as Prime Minister Netanyahu's spokesman, and is at present the Israeli Consul in Miami, Florida.

There was one item that was not brought to the attention of the assembled, perhaps the most important item: the date when the campaign would actually start. We very much wanted to begin on Tu BeShvat 5754 (1994).

But the Yesha Council refused to allow us to set a date. "Prepare the file," they said, "and we will set the date" – as if what was involved was the preparation of building materials or office equipment. But the main thrust of our work should have been preparing the public, making sure they were aware of the details of the scheme, inspiring a 'desire for action'. If no date is set, even the most fervent advocates will quickly lose their zeal and our efforts will go down the drain. We hoped that the readiness of our public for concrete action would prod the Council into setting the date.

Meanwhile we proceeded to detail every step of our initiative. Close by each settlement, the spot that was to be taken over was pinpointed, and the needed equipment was stored. Rosters of guard duty to man the various points were drawn up, and lists of additional volunteer manpower from without the Yesha areas were compiled. In order to maintain operational readiness and zeal, we continually faxed updates to all our activists, made sure they all participated in the variety of preparations, and gave them all the feeling of being involved in a campaign on a very wide front. The staff of volunteers in Neveh Aliza already consisted of dozens of members, all of whom were outstanding professionals who contributed in their areas of specialization: in computer work, management and organization, graphic work and the like. Computers, fax machines, and office equipment streamed in from all quarters, and most of all, readiness to man our small headquarters, which was established in an abandoned caravan on the outskirts of the neighborhood. The cost of all this was covered out of our own pockets. Not one cent was received from the official institutions of Yesha, although in all the press publicity, the Yesha Council made sure to appear as the organizing body behind the venture.

Preparations for the operation accelerated greatly. We felt that the fruit was definitely ripe, and that it would rot if not plucked in time.

We devoted much of our time in that period to attempts to convince the Yesha Council to proceed, which meant endless trips to the Council's Jerusalem offices. We explained the crucial importance of setting the date; we illustrated, by citing specific incidents, the readiness of the public for action – but to no avail. We felt like artillerymen who have loaded an awesome shell into the muzzle of a cannon, the firing of which is given over to the Yesha Council, a body which, due to its inherently faulty structural basis, could not rise to the occasion.

The Yesha Council is a sort of 'Union of Municipalities' comprising essentially local council heads who receive their budgetary allocations from the Ministry of the Interior, and therefore cannot, and should not, go forth in frontal attack against the establishment in which they function. The problem lay in the fact that the Yesha Council refused to acknowledge these restrictions, and viewed itself as the body responsible for public expressions of dissent and opposition, and not only for the welfare of the residents. On the one hand, they themselves could not enter the fray, while on the other hand, they were averse to passing on the credit for a struggle and consequent media attention onto others. This dilemma militated against any actual struggle taking place, apart from useless public meetings and declarations. Private initiatives were silenced, the Council exhibiting inattention to the frustration felt by the public whose interests it was ostensibly representing. To this very day, the Council's activity focuses mainly on mailing off letters and position papers, holding press conferences and endless meetings, and raising funds which mostly serve to perpetuate their own apparatus.

As a body whose main strength lies in its tongue, the Council's spokesmanship became its main function. Thus the Yesha Council maintained a spokesman and deputy spokesman (Aaron Dompa and Shai Bazak) in salary, cars, cellular phones, and other accouterments.

We quickly learned that Aaron Domb, spokesman of the Council, was much more influential than the executive secretary. Even when we succeeded in making some progress with Uri (who tried somehow to maneuver between conflicting interests, and at times seemed to really mean what he was saying), it was 'Dompa' who always turned the wheel back.

Eventually Dompa became executive secretary, an unusual jump in rank, but understandable in the Council. The fact that parallel to the existence of the Yesha Council there arose, during the period of the leftist government, a myriad of independent confrontational bodies, indicates the negative function it performed by blocking any practical measures, and the need felt by the public to create alternative channels of demonstrative opposition. In reality therefore, the Council served the leftist government as an invaluable asset (much greater than the 'Peace Now' movement) which acted to quash any burgeoning attempt at real opposition to the government's activities.

Uri Ariel probably never dreamed that those 'Americans' would stick in the Yesha Council's throat like a bone. To swallow it is impossible, for the aforementioned reasons; to throw it up is equally impossible, for what will we tell our public, which is waiting impatiently for the struggle to begin? The only solution is to tire those Americans out (they 'who did not do military service..., who do not appreciate the values of settlement, and in particular, where were they when we braved the

Revealed: Secret Operation by Yesha Council to Rapidly Erect 130 Settlements

OPERATION'S AIM: TO HALT WITHDRAWAL

The Statement of Purpose opens with the words: "The Israeli Government is determined to relinquish the areas of Yesha, the Jordan Valley, the Old City of Jerusalem, and the Golan, to alien sovereignty. The Government's intention is to wipe out Jewish settlements in these areas." The operation, to be known as "This Is My Land", will be carried out with military precision. This Friday at Ariel the activists will receive detailed folders, including maps and instructions.

Insert: First page of guidelines for the activists

Yediot Acharonot, December 1, 1993

authorities and settled in Sebastia?'...) using the tactics of the Histadrut, that is, the bureaucracy: "We will discuss the issue next week..."

We wait, update the settlements, and then go up at the designated time to Jerusalem (a ninety-minute journey each way).

"The meeting has been postponed until Monday because Uri had to go..."

We note the postponement, inform the settlements, and come back on Monday...

"A big deal is under way right now by which we can get hold of fifty more dunams. You must wait."

We wait.

"Something is brewing which we cannot reveal – but believe us, now is not the right time."

When then?

"We'll keep you informed. Meanwhile, keep the settlements in a state of readiness, and make sure the action file is ready..."

We go back to Karnei Shomron – and continue with our preparations…

"We would like to know the names of those who will man the various points every single day..."

But how can we do that if we do not have an exact date for the project's realization?

"Prepare an alternative list for each day of the week..."

Between one postponement and the next, the Council saw to it that our good name was being furtively besmirched. When someone called up the Council and asked to join the operation, there was someone ready to enlighten him to the fact that the initiators were a bunch of inexperienced Americans, and that it would be wise to distance oneself from their plots.

One of the brilliant ideas thought up by the Council in order to crush us under their bureaucratic wheels was the following demand: "Under no circumstances may you take possession of lands that are not state-owned."

"Right," we replied, "we have written that and explained that to all who are involved. The settlers know exactly which lands around them are available..."

"We want a detailed file from each and every settlement, including a topographical map (preferably on a 1:20,000 scale), the exact spot to be seized, clear indications of access roads to the spot, alternative spots in case the suggested ones are not ratified by us, etc. etc."

This request was meant to get us embroiled over our heads in insurmountable tasks, but the 'Americans' did not accept defeat, and overnight the improvised headquarters of 'Zo Artzeinu' became transformed into a branch of the Israel Lands Administration... The residents of the communities raised their eyebrows when they were told to fill out forms, take measurements, supply verification and maps, but, as was their wont, discharged their tasks with alacrity. Within a short time, we were able to return to the Council with cartons filled with files, a file for each settlement, which contained topographical maps, properly arranged lists of manpower allocations, lists of equipment, and the signature of the authorized person in each community.

And so the days flew by with fruitless planning, and the initial enthusiasm began to dissipate. Throughout all this time we refrained from attacking the Council through the media. We knew that such a step would play directly into the hands of the Left, and we were determined to preserve unity, at least outwardly. This was not the way Dompa acted. From the moment that he realized how important unity was in our eyes, he did not hesitate to exploit this 'weakness', and even explicitly threatened to turn against us in the media if we dared deviate from their path.

On the tenth of Tevet 5754 (looking back, it seems that our operation proceeded from one fast day to the next), we finally carried out a step that broke the rules of the game. The need to activate the set-up that we had built up became critically urgent, in order to preserve the loyalty and commitment of the activists. We decided on a move that would give expression to our organized power and would also prove to the Yesha Council that our plan was feasible. We still deluded ourselves into believing that the delays stemmed from their fear of failure.

We repressed recognition of the fact, which gradually became clearer and clearer, that the postponements stemmed from – fear of success...

We unilaterally announced the date of implementation of the 'dress rehearsal' before the 'actual performance', in the course of which the activists would go forth to the designated spots, mark the paths, make sure that everyone became familiar with the area, and then disperse.

This was not to be the main event, but it would demonstrate our ability to summon dozens of settlements to dozens of spots simultaneously, in perfect coordination and with orderly records; in short, it would show that we had the manpower, leadership and means of control.

The move was successful, and proved our capability for meaningful action.

On the day of the action, a television reporter, Nitzan Chen, got in touch with me and asked for an interview, against the backdrop of the ascent of the residents of Karnei Shomron to their spot. I had no idea what would take place, and preferred to be interviewed inside our caravan. Finally I was convinced to hold the interview at the encampment. This was my very first television interview ever, and it taught me a thing or two about media reportage.

Nitzan's first question was: "So Dompa is now eating his hat, eh?"

I understood from that opening that the dirty laundry had already been hung out for all to see (by Dompa, of course). It was also obvious that Nitzan Chen wanted to provoke my anger in order to draw me into nasty criticism of the Yesha Council, which would have provided him with the headline he sought... I played the innocent and responded: "Today is a fast day; no one eats and no one feeds." I ended the interview and returned to our headquarters. From every corner detailed reports arrived about the ascent of settlers to new points of settlement. Everything was done and painstakingly recorded on the forms that had been prepared in advance. At the close of the exercise, we totaled up the number of participating settlements, and it transpired that it added up to 68! This proof of our ability raised our spirits immeasurably. We were convinced that if it were not for the procrastination of the establishment, we could have carried out 'the actual performance' that day, instead of its being just a dress rehearsal, and could have already set forward the process that would lead to the abrogation of 'Oslo'. But very quickly this taste of success was replaced by great disillusionment. Our independent activity brought 'out of the closet' the opposition of the Yesha Council to our operation. From every quarter, the settlements began receiving faxes like the one reprinted on the opposite page.

Meanwhile Dompa issued notices to the media to the effect that the operation had been called off. Activists who heard on the news that the operation had been canceled called us up angrily to clarify what had happened, and upon hearing that this cancellation was not our doing, they became quite furious, but then lost all interest in pursuing the matter further. Reports in the press that had been planted by the Yesha Council removed all doubts as to their intentions.

From that point on, the heads of the Council turned against us openly. The activists in the various settlements lost their fighting spirit and withdrew from further participation. The fifteen settlements which stayed on with us were mainly newer ones, whose leaders had not emerged from the ranks of the Gush Emunim establishment and who therefore did not feel bound by the dictates of the Council.

The dilemma I now faced was intolerably painful. If I proceeded to act with only the remaining settlements, it would beget a conflict leading to disunity. If I called everything off, that would mean an end to the struggle, and would leave us no other

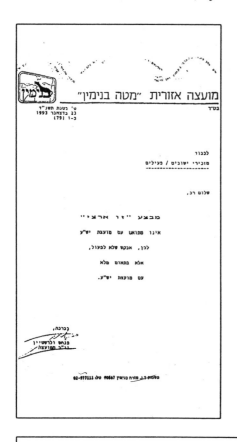

מועצה אזורית "מטה בנימין"

ט' בטבת תשנ"ד
22 בדצמבר 1993
ב-1-1 (179)

בס"ד

לכבוד

מזכירי ישובים / פעילים
....

שלום רב,

מבצע "זו ארצי"

אינו מתואם עם מועצת יש"ע

לכן, אבקש שלא לפעול,

אלא בתאום מלא

עם מועצת יש"ע.

נברכה,

פנחס וולרשטיין
יו"ר המועצה

ד.נ. מזרח בנימין 90607 טל. 977111-02

הנהלת מועצת יש"ע החליטה לעכב את "מבצע מכפיל"

– מאת צבי זינגר,
כתב "ידיעות אחרונות" –

בי'רוגע האחרון ביטלה אתמול הנהלת מועצת ישע את התאריכים של "מבצע מכפיל" – לאחר שכבר נשלחו לכל הישובים הודעות עם התאריכים.

המבצע היה אמור להיערך בשני שלבים: הראשון – ביום שישי הקרוב, ובו היו אמורים תושבי הישובים לצאת לנקודות שנבחרו להקמת 130 התנחלויות ולהניח בהן אבני-פינה. השלב השני היה אמור להיערך ב-5 בינואר, ובו היו אמורות ההתנחלויות לקום. בהנהלת יש"ע אומרים, כי המבצע נדחה בגלל עיתוי לא נוח, וכי תאריכים חדשים ייקבעו בקרוב.

בצמרת מערכת הביטחון בוחנים עתה את ההצעה מהפכנית להתקין מערכת אלחוטית לאיתור מכוניות במצוקה בכל מכונית ישראלית ביהודה, שומרון וחבל עזה. בין השאר נידונה ההצעה עם יועץ ראש-הממשלה לענייני טרור, יגאל פרסלה: עם אלוף פיקוד העורף, זאב ליבנה; ועם גורמים נוספים.

על-פי ההצעה, שהגישה מועצת יש"ע, יש שתי מערכות אלטרנטיביות: הראשונה – היקרה יותר – מצויה כבר באוטובוסי "אגד" מזה מספר חודשים. עלות היחידה – כ-700 דולר.

המערכת השנייה היא פרי פיתוחה של חברה ישראלית, ועלותה – כ-300 דולר, אולם היא תהיה מבצעית רק בעוד כשמונה חודשים, אם תונח לחברה ההצעה כראיית מבחינה כלכלית. מערכת זו מופעלת באזרה"ב. על-פי הצעת מועצת יש"ע, תמומן מחצית הפרויקט על-ידי מערכת הביטחון, רבע על-ידי הרשויות המקומיות ביש"ע, ורבע על-ידי בעלי המכוניות.

(right) YESHA COUNCIL POSTPONING 'DOUBLING OPERATION'
Yediot Acharonot, December 21, 1993

(left) Letter sent on December 23, 1993, to all settlement heads, stating that the Zo Artzeinu 'This is Our Land' Operation was not coordinated with the Yesha Council, and asking them to refrain from participating. Signed by the Chairman of the Yesha Council, Pinchas Wallerstein.

---

option but to revert to the former useless public demonstrations. I felt that too heavy a burden was resting on my shoulders, and that I could not make a decision by myself. In the middle of that night I drove to the Chairman of the Committee of Yesha Rabbis, Rabbi Melamed, whom I had never met before, but who, I assumed, by virtue of his position, was the one most likely to help me in such a difficult situation. The Rabbi heard my predicament, reflected for a few minutes, and said: "Unity is indeed extremely important, but it cannot outweigh the struggle. Try to get the members of the Yesha Council to come here, and we shall discuss the matter. Let us not call this a *Din Torah* (adjudication by Torah) but something a bit less threatening, like a *Torah consultation*.

I thanked the Rabbi, and some time afterwards we did indeed gather in his residence in Bet-El. Those present included Uri Ariel, Ze'ev Chaver (Zambish), Shmuel, Rabbi Melamed and his confidant, Ya'acov Katz (Ketzele). Shmuel and I outlined all our proposals, while Zambish and Uri argued that they still had the opportunity of bringing a number of caravans to some settlements. The thrust of their argument was that it was preferable to keep a low profile in order to achieve results on the ground, which is what Zambish, who was then the head of *Amanah*, the settlement movement of Gush Emunim, had indeed accomplished to a certain degree. This argument once again proved that the Yesha leadership still did not comprehend the position they had been led into, and that it was still fighting the battles of the past. Even if Zambish were to erect ten new settlements (actually, he did not establish even one new settlement) without anyone's noticing the fact, would that have any effect on the political process? Would that impede the process of delivering all of the land into the hands of the PLO?

In other words, in the name of the traditional values of settling the land, the Zionist myth of 'another dunam and another goat', Yesha had called out its forces against an operation meant to save the entire structure, leaving the settlements defenseless in the face of the process of liquidation being forced upon them.

Hadn't the method of 'another dunam and another goat' proved itself in the past? Certainly, but that was when it applied to the ascent to the top of the mountains, that is, when there was a worthy, attainable goal, but not at a time of imminent decline and collapse.

When a building is erected, every brick counts. But when a cannon is directed at the house, one does not persist in building yet another story; instead, one digs foxholes and goes out to do battle. Otherwise, the cannon shells will, without extra effort, and without meeting additional resistance, demolish even the newest floor added.

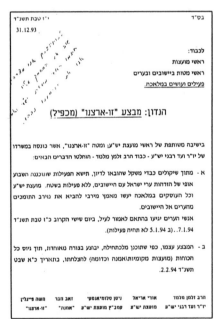

The pledge of harmonious coordination, December 31, 1993

The names of the five signatories and the bodies they represent appear at the bottom.

"And how long will it take you to get those caravans to their destinations?" asked Rabbi Melamed. Zambish specified the time, and thus, quite elegantly, nothing was left of their procrastination. It was then agreed that at the end of the period required by Zambish, our operation would proceed hand in hand. Shmuel and I, who no longer had much faith in the word of the gentlemen sitting opposite us, made sure to put the conclusions in writing, and to have all those present sign, including Rabbi Melamed. We assumed that if the Yesha heads signed such a document, next to the signature of the Chairman of the Committee of Yesha Rabbis, they would not dare violate their commitment. It had required quite an effort, but once the paper was signed, I could again feel the stirring of hope.

The designated date elapsed, and again we made our way, for the umpteenth time, to the Jerusalem offices of the Yesha Council, in order to coordinate our steps. We were asked to wait outside, but we could not help hearing the thundering voice of Dompa. A loud shouting match was taking place within. I gathered that once again the whole deal was going to fall through. After a full hour, we were ushered in. In the room sat Uri Ariel, Aaron Dompa, Nissan Slomiansky, Shai Bazak and other permanent personnel whose precise function I never knew. The participants hung their faces in shame, while Dompa took the floor. "We have had differences of opinion," he said, "and since I admit that I led the opposition to the operation, I am exercising the right to speak. I know that Nissan (Slomiansky) is finding it hard to accept what I am going to say, and that's why he is hiding in that corner," he continued, in an attempt to soften the impending blow by injecting a bit of banter. By the end of a few more sentences, it became evident that Dompa had succeeded in bringing us back to square one, and that all the understandings arrived at in the Torah consultation, the signed documents, were meaningless. Dompa had led the Yesha Council to a total denial of its commitments.

I had intended to let him finish his words and only then respond, but Shmuel, who could no longer contain himself, got up and left, and so I too went out after him.

The 'Doubling Operation' – First Arrest
(or: The Queen of Hearts and the card soldiers)

Chapter 6

In utter silence we plodded along the streets of Jerusalem, distancing ourselves from the offices of the Yesha Council. We had embarked on a struggle to prevent the relinquishment of the heart of the country to the PLO. We had devoted all our energy, time and money to this cause, but found ourselves butting our heads against the impenetrable wall of the existing settlement establishment.

The months of attempts to propel a fundamental change of policy through the agency of the establishment bodies, those that label themselves 'the national camp', I now view as the most intensive, concentrated course I have ever taken. When I first began that course, I naively believed that establishments conduct themselves in the interest of their enunciated goals, and in the service of those they represent...

I believed that disagreements, if there were any, would be substantive, and would be ironed out amicably in light of the common objective. I had a basic faith in people who took upon themselves leadership and responsibility. By the end of the course, I understood that the world is divided, essentially, into the establishment – and whatever is not part of it. The value defended by the establishment above all others is self-preservation. Just like the principle of human survival, the will to continue to live, is to be found in every living species, plant, and even inanimate nature, so the establishment, as an autonomous body, is preoccupied with assuring its own survival.

The man in the street thinks that the establishment was set up for the express purpose of serving those who created it and support it financially, but that is not the case. The objective of the establishment is to preserve its own existence and maintain its sources of income and strength. Secondary to that is the goal of satisfying the wishes of its constituency, since by doing so it ensures its own survival. But should the self-interest of the establishment's own survival require action directly contradictory to the interest of its constituency, the establishment's interest will take precedence over those of the public.

Furthermore, the various establishments, even if they represent conflicting ideologies and are seemingly in confrontation with each other, do so merely to justify their existence, and will always prefer each other rather than outside factors challenging the establishments, even if these dissidents share the same basic ideology with them. It is as if they were fish, preferring to fight each other in water, their natural habitat, rather than join up with land animals, be they the most trustworthy, successful and efficient.

The Yesha Council, which inherited the good name of the extra-establishment Gush Emunim, became an established organization, which prevented it from entering into the fray that would have meant – putting its survival at risk. That explains why the Yesha Council had become a major factor in obstructing any real struggle against the government's policy, actually an asset of great importance for the Rabin administration, an importance much greater than that of 'Peace Now' for example...

The general public looked upon it as the leadership of the settler movement, the undeviating extension of Gush Emunim. The profuse communicativeness of Dompa, Shai Bazak and Co. reinforced this image in the eyes of the public and no one tried to challenge this leadership.

The members of the Yesha Council were adept at exploiting the aversion displayed by the settlers to internal dissension. The settlers were an idealistic public that always preferred accomplishing things to engaging in internal skirmishing. None of them was inclined to challenge the leadership of the Yesha Council, because no one was really eager to take on that role.

The fact that the Yesha Council members had never stood for election, and had rejected that suggestion whenever it was raised, did not overly agitate the public. I, too, as an individual member of that public was not bothered by the matter. As long as I had the impression that there was a leadership, and due to previous training, gave them my trust, details didn't concern me, not even the strange fact that they were managing public funds without any formal sanction.[1]

It was, politically speaking, a most sensitive period. The furtive consultations at Oslo and the official recognition of the PLO had been revealed, but the practical provisions of the agreements had not been signed. Rabin had not yet shaken the hand of Arafat, and the Israeli public had not yet digested the total change of direction in Zionist thinking.

Every Israeli had been conditioned from early childhood to view Arafat as the incarnation of the devil, and with good cause. The murder of women, old men and children – this was the daily fare of the man and of the terrorist forces that he had unleashed. His political program called for nothing less than the total destruction of the Jewish state, and the establishment of a Palestinian state on its ruins. Against such a satanic total enemy, Israeli public opinion was of one mind: total rejection. There were, it cannot be denied, some eccentric leftist extremists who actually justified his stand, and espoused entering into discussions with the man, individuals like Uri Avneri, Abie Nathan, and Yossi Sarid. There were also the members of *Matzpen* who identified with the PLO's doctrine and stood for the elimination of the Zionist entity

---

[1] The Yesha Council is funded primarily by allocations from the budgets of the various community councils (that is, from funds provided by the Ministry of Housing, and the individual property-tax-paying settlers, who had never elected it).

and the establishment of a multinational and socialistic state in its place. These extremists, like Chaim HaNegbi of Matzpen (who has his own regular column in the daily *Ma'ariv*), represented at that time a fringe minority in Israeli society, but were very good at worming their way into the mass media, and using them to promote their own agendas.

The proportion of key men in the world of the Israeli media who had come from those extreme leftist schools of thought is simply amazing, and bears no relation whatsoever to their standing in the citizenry. An outstanding example might be Moshe Negbi, a man who justified, in broadsides published by the movement *Yesh Gevul*, an all-out civil war (!) in the event that their 'red lines' were crossed (the 'red lines' to be determined by Negbi, of course). This same Moshe Negbi currently serves as the legal commentator of the (government-supported) *Kol Israel* radio station.

This accounts for the fact that when Rabin startled the Israeli public with his Oslo move – which was no less than the adoption of the post-Zionist ideologies from the schools of the extreme leftist movements – he and his government earned the full support of the Israeli media, out of all proportion to the degree of support to be found in the flabbergasted public.

The average citizen, who detested the disgusting, pistol-packing murderer with the bristly face, suddenly found himself exposed to a new 'politically correct' line. The king is indeed naked! He is still as loathsome as he has always been, but from all sides he was being lauded, and so the man in the street attuned himself to the media outpourings. The general mobilization of all the electronic and written media with the objective of changing the public's perceptions and an all-out assault on the conventional attitudes regarding the PLO began to make their mark.

Rabin, who, in order to be elected, made sure to promise unequivocally that he would never talk with the PLO and would never discuss the establishment of a Palestinian state, did not have to deal with pesky media carrying out their democratic task and posing troublesome questions. On the contrary, the media tried in every possible way to portray Rabin and his associates as 'heroes of peace', while those elements that dared raise their voices against 'post-Zionism' (the 'peace process') were labeled 'war-mongers', the 'extreme right', etc. Demonstrators from the Right wing were invariably characterized as 'the extreme right'– implying fascist aspirations, while the demonstrations of supporters of the process were consistently described as actions on the part of 'the peace camp'.

It was not at all pleasant to be counted in that period among the opponents of government policy. The various élites, in the army, the police, and academia, hurried to fall in line with the government and the media, and provided mutual support for approval of 'the process'.

Thus, for example, then-Chief-of-Staff Ehud Barak issued politically tainted proclamations, such as the one favoring 'peace' as a strategic asset that outweighs the importance of Ramat HaGolan, a pronouncement with clear political overtones, a breach of his military responsibility.[1] The media rushed to publicize such statements broadly, and as a result, this mutual nourishing created an effect that left the man in the street with little chance of analyzing the pertinent data for himself.

In such circumstances, an ordinary, sane member of the community joins the bandwagon and ecstatically praises the magnificence of the king's new clothes, and no one will dare call attention to the king's nudity.

The shaping of public opinion, that snowball which began to roll down the mountain, gathered speed in the direction of general acceptance of the PLO, the 'necessity' of entering into negotiations with it and handing over parts of the country to it. If at the start, when the first contacts that were made with the terrorists became public knowledge, the snowball was stuck at the peak of the mountain and it was not clear in which direction it would roll, as time elapsed and the arena remained empty of any counter-activity, the snowball swelled, gained momentum, and without any chance of being arrested in mid-course, crushed all the venerable Zionist values.

Public opinion, that elusive, capricious concept, requires elucidation at this point. It would seem, according to what has already been reported, that 'Zo Artzeinu' tried to act in opposition to public opinion, which began to incline in favor of the Rabin government's stand. This was not the case. To understand the situation, it is worthwhile to recall exactly what happened in the tale of the king's new clothes. Every one of those who lauded the appearance of the naked monarch knew in his heart the shameful truth. But to anyone on the sidelines, it appeared that public opinion was of one mind, that the king was splendidly attired. It was up to a small child to come with his pin and puncture the ridiculous balloon. Only then would the crowds come to their senses and true public opinion assert itself. With every television screen and newspaper headline hailing the acceptance of yesterday's hated enemy, it was inevitable that this superficial public opinion would overwhelm the public's perspicacity. In this one-sided media reality, ordinary demonstrations did not succeed in exploding this balloon. What was needed was the pin of civil disobedience by 'Zo Artzeinu' to get the masses to wake up.

But it was not only in the area of Israeli public opinion that the government of Israel faced an unclear reality in the early stages. Even vis-a-vis its 'partner', it had to overcome many hurdles of suspicion. At first, Rabin steadfastly refused to meet personally with Arafat, and did not yet dream of shaking his hand. Any hasty step by one of the parties was immediately interpreted as laying a trap for the other side, so

---

[1] Like most of his fellow officers, Barak enlisted in the Labor Party as soon as he was discharged from service.

that at that stage there was a great potential for neutralizing the entire process by settlement demonstrations.

As we walked along the streets of Jerusalem we felt, Shmuel and I, that it was a critical time. We thought that if we submit at this stage, the Oslo train would go forward without any substantial opposition, ignoring some feeble, inconsequential carping, and the road would inevitably lead to the loss of the heartland and all that would follow. We felt that it was not too late, at this unstable period, to put a lid on Pandora's box. Yes, it would take a formidable effort and unification of forces, but at this point in time, it was still feasible. We returned to Karnei Shomron, with the determination to attempt to persevere and maintain the struggle at all costs.

★ ★

That night we faced a difficult choice. Very little was left of the original operation. Of all the dozens of settlements that had been eager to carry out our plans there were now only a few still prepared to do so, after all the tiffs and run-ins with the Yesha Council.

It was then that a thought occurred to me:

See here, Shmuel, we are left with only five bullets out of a full magazine of 100 (communities that had been willing to go ahead). We can no longer discharge bursts of automatic fire, as we had planned. So, let's fire instead single shots.

Every night we will put up a single encampment site.

True, the army can muster all its forces there and we will be moved out even before we manage to drive a single peg into the earth. Nevertheless, such an attempt every night will inevitably resound throughout the country. And perhaps, if we succeed in arousing public reverberations, additional settlements may be prompted to take part in our endeavor. Settlements that have tried to take root and have been removed from the land will return, with new groups joining the action. Thus, despite everything, we may be able to exert real pressure on the establishment, which will be hard-pressed to deal with many such 'trouble spots' at the same time.

The idea did not carry the same appeal that the original plan did, and also, the original fighting spirit had evaporated with disappointment. However, we dared hope that it was still possible to erect what had been toppled and breathe a new spirit into the ranks, and that those who had abandoned the struggle would return to the fray after a week of repeated struggle on the land.

With many 'butterflies in the stomach', we proceeded to execute our plans, which were on a much smaller scale than the original conception.

We carefully considered exactly what forces were available to us.

They were all settlements and individuals of the second round of settlements, those which were not identified with the historic *Gush Emunim*, and felt no personal commitment to the Yesha Council clique, but to the struggle itself.

These were Karnei Shomron (no surprise), Ma'aleh Adumim (some 'Americans' resided there), Kiryat Arba (they were always antagonistic to the Yesha establishment), Bat Ayin (penitent returnees to Judaism, totally isolated from any establishment body), Tapu'ach (see Kiryat Arba), and a few others, about whose reliability we were uncertain.

We decided to begin with Kiryat Arba. In view of our situation, we preferred to begin with our big guns at the very start...

On the second night, it would be the turn of Bat Ayin to take hold of a site for settlement. (We relied on their faith; they would go forth even if the first night's attempt flopped.)

Karnei Shomron would do so on the third night (that's where Shmuel and I were, and we knew things would be O.K. here).

Tapu'ach on the fourth night.

Hashmonaim on the fifth night.

Yakir on the sixth.

Ma'aleh Adumim in the following week, and by then, other volunteers would be joining – hopefully...

We immediately contacted the various settlements. In our talks with them, we learned that the despair we experienced in our dealings with the Yesha establishment was shared by many others, as a result of their own encounters on different occasions, so that we did not have to elaborate on what we had gone through.

The date for the first attempt at encampment was set for Tu BeShvat, 5754 (January 26, 1994).

The residents of Kiryat Arba agreed to be the first. There was no need to explain to them what had to be done. Kiryat Arba, a settlement that had always been in the forefront of the struggle and had been the most grievously besmirched by the Left (and to our mortification, even from the leadership of the Right), was quite accustomed to similar ventures, and was delighted that this time it was not alone in the battle.

"Don't worry," I was reassured by Yehoshua Shani and Shalom Sarel, two of the prominent figures in the Kiryah, "we will have ourselves a real shindig." And that's what they did. They planned everything down to the smallest detail, and although the authorities thought they knew exactly where and when the action would take place, the yishuv managed to outwit them. They even did not let me into their secrets... and I acquiesced, rightly.

Motti Karpel and his buddies at Bat Ayin organized the settlers for the encampment due to take place on the second night.

My acquaintance with the people of Bat Ayin instilled in me a deep feeling of self-depreciation vis-a-vis these men of truthfulness. The entire settlement consists of newly-penitents, people who did not find what they were seeking within any other settlement framework. They built their homes with their own bare hands, eschewing the hiring of Arab employees. They all have piercing deep eyes, and an outlook combining pure and optimistic faith with an attachment to nature and practical living. One of them raises goats in his yard, the other runs a famous clinic in the city, and another spends his days studying in the Beit Medrash. Their houses, which blend so perfectly with the natural terraces, can barely be seen at first glance, and their children look as if they had just come back from watching the combat between David and Goliath.

Karnei Shomron also girded itself for the operation, as did the other settlements, although no one came near the level of the 'operational efficiency' of Kiryat Arba.

We informed the media of our intentions, and we publicized the dates of action and where we intended to strike roots. Had the media ignored us, and had the IDF looked the other way and refrained from approaching the areas, it is highly doubtful that we would have achieved any effect whatsoever. In that case, we planned on turning these symbolic encampments into real, full-fledged settlements. We also had plans for mobilizing volunteers from within the borders of the 'green line' and for launching an all-out drive for broad settlement, a step that could not possibly be ignored. But all this uncertainty came to an end as a result of the harsh response of the Rabin government.

The disproportion between the number of forces sent to remove the miserably small encampments and the actual size of the disputed areas was simply ludicrous. When I saw the troops advancing on the forlorn tent and the flag which the residents of Bat Ayin had put up, I became totally convinced of the correctness of my original calculations. My estimate of the sensitivity of the process at that point in time, its utter dependence on the conduct of the settlers, and the anticipated behavior of the authorities, was validated.

I had been proved right, and with hindsight I dare state that, were it not for the Yesha Council, we could have begun a process that would, once and for all, have buried the snake pit opened at Oslo.

Precisely upon the start of the operation, I was called up for a three-day reserve duty exercise, and thus was prevented from actively participating in the encamping by the Kiryat Arba residents. I comforted myself with the realization that the people of Kiryat Arba would manage very nicely without me, since there was no dearth of local leadership. Shmuel joined them that night, and what took place I heard via the small transistor radio that was attached to my ear during my reserve stint.

The inhabitants of Kiryat Arba had no illusions regarding the army's determination to clear them out of any new settlement point. They were accustomed to staging independent demonstrations. From the outburst of the intifada by the Arabs, Kiryat Arba was always in the forefront of the bloody struggle between the two nationalities over the land of Israel.

The descendants of Abraham focused the struggle over the land promised to him around his burial ground.

The legitimate heirs of the first monotheist, Isaac, Jacob and their wives, are also buried in that remarkable site, the Machpelah Cave, and their descendants maintained their presence there for thousands of years, until their horrible massacre in 1929, and the expulsion of the survivors, by the sons of Ishmael.

Following the liberation of that city in the Six Day War, Jews began returning to the city of their forefathers. But the local Arabs, who quickly recovered from their humiliation and realized that there would be no policy of retribution for their satanic, murderous past, had no intention of resigning themselves to this. Clashes were a matter of common occurrence, and brutal acts of murder became a recurrent ritual.[1]

The list of murdered victims among the Jews of Hebron who returned to the houses of those butchered in 1929 continued to expand. In response, the authorities tightened their supervision – over the Jews...

---

[1] Sheik Jabari, the mayor of Hebron at the time of its liberation, did offer the victorious IDF forces payment of compensation for the families of those killed in 1929, full rental fees for the entire period during which their homes had been occupied by local Arabs, and invited the Jews to return and settle in Hebron (*Ma'ariv*, 15/6/67 – as quoted in *Nativ*, May 1997). But shortly after, Jabari and his associates realized who they were dealing with, and the traditional Arab bloodshedding resumed.

The protests of the inhabitants of Kiryat Arba were of no avail. The IDF viewed them as a provocative factor in an Arab zone, and the government considered them a hostile element. During the Rabin administration, Kiryat Arba became a harassed town. People hardly dared communicate by phone, even on mundane matters. Large contingents of the army and police continually checked every nook and cranny in ceaseless efforts to locate potential demonstrators. The general apprehension concerning the Arabs shifted into growing violence against the Jews. The media joined the fray, and depicted the Jews of Hebron and the Kiryah as dangerous fanatics, *Houmanis*, a thorn in every Israeli's backside, for whose protection 'huge' army forces are required to sacrifice their lives and for whom the general public is required to waste its financial resources. The residents of the Kiryah, who stood in the front lines of the struggle, bore the full brunt of Arab terror, and in addition, a disproportionate share of the media incitement and of the persecution of the government and its branches.

The Yesha Council, the established leadership of the settlers, washed its hands of the residents of the Kiryah, and adopted the infamous line espoused by its spokesman Dompa: "We are respectable; it's only *they* who are trouble-makers." The pearls of wisdom of the spokesman of the Yesha Council regarding the 'wild weeds' growing in Kiryat Arba were echoed with great relish in all the media, and thus served as a major tool in the castigation of the people of Kiryat Arba.[1] Israeli citizens got the impression at that time that Kiryat Arba, with its 6000 inhabitants, was a bastion of the terrorist Hamas, more or less a twin of the Shechem Kasbah. The Kiryah became a social pressure cooker, and it became very hard to live there, even without the grave security problem created by the Arabs. There were residents who had withstood all the turmoil and clashes with the Arabs, but could no longer take the national demonization of the community, and left.

For the people of Kiryat Arba, the very fact that an outside factor ('Zo Artzeinu') was carrying out a Yesha-wide operation in which they were but one link, without their shouldering sole responsibility for the venture, was an exhilarating change. The fact that the Yesha Council was left out of the picture delighted them even more, and it was totally unnecessary to fire them with the desire to participate.

---

[1] At the time these lines are being written, we have learned that Dompa – now secretary-general of Yesha Council – announced at a convention of 'Peace Now' that "there are people in Hebron who are capable of emulating the deed carried out by Dr. Baruch Goldstein". Anyone who knows the Jews of Hebron and their remarkably moderate stand vis-a-vis the mad reality forced upon them can imagine the extent of the harm that such a statement could bring upon them, particularly when expressed by an ostensible leader. No one has ever heard any 'Peace Now' leader lash out at any member of the 'peace' camp. 'Peace Now' needs no legitimatization by those in Israeli society that confer it. The leader of the Yesha Council feels the need for legitimatization, and tries to achieve it by casting aspersions on people who belong to his own camp, and this, not in the framework of internal clarifications but at a convention of 'Peace Now'...

IMPRESSIONS -- Drawing by a resident of Kiryat Arba

Hundreds of participants were organized, and it was planned to take over an abandoned structure near the Glass Junction at the edges of the Kiryah. The selected point was to be named the 'Lapid Hill', in memory of the father and son of the Lapid family, who had been murdered nearby a short period earlier. None of the 'recruits' knew the destination in advance. Plans were strictly classified, and a clever feint had been concocted.

Yehoshua Shani, Shalom Sarel and their buddies knew the IDF was keeping a very close eye on their every move throughout that evening, and would try to snuff out any attempts at the very first sign. They had to devise a way of misleading the army, in order to arrive at the targeted place and establish their presence there, accompanied by journalists, but without the army. And that is what they did.

A small band of fifty men set off first, and staged a 'settling-in' on a remote corner of Kiryat Arba. No sooner had they done so that all the military forces in the sector streamed to the spot, and started evacuating the dummy settlement. Additional forces blocked off all roads leading to the area, and confusion and utter chaos reigned. No one knew what was going on, communications networks were inundated with reports, and all the generals, accompanied by their adjutants, drivers, etc rushed to where the video cameras were photographing.

While all this was taking place there, hundreds of other settlers managed to evade supervision, reached the abandoned building at the edge of the Kiryah and established themselves in it, accompanied by Gil Littman of Kol Israel and other media personnel.

The surprise was complete. It took the armed forces a long time before it dawned on them that they had been duped and had failed to pinpoint the main target of the operation, and still longer to organize for the removal of the settlers from the building. The evacuation itself did not entail much effort, since all the activists were very careful to maintain absolute passivity and not to forcibly resist their removal.

Dozens of detainees were led that night to jails in Bethlehem and Jerusalem. Shmuel, too, was arrested that evening with the residents of Kiryat Arba, but released the following day. Among the detainees there was a young lawyer, a new immigrant from England by the name of 'Shoan' Kasper. Kasper was to accompany us for a long time, voluntarily arriving in the middle of the night at forsaken jails all over the country in order to arrange for our release.

Next in line of duty were the inhabitants of Bet Ayin, and I got ready to join them upon being discharged from my reserve service.

I arrived at Bet Ayin on the evening of their encamping.

It was very cold on the hills of Gush Etzion. The members of the settlement gathered in the synagogue which they had themselves built, and organized their setting forth to the new settlement point. There was no sign of any army units in the area. No one knew how things would turn out. I sat down in a rear corner and listened to the instructions given by the leaders of the small community. I was asked to say a few words, which I did. I replied to a number of questions, and we set out.

מבצע מכפיל

בשבוע הבא: יקיר, קרני שומרון, מעלה עמוס, תפות, יקיר, מעלה אדומים

– מאת שיולי נחום ונבי וינגר, כתבי "ידיעות אחרונות" –

THE 'DOUBLING OPERATION'

Setting up an encampment at Bat Ayin in Gush Etzion. Eight settlers who tried to encamp near Kiryat Arba two days ago were released yesterday on bail of 1,000 shekels. They undertook not to enter a closed-off military area. Twenty-two others refused to sign such a commitment, and will therefore remain in custody for 48 hours, after which their cases will be brought before the Jerusalem Magistrates' Court.

Insert: NEXT WEEK: YAKIR, KARNEI SHOMRON, MA'ALEH AMOS, TAPU'ACH, MA'ALEH ADUMIM

I tried to be present at each of these actions. I did not consider myself the leader, and never conducted myself in that manner, but I realized that the locals needed leadership, and so I assumed a conditioned behavior. I always left it to the local leadership to direct the activities, in the hope that they would not need my intercession. I avoided interviews with the media. I preferred that television viewers should see different faces each night. But the residents were aware of my presence, probably drew encouragement from it, and appreciated this kind of conduct.

As in the case of Kiryat Arba, the new target spot was given a name. Bet Ayin labeled it the 'Stronghold of the Follow-up Generation'. On the way there they carried tents, boards, flags and various tools, and trudged down the hill to the target area. The

'Stronghold of the Follow-up Generation' was established in a secluded place, where, were it not for the media exposure, it would have been possible to erect another Shalom Tower (thirty floors high) without anyone ever being aware of the fact.

When we arrived, night had already fallen, and we were drenched with rain. We began construction. On a flagpole hoisted atop one of the rocks a flag was raised, and the settler who was responsible for this was featured the following day in the newspaper headlines.

Media people swarmed about us, and in those days I had no idea as yet as to who was what, which networks were present, which were local and which foreign, which was radio, and which newspapers...

A lieutenant colonel arrived at the scene and informed us that we were to vacate the area. An argument broke out around his military jeep, but I cut it short. I urged the residents not to engage in an argument but to ignore him and proceed with their plans, which they then did.

Shortly after, we learned that large forces of military police were deployed in the area. A little later, hundreds of unidentifiable figures began to appear. The darkness, the rain, and the mist blurred our vision. Naturally, we assumed that they were army forces, but they were still about half a kilometer away, and we pretended not to have noticed them.

The figures gradually came closer. One of the television men shifted the projectors of the TV cameras in their direction. The sight that greeted their eyes led to a general burst of laughter. The hundreds of soldiers of the military police, assembled in order to evacuate us, had been brought directly from their training course somewhere in Tzrifin. They were thoroughly prepared for their task, and were outfitted with red-and-white jackets that reflected light. The hundreds of military police swarming down the incline towards us were suddenly lit up in the glare of the projectors, and their light-reflecting jackets suddenly shone a glowing red against the background of the mists and the heavy darkness.

One couldn't see faces, uniforms, feet or hands – all that was visible were those hundreds of shining jackets suspended in space and marching towards us down the slope. It looked as if the 'Queen of Hearts' of *Alice in Wonderland* was sending us a battalion of her card soldiers...

The contrast between the large size of the forces sent to this forgotten hill slope and the small number of settlers, the forlorn tent, and the tattered flag, was striking. Evidently the threat posed by 'Zo Artzeinu' had been taken most seriously, and someone had decided to quash the operation resolutely at the very outset. The number of specialist forces assembled at this spot was staggering. Also, the types of forces deployed were of a breadth I had never seen before. I had assumed that the regular IDF forces were the ones assigned to evacuate us. But the army had brought up professionals, all the available military police, apparently because of their wider authority, which subsequently enables easier initiation of legal processes.

The following day the newspapers reported the ridiculous explanation offered by the top political and army echelons in an attempt to besmirch the settlers. "The settlers compel us to deploy forces for a confrontation with them, instead of defending them," asserted 'senior' military sources. It was obvious that this humbug emanated directly from the Prime Minister's office. The military police that evacuated us had never assumed the task of 'protecting the settlers', but even if they had, this claim would still have been groundless, and its sole intent was to deny the settler community legitimatization.

When the Histadrut (The General Federation of Labor) or the 'peace' organizations demonstrate, no one among the 'senior police sources' will claim that the disturbance prevents their dealing with thieves and murderers. The police are obligated to deal with violations of public order in all of society's strata, and it is with that in mind that they deploy the forces deemed necessary.

Suddenly, when the issue is a struggle on the part of the settlers, the matter becomes a burden falling upon the armed forces. Which is to say, the authorities play on the heartstrings of the public's loyalty to the IDF and try to direct it against the settlers and their campaign of resistance. The senior commanders portrayed matters even more acutely by asserting that by having to evacuate settlers it becomes more difficult for the IDF to protect them adequately. In other words, the settlers even spit upon the hand that tries to defend them, and are thus themselves responsible for the neglect of their security.

This propaganda was fiendish, particularly in light of the abdication of authority in the areas during the recent years and the IDF's practical renunciation of responsibility for security.

If the military commander of the northern region of Israel were to declare that the inhabitants of the north were a burden upon the IDF, he would find his career at an end that very day. But, as stated, the settlers were fighting for their very right to legitimatization by the public. The IDF and the government knew that, and tried to exploit the situation to suppress such legitimatization. In this confrontation, the settlers were and remained the underdogs.

★ ★

The surrealist jacket scene straight out of the Wonderland of Alice quickly dissipated, and we were brought back to the realities of the Jewish Wonderland.

After a brief argument, the military police evacuated the residents from the spot without much difficulty. The tents were taken down, the flags were furled, a large number of men were sent to jail and with that the episode came to an end. The local commanders acted under such strict orders that some newspapermen were even beaten and some even arrested. This boomeranged against them in the following day's media coverage.

I was not arrested that evening. Perhaps I was spared that pleasure due to the inconspicuous position I adopted. I was not yet easily identified as a big fish. I also knew that this evening was only our opening volley and that our main effort lay ahead. I felt it important that I remain unhampered another day or two, and therefore did not make any particular effort to get myself arrested at this stage.

I returned home late at night. I had no idea what effect we had made, whether matters would begin to take shape as anticipated, or whether it would all turn out to be quite meaningless.

It would seem that the evening's objective had been fully met. Dozens of individuals were under arrest, we had a fully documented struggle on the ground, and the government had not failed us, behaving precisely as we had expected. But would the whole project gather steam or slowly peter out...?

I waited impatiently for the morning newspapers, and was not disappointed. The many reports and the great journalistic interest proved to me that I was indeed playing on the sensitive chord that I had been aiming for. Unintentionally, this media coverage encouraged the other groups that were organizing for the next steps.

The next night it would be our turn, the residents of Karnei Shomron.

We selected a bare slope not far from the industrial zone of Karnei Shomron. The place was of special importance. It was privately owned land, the property of Moshe Zar, one of the residents, so that actually any move to this spot would be legally tantamount to inviting friends over to a garden party on private land. We hoped to create a legal conundrum over our being ejected from the place. I had few illusions. I had never placed much blind reliance on 'equality before the law' for all Israelis, but nonetheless we made sure that we had in our possession all the documentary certification of ownership of the land in question, and a written invitation by its owner to come.

Our documents carried no weight when the forces arrived to evacuate us. The brigade commander of the area declared the entire zone from Shechem to Kfar Saba, including Karnei Shomron, Kedumim, and every point within, 'a closed-off military area', and

REPORTERS ARRESTED

Last week the IDF arrested 8 newspapermen covering events in the territories. Following severe criticism, Major-General Yatom ordered a stop to such arrests.
Last week saw an intensification in the army's confrontation with the media in the territories. Eight reporters have been arrested since last Wednesday while attempting to cover the 'Doubling Operation' organized by the settlers...

Left insert: A SCANDAL and SERIOUS VIOLATION
The national Union of Israeli Journalists yesterday demanded that the IDF call an immediate halt to preventing newsmen from the performance of their duties in the territories...

Right, first item: SOLDIERS' ORDERS (to reporters): "YOU MAY NOT SPEAK or OPEN the WINDOWS"
"... For two hours we sat in the bus with the settlers, while the soldiers and officers kept approaching every two minutes to make sure we were obeying their orders (not to engage in conversation...). It seemed that their purpose was to prevent any media coverage, rather than keep an eye on the settlers..."

Right, second item: NOTHING LEARNED from YAMIT EVACUATION
"... Wherever the IDF confronts a civilian population, and particularly an Israeli one, declaring an area a 'restricted military zone' out of bounds to Israeli newsmen is not at all feasible, and moreover, is reprehensible and superfluous..."
Commentary, by Alex Fishman

---

gave us very short notice to vacate the place. Inhabitants who had no idea what was going on and who had come to shop at the nearby commercial center found themselves escorted to the police van which was at the ready. A new immigrant who exited from the supermarket and, seeing what was going on, took out of her handbag a camera in order to film the event, was attacked by the military police's operations officer, who struck her in the face and grabbed her camera from her hands.

The ridiculous situation whereby the living room in the home of residents becomes a closed-off military area did not trouble the legal authorities. The IDF's wholesale utilization of this device – to declare a place a 'closed-off military area' – deprived it of any substantive significance, and simply turned it into a political tool. The term 'closed-off military area' normally indicates a zone having some special security sensitivity as a result of training practice, operational activity, or some kind of strategic importance. In our case, we did not enter a closed-off military area; what had happened was that the closed-off military area had 'come to us'...

The soldiers of the military police dragged us one by one to the screened vans. When my turn came, the soldiers approached and began with the usual admonition before the actual arrest. I asked them to cut it short and carry out their duty. They proceeded to drag me to the van while engaging in a bit of revenge by allowing my back to scrape against the rocks and thistles. With all the excitement around us, I hardly felt any pain and ignored it. These were just 19-year-old boys who, in a moment of weakness, let out their frustration ... on my back. I had forgotten all about it until a few days later when I heard a shriek from my wife, when she suddenly saw my exposed back. I had forgotten that my back had given the rocks a good 'brush', but now, after the bruises had healed, it looked as if I had undergone a thorough lashing. Seeing this evidence of violence against us, Tzippy lost her normal sense of humor, and my attempts to soothe her failed to dispel her rage.

Dozens of men and women protesters were jailed that night. Among the jailed sat a quiet, whimsically smiling person, the prominent former Russian Prisoner of Zion, Dr. Yosef Begun, who identified with our struggle, had joined the activists, and was arrested with all the others without being recognized.

The packed police vans set off on a tiring journey around the various jails in the country. The residents of Bet Ayin and Kiryat Arba were still in detention, so that the entire jail system was hard put to cope with the crush. The need to keep the large group together so that it would not become necessary to transfer detainees from all over the country for joint court hearings for further remand required finding a suitable detention center. Finally, towards morning, the convoy arrived at the jail at...Tiberias.

A supportive demonstration by the residents of Tiberias in the presence of many representatives of the media awaited us. We were jailed, and, as we had decided, we informed our interrogators throughout our cross-examinations that "this is a political investigation and we have nothing to say".

We were assigned to the various chambers. The cell in which we were placed was already filled up, when the iron grating of the cell opened and Yosef Begun came in carrying a standard, foul mattress. The capacity of the cell was over-extended, so that Begun had to find space to sleep on the floor. I offered to exchange places, so that he should occupy my bed. "But you are the commander of the operation..." he replied with a smile. "Fine! Therefore, I do hereby order you to switch to my bed...," I answered. He acquiesced, and we exchanged places.

Shmuel, who as a student in the USA had been jailed a number of times for demonstrating on behalf of Begun's release from the Russian prisons, found the situation particularly amusing. "See here," he remarked to Begun, "you were imprisoned in Russia, I was imprisoned on your behalf in America, and now the two of us are jailed together in Eretz Israel..." Begun smiled wryly, with both good humor and a trace of bitterness.

We spent the two days jailed in Tiberias comparing the prison conditions in three different locations, listening to jokes told by Shmuel (who insisted on trying to dig an escape tunnel with the help of a plastic teaspoon stolen from the mess-hall) and studying Torah in pairs.

At night, getting ready for sleep, I took out of my knapsack my pajamas and toiletries, which I always carried about with me, and made ready for sleep on the floor of the cell as if it was a deluxe hotel. All the other occupants, who slept in their clothes, burst out in laughter, and to this day recall with a smile my snappy but meticulous adaptation. "You'd better start getting used to this," I retorted, "this setup is going to become your second home..." Two days later we were released from custody, and our trial is presently taking place.

★ ★

At this point I anticipated that the inhabitants of Bet Ayin would again go up to their designated spot, according to our original plan, but it transpired that my expectation was unrealistic. Most of the men in the settlement were under arrest or had just been released. They were apprehensive about their economic situation, since they could not count on financial support of the kind assured by kibbutzim to their members who engage in political activities. A few young fellows did try once again to settle the targeted spot, but to no avail.

It was thus that the Achilles' heel of all the operations of 'Zo Artzeinu' became exposed: the inability to persevere in the struggle, to maintain pressure at the very same spot, enabled the establishment to wear us out with their overwhelmingly large numbers. Our strength manifested itself in our ability to split up and thus require the authorities to deal with many fronts simultaneously. But the moment we stood in straight lines and failed to refill the lines following the wearing away of the front lines, it was only a matter of time before we would lose momentum and the struggle would peter out. We failed precisely in this respect in the great operation held a year and a half later, when we blocked off dozens of major highway intersections throughout the country. We thought that the public was sufficiently fired up to come out repeatedly for further engagements of the same sort. But it transpired that those who participated in the initial stage tended to make do with that (especially since police behavior proved that such participation actually endangered one's life and limb). Thus we succeeded in returning to the areas just a few more times, and the operation came to an early end.

We never formed an established organizational apparatus. We were unable to supply practical assistance to the detainees and their families. We did not solicit men of wealth for financial support, nor did we organize for an extended, protracted campaign. This fact proved to be our undoing in the long term, although there were certain operational advantages to having a limited setup and a lack of a bureaucracy.

★ ★

According to the original plan, ten more settlement points were to have been established, among them at Yakir, Ma'aleh Amos, Ma'aleh Adumim, and others. Indeed, during the three weeks of the campaign, there were repeated attempts to carry

(1) *(top)* 'DOUBLING OPERATION' : THE IDF LEFT -- THE SETTLERS RETURNED (to Bat-Ayin)

(2) REMAND OF GUSH ETZION SETTLERS EXTENDED; REFUSED TO UNDERTAKE NOT TO ENTER CLOSED-OFF MILITARY AREA

(3) 'DOUBLING OPERATION' CARRIES ON -- IN DRIVING RAIN 3 MORE OUTPOSTS ERECTED
The area has been declared a 'closed-off military zone'. Senior Security Sources: The settlers are harming our struggle against the terrorists.

out the original scenario, and many encampments were set up and then forcibly evacuated.

There were also attempts by organized supporters in the large cities, and in this battle of opposing elements, it was not yet clear which side would force down the opponent's arm.

POLICE COMMANDER: WE MAY ERECT DETENTION CAMPS FOR SETTLERS
Twenty settlers who participated in the 'Doubling Operation' in Samaria have been arrested

(Photo shows one of them being led to imprisonment.)

Despite the fact that the tiny 'Zo Artzeinu' secretariat functioned with both legs tied and one arm neutralized, despite the fact that it was able to activate only a fraction of all the willing participants before the Yesha Council withdrew its support, and that it carried out its operations without any financial backing, the campaign succeeded in destabilizing the authorities' self-confidence. The heads of the police were already at work planning detention camps for the settlers, an unprecedented step that would have exposed the undemocratic character of the leftist government, and garnered large support for us in public opinion.

The government could not afford, at this sensitive stage, to allow even a single encampment to remain on the spot without evacuating it the very night it was undertaken.

The operation reinforced the original assumption that the authorities' ability to cope with such a phenomenon was quite limited. Also without doubt, had we enjoyed the requisite cooperation and been able to carry out the original plan to establish 130 temporary encampments simultaneously (or even a quarter of that figure...), it would have been impossible to handle the situation, and the operation would have achieved its goals.

In actuality, in this testing of stamina between IDF forces, a jammed imprisonment network and the other muddled government systems, and a handful of settlers trying to do battle both with their government and their own ostensible leadership, the settlers' zeal began to dissolve. The need to deploy depleted numbers of inhabitants in a way that enabled the authorities to deal with them by means of the 'salami' strategy, instead of confrontation on a wide scale with all its advantages, took its toll. The authorities and their agencies wore down the few dissidents struggling against them, and the operation ran out of steam. It is true that the settler public as a whole showed an increasing tendency to side with the activists. Many of them who had been opposed to the operation and followed the line set by the Yesha Council began to have second thoughts, and even gave open expression to the change in their position. The general empathy with the organizers increased. It was clear that someone was finally taking the struggle to heart. But these manifestations of support, and the flow of new adherents, were not enough to sustain those in the forefront of the actual struggle, and the operation began to die down.

Shmuel and I decided to announce a halt in the settlement operation, a halt that would prevent the total crushing of our forces. We intended to engage in a broad campaign of re-mobilizing the settlements that had reneged and renewing the original program in its entirety at a later stage.

Our initial successes canceled the possibility of carrying out surprise steps, but reinforced the basic assumptions and proved that the plan was feasible. Our reputation soared in the various settlements, and the reorganization stood good chances of success.

The decision to call a temporary halt took into account the fact that the activists were exhausted and had begun to lose their enthusiasm. And we too, despite the impressive display of competence, were quite spent. A week later, on the morning of the Feast of Purim, an event occurred that staggered the whole country, wrecked our plans, and prevented us from carrying out further designs.

In those days, Kiryat Arba and neighboring settlements were under the heaviest pressure. The number of killed and wounded increased, while governmental and public backing was given to the opposing camp.

At that time, a young physician, an immigrant from the USA by the name of Baruch Goldstein, was serving as district doctor.

During his lifetime he had became a legend among his neighbors. His total dedication to the health of the area's inhabitants knew no bounds, surpassing by far the call of duty. He befriended every poor and depressed person, dealt with utter devotion with the most sensitive problems of the citizens, and did not give up on even the toughest cases. He regularly worked with retarded children, achieving successes in cases in which other professionals had given up. He exhibited the greatest degree of love and patience when sitting with a retarded child, whom he had picked up somewhere, and drawing pictures with him. Next to his pillow there would always be his cellular phone, which did not stop ringing throughout the night. Goldstein could not suffer losing even one precious instant in the event that a resident was in sudden trouble, and kept himself in readiness even during his sleeping hours.

Every inhabitant knew that if he or she were stuck in the middle of a snowy night in an accident or hurt in an ambush, Baruch would arrive at the scene, and all would be well.

There was hardly anyone who so directly experienced the effects of the bloodletting in Hebron and the failure of security as he was. He was also not the type of individual to draw a line (which is so vital) between his professional anxieties and his private life.

In the small settlements to the south of the Hebron hills, the line of waiting patients in the dispensaries would invariably expand when everyone learned that on that day it was Baruch's turn to appear. "Everybody wanted to be sick and require his attention when they learned that he was due to arrive at the dispensary…, " told me a member of Beit Yatir.

Dr. Goldstein did not content himself with providing medical aid to the Jewish inhabitants; he devoted his special medical skills to the Arabs of the vicinity as well and of course to the IDF soldiers in the district. His professional competence and unrivaled dedication earned official recognition and Kupat Holim awarded him the designation of 'Doctor of the Year'.

Dr. Goldstein had strong roots in the city of Hebron. His family had lived there before the harrowing events of 1929. The calls to "Slaughter the Jews"' (*"Itbach al Yahud"*) which recurred in every corner of the town and at every occasion, reverberated throughout his being, reminding him of what his own family had undergone at the hands of the murderous mobs of Hebron.

A short time before Purim, persistent rumors circulated of impending slaughter by Hebron Arabs of the Jewish residents of the town. These rumors fitted in with the unbridled incitement in the mosques. There was an overall, threatening atmosphere of unsheathed knives.

Should one think that these were hallucinatory imaginings and meaningless bombast emanating from the muezzins, along came the following incident to reinforce the dread of an approaching massacre of the Jews.

On the eve of the holiday, the supreme command of the city held a coordinating session of all those carrying official responsibilities in the district. Dr Goldstein, in his capacity as district medical officer and with a vital function to play in any emergency, was among those present. Others with vital roles to fulfill participated, and it is from them that I learned what went on. The assembled were informed that murderous attacks on the Jewish residents of Hebron were in the offing, assaults on a scale greater than what we had become 'accustomed to'. Dr Goldstein was told to alert the emergency battalion aid station and to report any lack of blood, plasma, and other medical equipment. Dr Goldstein asked the senior officers why they did not declare a general curfew in Hebron, knowing as they did of these intentions. The answer was brutally direct:

"It is impossible – we now have a peace process..."

In Kiryat Arba, the expression coined by Shimon Peres, 'sacrifices for peace', took on a very 'practical' connotation, and Dr Goldstein was the one who daily had to confront the cost of the Oslo adventure. There is no doubt that for Goldstein the response that he got at that meeting was tantamount to a simple and clear announcement of a death sentence imposed on a number of Jews, sacrifices to be offered up on the altar of 'the peace process'.

On the evening of the Purim holiday, Dr Goldstein went down to the Machpela Cave (the tomb of our ancestors) to listen to the reading of the Purim Megillah. A mob of Arabs surged out of the building with cries of *"Itbach al Yahud!"*. The soldiers stationed at the spot just stood there and looked, and when Goldstein asked them why they were not taking any action, they simply shrugged, betokening their lack of authorization.

The selection by lot, described in the Megillah, of the day for the annihilation of the Jews became a very true, vivid reality that evening... It does not require a stretch of the imagination to see how the imminent danger to Jewish survival in Shushan and the rest of the Persian empire, which boomeranged into a reprisal against the enemies of the Jews, became a living reality in the soul of Dr Goldstein. He had just finished the reading of the Megillah, left the Cave of Machpela, saw how the rumors, the army predictions, and the blood-drenched history of the City of the Fathers were being actualized before his very eyes – with no savior forthcoming.

He left no explanation for why he chose the dreadful path of massacre of Moslem worshippers to overturn the threat. Perhaps he thought that any lesser step would fail to lead to the tumultuous disruption that would bring about the necessary general curfew. Perhaps he had become imbued with some mystical notion and chose precisely that spot and that awful method ... no one will ever know.

People who knew Dr Goldstein and who were aware of the situation in Hebron on the eve of that terrible massacre as well as the man's devotion to the welfare of the individual and the public as a whole find it difficult to condemn him wholeheartedly. It is hard to condemn someone who sacrificed his own life in order to save you from impending extinction, even if he had taken such a dreadful step.

I personally had never made his acquaintance, and when I learned the following morning of the murder in the Cave, my instinctive reaction was – a mad killer, a despicable person... My close relations with the local inhabitants have since then made it possible for me to learn the relevant facts that have been systematically concealed by the local media. These facts created an inner conflict in my relation to the man – on the one hand, utter rejection of and revulsion against the murderous deed, and on the other, his wonderful prior professional record.

The authorities refused permission to bury Dr Goldstein in the old Jewish cemetery in the city of Hebron, and he was temporarily laid to rest at the entrance to Kiryat Arba. His temporary burial spot became a permanent grave, and achieved the opposite effect. His separate and prominent burial site became a symbol of Hebron's distress, and attracted people who identified with his deed or felt a moral debt towards him. His personal sacrifice, and the deed that was reminiscent of Biblical episodes, became entwined in mystical motifs, and part of the public began to relate to the grave with the respect reserved for truly holy martyrs.

Goldstein was and has remained for me an unsolved enigma, a profound contradiction between my entire essence as a human being, as a Jew, and the objective conditions in which he found himself.

Was there really no other way? Is it possible that irrelevant messianic stirrings were what had prompted him? Could he not have chosen another step?

On the other hand, what would have happened had he not acted the way he did? After all, he was no sadist who enjoys torturing Arabs. He healed them.

There is no doubt that he was an extremist, and his outlook lacked a certain dimension of depth. He was devoted to his patients to an almost obsessive degree, and perhaps there was something non-human in that uninhibited dedication... It is also evident that he was not one of those martyrs who proclaim themselves messiahs and try to enter the pages of history by committing a mad act. He did not carry out the massacre in the Cave in order to halt the political process. There was no attempt to deflect political currents, which of course he viewed as catastrophic but with which as an individual he never tried to interfere. Dr Goldstein did not intervene in a political process, but rather in a clear and imminent danger affecting the lives of many of the Jews of Hebron.

All right, I shall stop at this point – I am not a psychologist, and actually... I write out of a state of bewilderment ...

One may assume that over the years the violent emotions will subside, and the facts of the case will become public knowledge, making it possible to properly relate to his conduct.

★ ★

Throughout the country and the world at large, the massacre in the Cave was exploited for an unprecedented assault on the settlers. No one remembers the name of the murderer who caused the deaths of the passengers on the bus on Dizengoff Street in Tel Aviv. No one remembers the name of the Arab who murdered the passengers on Bus 18 in Jerusalem, neither the first time nor the second time. No one remembers who committed the murders at Dizengoff Center in Tel Aviv, who killed in Afula, who machine-gunned and who killed furtively. But everyone remembers Baruch Goldstein.

In Gaza, on the other hand, they all remember the most outstanding murderer to come from their midst, but in quite a different manner. The name of Yichye Ayish, the engineer, is well remembered.

In an official ceremony, their leader named one of the main streets of Gaza after him.

The unprecedented self-flagellation that followed Goldstein's nefarious deed was immediately accompanied by widespread condemnation in the Security Council and the entire world. To this very day, four years after the event, Israel has not dropped the issue. Members of the Knesset from the Left demand that Goldstein's corpse be removed to a remote spot, where it will be impossible for anyone to maintain a vigil in his memory. The topic constantly resurfaces in the media, which treats it from every possible angle, while behind all the verbiage, all the relevant facts revealed above are still repressed and concealed.

The massacre in the Cave dealt the image of Israel a grave blow.

The Israeli had always viewed himself as proper, as moral, as one who takes drastic action reluctantly because there is no alternative, the exact opposite of that innate ruthlessness that characterized the other nations and which was so sadistically applied to the Jewish people throughout the generations.

Zionism led to a crack in this image, as it depended primarily on the physical strength of the Jews for the realization of its political objectives. This inevitably created a conflict with the dwellers in the land, so that for the first time in many generations the Jews found themselves in the position of the strong, the dispossessors, who subdue the weak. For this reason, the extreme Left was always antagonistic to the very existence of the Zionist state, viewing it as an exploitative colonialism no different than any other.

At first there was indeed broad rejection of such attitudes, but with the passing of time, and primarily after the Six Day War, the Left, for all practical purposes, adopted the basic principle that Zionism does not express a moral doctrine, but merely an existential one.

In reality, from its very inception, classic Zionism contained within itself this innate flaw. It was not a Zionism of national destiny, but a Zionism of physical existence. The impetus for self-perpetuation has always been dominant, and drives the public much more easily than the ideological pull. The Zionists who began that incredible process of rejuvenating a dead nation and restoring it to its homeland chose the easy path. But there is no doubt that in the flight from contending with the nation's historical destiny there was also a basic desire to avoid an obligatory confrontation with the true significance of Jewish identity.

Zionism therefore erected itself solely on an existential foundation, and even if they spoke of the new Jew being created in Eretz Israel, they did not invest much thought in the matter and assumed that it would eventually work out.

The new Jew, the generation that grew up here, for whom the question of self-preservation ceased to be of paramount concern, found himself in a difficult conflict. The hatred towards him displayed by his neighbors did not decrease, while the moral justification for our presence here was no longer as manifest as it had been.

A broader acceptance of the 'truth' propounded by the other side, as it first found expression in the ranks of the extreme Left, the *Matzpen* organization, has now become characteristic of every leftist, and even every moderate, who prides himself on objectivity.

The Israeli who lacked any ideological basis for living in Eretz Israel did his utmost to lend credence to the theory of self-preservation.

The Israeli must remain a sheep, and shun any identification with the image of the wolf.

The compulsory visits at Yad VeShem, emphasis on the feeling of 'no alternative', unreasonable instructions to soldiers serving in densely occupied Arab areas, readiness to hand over to the Arabs any area considered meaningless in terms of security needs, basing our entire existence in this land solely on security concerns – all these were designed to maintain that image of a sheep and the simplest moral justification, free of crucial questions.

For a sheep must always be right – so note to what degree we behave like sheep.

But then Baruch Goldstein arrived on the scene, behaved like a real non-Jew, without any inhibitions, while prayers were being conducted, from behind... and with one stroke toppled that tower of cards, demolished that sheep image which we had tried so hard to develop and upon which we leaned.

The fundamental basis of the existence of the State of Israel, existential Zionism, was grievously undermined. It could not digest this, it could not forget, it could not forgive.

But it was not the slaughter of innocents that really upset the Israelis. They care for the Arabs as they care for the snows of yester-year, and their widespread public self-flagellation is out of all proportion to the reaction of other nations to a crime committed by one individual. It is imperative that we recover the image of a sheep amongst seventy wolves; otherwise, by what right are we here?

★★

The apologetic self-censure, the flood of hatred that burst forth from all strata of the Left, the establishment of a committee of inquiry covered by live media reportage, all these created an atmosphere which prevented any possibility of a re-enlistment of the settlers, and an extension of the campaign of 'doubling settlements'. Our target public dug itself deeply in defensive positions vis-a-vis the vehement assault, and no one contemplated baring himself in a renewed struggle at that time.

Our private financial resources had meanwhile dwindled. Shmuel and I simply had to get back to work and support our families.

Thus, with heavy heart over the missed opportunity, we shut down the central headquarters, with the feeling that we had done our share, and with the determination that never, *never*, would we again knock our heads against this stone wall.

It would seem that a great deal of effort had gone down the drain wastefully. But in actuality we had acquired a reputation which was not erased, and which a year and a half later enabled us to return, and on a large scale.

And there was yet another 'small' profit achieved by the 'doubling operation'.

The spirit and the enthusiasm kindled in the hearts of the settlers and the realization that one can take matters into one's own hands led in some places to an independently and quietly executed continuation of the campaign. Unclaimed public lands and strategic points were settled and developed.

The new places turned into flourishing neighborhoods, and Shmuel and I are periodically invited by the settlers to celebrate the 'birthday' of the campaign which led to this unauthorized development.

★★★

Tzippy's Cookies

Chapter 7

"Where did you usually meet?" asked the prosecutor.

"We always met at Moshe's house," answered Shmuel Sackett calmly in the heavily American-accented Hebrew that never failed to reveal that he was a fairly recent newcomer to Israel.

The prosecutor sensed that he was about to take hold of the tail of a big fish. Number Two in the organization had just implied the existence of an 'underground hierarchy'. Moving in for the kill, he asked the next leading question:

"And why did you always meet at Moshe's house?"

"Because Moshe's wife Tzippy baked much better cookies than my wife," answered Shmuel with characteristic openness.

The judges were unable to resist joining in the laughter that engulfed the courtroom, to the dismay of the prosecutor. For a moment, the seriousness of the situation was forgotten. Shmuel's frank answer had revealed the real reason for the choice of our home for the meetings of what the government and media believed to be the 'terrorist organization', which was to bring the country to a halt in Israel's first experience of the democratic tool known as nonviolent civil disobedience.

> R. Yochanan said, "Jerusalem was destroyed only because they gave judgments therein in accordance with Biblical law," i.e., they based their judgments strictly upon Biblical law, and did not go beyond the requirements of the law.
>
> (Bava Metzi'a 30:)

> Good men must not obey the laws too well.
> – Emerson

R. Yochanan and Emerson, who lived seventeen centuries apart, both enunciated the necessity of viewing the law in proper perspective, for otherwise it might, for all its importance, turn into a legitimate tool in the service of arbitrariness, callousness and cruelty.

The question of the limits of obedience became a topic of discussion and debate during the previous Likud administrations, a long time before the appearance of 'Zo Artzeinu', when the Left found itself, for the first time, under a government whose policies were not to its liking. Leftist academics, pundits, commentators and politicians had argued the pros and cons of civil disobedience and, by and large, concluded that it was a legitimate form of expression within the bounds of democracy. However, theory was one thing, and getting the masses to put it into practice was another. The most that was accomplished was that groups like *'Yesh Gvul'* were able to get a few individuals to refuse to serve in the army altogether or to refuse to serve specifically in Yesha areas. Their effect was negligible, perhaps because these movements did not represent the deep feelings of the nation, and so remained no more than insignificant brooks alongside the main stream.

On the other hand, Shmuel and I did not need longwinded debates in order to understand something obvious to every thinking person. It is self-evident that there are limits to obedience; otherwise a government can use its authority and power to interpret and enforce laws in an evil manner. The question, therefore, is not whether there is a limit beyond which disobedience is the moral imperative. The real question is where that line must be drawn, and in the event that it must be crossed, how this can be done without undermining the foundations of the society. To us, it was apparent that the government had already gone beyond the point at which obedience was required. We felt that the basic principles upon which the entire vision of Zionism was based had been totally shattered, that the policies of the Rabin government were bringing Israel to the brink of a catastrophe that could result in the destruction of the state. Consequently, our discussions concerned the operational aspects of organized disobedience rather than theoretical discussions of morality. In retrospect, it became clear to us that the fundamental principles which had been shattered had not really been considered fundamental principles of the Israeli judicial system.

How then were we to violate the law without 'throwing out the baby with the bath water'? That is, how could we avoid a state of anarchy?

We established several guidelines which were never to be violated:
First, there was never to be any violence of any sort, neither physical nor verbal. Second, we would always take steps to minimize any danger to ourselves and others that could possibly result from our actions. This included participants, bystanders, and even the police, who we knew would be used against us. Third, we had to be fully prepared to accept the legal consequences of our actions. This acceptance was very important, since it meant that we respect the law and do not try to evade it; on the contrary, we meekly accept responsibility for the results of our actions in light of the law which we have breached. A rebel is punished for his deeds in the event of failure, while anyone engaging in civil disobedience will be punished in any case – even if the government should change hands (as did indeed occur in our case).

Within the constraints of these guidelines, all was fair and proper in the attainment of our objectives. We were propelled by a painful sense of existential danger, and thus did not stop to weigh the precise legal implications of every word.

Undoubtedly, we would be easy prey for the attorney-general, but we felt that the urgency of the hour did not allow time for all the legal niceties that could have prevented some of our subsequent problems. Words and statements that could have been, and later were, interpreted as calls for insurrection did appear in our publications.

The few interviews that were held with newsmen invariably began with the question, "Are you planning to break the law?" This question, which was always raised in amazement as if we were preparing to profane some ineffably holy entity, is indicative of the ambivalent Israeli attitude toward the law. On the one hand, there is no other democracy in the world in which the law is treated with such disdain as in Israel. On the other hand, no one would ever dare to proclaim such an attitude in so many words in public. When the head of a labor union is asked whether the law will be violated in a labor dispute over wages or against the dismissal of workers, the answer is invariably a self-righteous and shocked "No, of course not!!". And the next scene will be this same person leading his workers in traffic stoppages, tire burnings, locking the plant manager into his office, and/or destroying the furniture in the board of directors' meeting room.

The world's established democracies recognize that there are situations justifying a formal breaching of the law. Norms of conduct in such cases have become part of the foundations of modern democracy.

When disobedience to the law is committed by one individual, it is generally recognized as ideologically based and is called 'conscientious objection'. When the same behavior is followed by an entire group of individuals, it is termed 'respectful civil non-compliance'. Unfortunately, the commonly used Israeli translation 'non-violent civil revolt' has a much harsher and misleading connotation.

Massive civil disobedience carries a much greater message than individual refusal to comply with the rules. The very fact that large groups can no longer tolerate the wrongdoings of the authorities and are prepared to passively violate the law while accepting the consequences of such action is indicative of an extreme wrong into which an insensitive government has led its citizenry. The larger the number of protesters, the less the authorities can claim that only a marginal group is involved. The response of a government to mass protest is one of the true tests of a democracy. The average individual is not inherently disposed to violate the law, but rather to concern himself with normal pursuits, with his family and with earning his livelihood. The ordinary individual inherently wishes to be led by a leadership of his choosing and to obey it. Obedience to authority is an innate instinct in most humans, and breaking this discipline is, to a large degree, unnatural. A mass of normal citizens who take to the streets to protest in a controlled manner (in contrast to an unruly mob), and are prepared to pay the price for their readiness to transgress the strict letter of the law, should serve as a red light to a government, a red light declaring with glaring intensity: You have violated the rules of the game: not the formal rules, but the most fundamental ones, the basic underpinnings upon which the national fabric rests.

A government that ignores such a protest, even if the law is on its side, cannot boast that it is a 'democracy'.

One of the features that characterized the struggle of 'Zo Artzeinu' was the composition of the public that went forth into the streets, and not just the fact that this phenomenon was new to the country. The participants were primarily intellectuals, academics, businessmen, students, and heads of large families, in short, not a sector of the population that typically goes out on protests.

The function of a mass demonstration is to communicate a point of view, to arouse enthusiasm and group cohesiveness among the protesters, to attract others to join, and to impress upon the public and the authorities the point advocated by the protesters, the urgency of their demand, and the power and popularity behind it. A government disregards these messages at its own risk.

The participants in the civil disobedience activities that took place in Europe and the United States in recent decades were mainly blacks (mostly unemployed) or students who were not saddled with family obligations. True, at their head stood idealistic ideologues who sacrificed a great deal for their convictions, but the 'human milieu' consisted of an ever-ready public easily activated. Such was not the case with 'Zo Artzeinu'. The scores of thousands who actually took part in its activities represented a huge majority that normally refrained from physical participation in stormy events.

The initial response of the Rabin government was to ignore the protest movement. When it became apparent that it was wider than originally thought and was gaining support, the government switched to a policy of brutality. Violence, in violation of the law, against non-resisting demonstrators (often with tied hands demonstratively held above their heads to demonstrate passivity) became a distinctive feature of the protests. The government failed the test of democracy posed by the 'Zo Artzeinu' demonstrations.

In the United States, the fifteenth of January is an official holiday. It is the birthday of Reverend Martin Luther King. Reverend King changed the history of the United States and became a hero, by breaking the law and thus moving blacks toward achievement of equal rights under the law. On this day, Americans take a break from work to acknowledge the achievement of this 'law-breaker'. By honoring this martyred figure, Americans officially recognize that there are limits to the law, that the law is not an end in itself, but rather a tool for the achievement of the goals of a society in an orderly manner. And, perhaps surprisingly, Americans are more law-abiding than Israelis are; drivers do not turn the highways into arenas where the strongest and most aggressive survive, labor unions do not arbitrarily close down factories, and tax evasion is not perceived as a legitimate national pastime.

The drawing of a clear demarcation between the obligation to maintain law and order and the rare but mandatory imperative to break the law in certain circumstances actually strengthens both principles. A study of the history of the western democracies shows that every instance of civil disobedience served to advance that nation toward the complete realization of the ideals upon which it was founded, and decreased or eliminated defects and injustices. Civil disobedience has served as a balancing tool of inestimable value against arbitrariness by the authorities. Every basically healthy society that has experienced civil disobedience has emerged stronger and more just. It has never led to anarchy. Conversely, dictatorships (or 'dicto-democracies' like the Rabin government), which do not allow this kind of public expression, become more repressive; eventually such states burst out into rebellion, with consequences that cannot be predicted beforehand. The desire of the governing classes (both Right and Left) to raise the rule of law to the level of a moral imperative which justifies all steps, quite a natural inclination for those entrusted with the reins of government and the power to enact the laws, results in the reality that Israel is not characterized by a respectful attitude towards either the law or morality. The public in Israel does not share the German trait of total obeisance; the sons of Abraham are incapable of blind adherence, and the Jewish head is adept at figuring out ways to sidestep the law:

The law is inviolate – that is, until the microphones and cameras are removed...

Suddenly, into this ambience, a new and unfamiliar phenomenon emerged: rank-and-file citizens publicly declared that they were ready and willing to break the law. Public curiosity was aroused, while political opponents immediately branded them as hooligans, ruffians, criminals, and barbarians.

On a Friday in June 1995 (*Tammuz*, 5755), I invited Shmuel to my house for a serious conversation over coffee and cookies, freshly baked for the Sabbath by Tzippy. After so many long days and nights of intensive activity, we understood each other perfectly, and there was no need to waste words. The year that had elapsed from the time of the 'doubling operation' left us both quite frustrated. The feeling that the Oslo catastrophe might be averted if only a proper leadership led the struggle continued to throb in us all that year. We had both devoted the previous year to improving our neglected family financial positions, and we were both determined not to act any more as Don Quixotes, but our resolution was wavering. We could not shake off our awareness of the wretched reality that was getting constantly more acute before our very eyes, and the realization that we had once already succeeded in inducing a large public to take action. On the other hand, one year earlier, we were convinced that increasing Jewish settlement would bring the negotiations with Arafat to an end, but now we were not sure. The Israeli government was working so closely with the PLO that a telephone call from Rabin to Arafat was enough to assuage the terrorist leader's worries about settlement.

As Shmuel munched quietly on his cookie, I tried to paint a picture of the situation. There is no one, I explained, who is doing what has to be done. We have a certain ability to organize and inspire others to take the needed action. Consequently, we are left with no choice other than to go ahead and do what we can. You know the saying: "Where there are no men..."

Shmuel did not need to be convinced and his only comment, after pausing to finish the cookie, was "Too bad we waited so long. What do you have in mind?"

"I think that we should expand and develop the idea that we had last year.

"This time we must forget about trying to cause Arafat to break off negotiations, since it is already too late for that. This time the pressure must be put directly on our government, from both sides of the Green Line. The demonstrative activities on the hills of Samaria must become merely one part of a nationwide campaign that should involve every citizen of the State and thus undermine the legitimacy of the government's policies. This time we must learn from our previous mistakes and not give the impression that it is only a settler issue. And most important of all, we must not turn to any political factors, we must not coordinate matters with any establishment group, we must not depend on any political body. Involvement with Members of the Knesset is out."

"Okay," said Shmuel, "what exactly do we do?"

"There is no point in trying to establish new settlements. In the year that has elapsed since the 'doubling operation', relations with Arafat have become so much firmer that the government can ask Arafat to simply ignore our provocative activities, thus enabling them to deal with us discreetly, far from the prying eyes of the media. In order to create a situation where the government can neither ignore us nor keep others from being aware of our activities, we must try to establish something other than settlements which, as the Prime Minister said, "don't move" him. A better idea would be to set up prominent outposts, to take over the positions that the army was abandoning and establish new outposts, particularly along the main highways in Yesha, to ensure the safety of those using the roads. This would give the residents some feeling of security and, at the same time, signal a challenge to the process of withdrawal. The government would have to remove us, and the public would be aroused... It is most important that it should not be possible to label the problem as one affecting only the settlers (the 'two percent', 'the propellers', who do not warrant the same degree of security – as Yitzchak Rabin put it). So we have to initiate a widespread campaign on the inner side of the Green Line, an action that will turn our demonstration into a national one. Supportive demonstrators should go into the streets at exactly the same time that we take over outposts, and block traffic at key junctions throughout the land for two hours. Then, if we hold out at our positions, there can be shifts of replacements by having people come out to join us from the other side of the Green Line, and it will no longer be possible to ignore the urgency of the problem."

Shmuel, whose personality combines a healthy dose of faith, practicality and good humor, smiled. "It sounds rather grandiose and ambitious – but the country is on the road to ruin anyway, so what can we lose."

As I write these lines and recall that meeting, I still wonder where we got the nerve to even think that two young non-conformist punks, with no real experience, with families to support, no sources of funds and no help from any organization, could pull off a stunt that no one else had even tried. It was a combination of a number of factors: an awareness of the lack of any alternative course of action, a conviction that there was a silent majority out there waiting to be called to the flag, faith in our leadership ability, a remarkable naiveté, and above all – the guiding Hand of Providence.

Shmuel then suggested a characteristic move. "Let's start keeping a diary of what's happening." The previous year, during the 'doubling operation', everything was geared to take place on a particular date that was to be determined by the Yesha Council, which had given us the impression that they would lend us their full support. Everything depended on them and, to our chagrin, they did everything possible to cause us to fail. This time, we decided to choose a date ourselves and make all the necessary preparations without relying on anyone.

It was an invigorating feeling to free ourselves from the restraints imposed upon us by self-interested bodies. It meant that we could decide and act swiftly without being encumbered by committees or organizations whose intentions might not be the same as ours.

So now it was again time to make our intentions known to the public.

We were aware of the need to engage in a very intensive information campaign. However, with almost no funding, this was an almost impossible task, unless, of course, we could get the media to provide us free publicity willy-nilly.

From previous experience, we knew that the key to success would be holding an impressive mass meeting that could create general enthusiasm and show the public that there were leaders they could depend upon. In view of the public's deep frustration and despair, a successful convention would set off waves of response that would quickly spread. We opened a diary and searched for an appropriate date and place. The choice of venue was simple enough: The Eshel Hotel in Ariel. We were familiar with this location from our previous experience in the 'doubling operation'. It was fairly easy to reach from all over the country and, in addition, the symbolism of its being located in Samaria would add a certain flavor, while the rental cost was within our limited means. The choice of date was somewhat more difficult but we finally decided on the first day of the month of *Av*, 5755 (July 26,1995). This was a Friday, when interested people would normally be available, and the meeting could be held early, when everyone was still fresh, rather than at the end of a long workday. And the beginning of the Jewish month, which is a special date in itself, would also be meaningful.

After choosing the conference date, we turned our attention to the date of the actual planned action. We estimated that if the meeting was a success, the activists would then require two weeks to get organized. We initially selected Monday, the 11th of *Av*, 5755 (August 7, 1995). But then we learned that the rabbi of our community would be celebrating his son's Bar Mitzva on that date in Jerusalem. We figured that blocking the roads while our own rabbi and his guests were trying to get to Jerusalem for a festivity would not make us very popular with our own community. So we pushed it forward by one day to Tuesday, the 12th of *Av* (August 8).

We had only three weeks till the conference, so we began working feverishly. We decided that everyone who attended the assembly would leave with a complete kit of detailed instructions and the commitment to spread the word among all their friends who could not make it to the convention. Shmuel and I divided the work between us. I planned the details of the campaign, wrote the instructions and arranged all the material that was to go into the kits. Shmuel took care of the technicalities of organization and administration.

The kit was quite simple, and had two goals. First, to enable anyone interested to quickly join up. Second, to impress upon the participants, by the organization and format of the information, that they were dealing with dependable persons who knew what they were doing. The material could have been compressed into a mere three pages, but that would not give the proper impression. I therefore created a detailed brochure with relevant attachments that described all the possible scenarios and how they should be handled. It included an introductory chapter reviewing the political situation in which we now found ourselves, a detailed description of the planned activities and a number of attachments relating to the selection of the locations of the outposts, proper behavior vis-a-vis the forces of law-and-order, what to do if arrested, how to behave during interrogation, and all the other eventualities that our experience taught us could be encountered.

Our basic assumption was that we essentially represented the majority of the electorate. Civil disobedience is not an activity that a small radical group can engage in. Fringe groups of the political Left or Right such as *Kahane Chai* and *Gush Shalom* would not think of calling for civil disobedience because they know that they do not have a large following and would only make fools of themselves if they did so. We were prepared to go into the streets because we believed that we really represented the people, and that success would depend on capability for leadership and organization, and not on the basic agreement of most of the public, which was already assured. Since there was no point in wasting effort on preaching to the converted, we devoted relatively little space in the kit material to background ideological presentations. Our main emphasis was on a clear description of the nature and conduct of the campaign.

The main focus of the campaign was the establishment of outposts throughout the area. Most of the kit dealt with how the various spots were to be chosen, how to take hold, and the like. This time we did not intend to declare that our objective was to establish new settlements, as we had done in the 'doubling operation'. We had learned from bitter experience that all the elements required for establishing settlements were not available, so we were making do with 'outposts'.

Instead of searching for out-of-the way sites from which the authorities would have difficulty removing us, we looked for prominent areas along the main roads. We wanted the authorities to reach us without difficulty and, indeed, to remove us. We wanted to establish non-violent points of friction that would attract media attention. The idea was not to set up a new *yishuv*, but to settle demonstratively along the main roads in a way that would attract the attention of all passing motorists. We wanted to be a thorn in the side of the government, a thorn that would be an insufferable irritation. To ensure success, we concentrated on the choice of locations, the selection of small groups to occupy them, the preparation of other small groups to take over when the first had been removed, and the security of the active participants. Locations were therefore chosen that were neither adjacent to nor unnecessarily close to Arab villages, and instructions for safety and for maintenance of contact with nearby Jewish communities were provided.

★ ★

Actually, what we were trying to do (unsuccessfully) was to employ settlement tactics different from those used previously by the Gush Emunim settlement movement. We did not aim at having large groups of people going out to the various destinations, only to be evacuated time and again, until they finally gave up. We preferred small groups of no more than five people with a minimum of equipment who, if removed from one place, could rapidly relocate to another. We counted on flexibility combined with the support from the 130 existing settlements. However, in practice, matters did not turn out as we had anticipated.

Originally, the function of the city dwellers was to draw attention to the overall settlement campaign, but what really happened was that the blocking of the intersections attracted a tremendous amount of attention, while the 'outpost operation' fizzled out within a few days. The participants in the outpost actions were dazzled and enthused by the media reports regarding what was taking place in the main cities, and rushed up to the outposts in great numbers, instead of in the small numbers that we had planned. As in previous settlement attempts, building materials and additional equipment were brought up, but after they were all removed from the sites by the army, the activists lost the will to repeat the venture.

Everyone, including the government and the 'Zo Artzeinu' people, was overwhelmed by the successful blocking of the intersections. This success drew attention away from the failure of the 'outpost operation', and led us on a path somewhat different from the original one.

We realized that the convention hall in Ariel had to be full to overflowing in order to succeed. Actually, the number of supporters was not crucial for the execution of the program, but we understood that a fully attended rally would leave the strongest impression on those present. In order to move people to action, hope of success must be planted in their hearts. We were the nucleus of the struggle, and those coming to the meeting would be exposed to us and inspired by our determination. But the 99% of the public whom we hoped to bring out into the streets would be exposed to our message only through second-rank or third-rank go-betweens, and this meant that the impression taken home by those participating in the convention would be crucial. We could not afford the necessary publicity that would have determined exactly how the message would be transmitted, nor did we enjoy the support of any orderly distribution setup to deal with notification of the planned meeting. We could only do our best and hope that the word would spread and bring the hoped-for results.

It turned out that our methods worked better than expected; the success of the meeting at Ariel created a wave of self-fulfilling rumors.

In order to publicize the launching of the campaign and the preliminary convention, we had to set up a broad communications network as quickly as possible. In order to maintain our firm non-establishment image, we did not want to make use of the establishment and the available means of information disposal. We did not turn to any of the local mayors, heads of councils, or anyone who acted in an official capacity or received a salary from any governmental agency. We employed a simple method: we contacted persons all over the country, using the lists that had been drawn up during the 'doubling operation' as a base, and adding names that we knew or were recommended.

The method used for the major cities and larger urban areas was somewhat different. At that time, there were already many local ad hoc groups involved in protests, so that there was some rudimentary form of infrastructure that could serve as a basis. We made contact with them and the response was quite encouraging. Within a short time, we had a long list of active supporters who were willing and eager to do the fieldwork. These people did not 'belong' to 'Zo Artzeinu' (since there really was no such thing as 'belonging to Zo Artzeinu'). They were ordinary citizens who were seeking ways to protest the disastrous actions of the Rabin government. These people were depressed by the way that their protest actions had been totally ignored during the previous three years that preceded the founding of 'Zo Artzeinu'. They were looking desperately for some way of expressing their objection to the path taken by the government. These were worried citizens who, for several years, had stood at intersections, with dignity and restraint, holding signs and handing out literature. They had already logged hundreds of hours at the major intersections, generally taking up their positions on Fridays and Saturday nights. Ordinarily, they protested in small groups, except when a particular occurrence, such as a terrorist attack, would bring temporary reinforcements. The news media, which completely ignored them, prevented the general public from learning of their determined opposition, thus creating deep frustration and almost unbearable anguish.

Into this pressure cooker, 'Zo Artzeinu' made its entrance. The overwhelming majority of local protest groups greeted our program with undisguised enthusiasm. Some accepted all the parts of our program; others accepted certain elements, while some accepted none. This latter, very small group later admitted its error but, at any rate, we were not ready to waste precious time on fruitless arguments with those who differed from us. Time was short, and we figured that initial success would persuade the doubters that our path was the right one under the circumstances.

We did everything that time and strength would allow to ensure that the meeting would be a success. In each community where we had a contact, parlor meetings were arranged. Every evening, after our normal day's work, we went to these meetings and returned late at night. Some of these meetings were very successful and well attended. At other times, I would travel many hours only to find myself in an empty room, with only the bored local contact, who had turned out to be a good talker but a poor organizer. But the very fact that both Shmuel and I were running around made waves, and helped spread the word, which shows that the mere expenditure of energy can sometimes be indirectly effective.

The nucleus of the operation was to be the communities in Yesha, which would actually set up the outposts. The demonstrations in the large urban areas would provide the public platform from which the grave emergency facing the nation would be broadcast. We were now faced with a delicate psychological problem. The activists in the cities were unwilling to take action unless they were sure that the people in Yesha would carry out their obligations and actually go out and set up the roadside outposts. The Yesha people, on the other hand, had just the opposite fear. They wanted to be sure that demonstrations would take place in the cities simultaneously with their roadside activities. We had to convince each side that the other was ready to take action and was just 'waiting for you'. We did not distort the truth, but we were forced into a situation wherein we told the truth to each side, but not quite the whole truth. We were able to give each side the feeling that a well-oiled, smooth operation would take place and each one only had to do his part. Each person was made to feel that his individual role in the orchestra was important and that he must perform it properly and at the right time.

In addition to the other preparations, we decided to invest some of our limited funds in radio advertising. We asked persons whose voices were popularly recognized to make short announcements to be broadcast on Channel 7. The first one to agree was Rabbi Benny Elon, who had made a name for himself as an activist in all the causes that we identified with. The second was Adir Zik, a well-known radio personality whose program on Channel 7 had a huge following and gave expression to the feelings of frustration pervasive at that time. Our brief acquaintance has since flowered into a deep friendship.

The support expressed by Rabbi Benny Elon for a pair of controversial activists and his public identification with them was very meaningful and added respectability and credibility to our plans. Rabbi Elon was, among his other accomplishments, the head of a yeshiva in Jerusalem and a well-known and respected figure. At that time he was already in public disagreement with the Yesha Council as well as with the National Religious Party (NRP) and had some personal problems with the NRP's Hanan Porat concerning his yeshiva. It is true that his ongoing public controversies made it somewhat simpler for him to add an additional one with relative ease. Nonetheless, it took a measure of public courage to take such a decision. He was a welcome and important addition to our ranks, partly because he had special appeal to the religious public, who naturally sought rabbinical approval for their activities.

The continuous radio promotion by Channel 7, together with our efforts to visit as many communities as physically possible, created an atmosphere of expectation. The tension we felt, as the date of the assembly approached was much more intense than any we had experienced before any of our previous operations. This was because the meeting was not only the beginning of our most ambitious campaign, but also because this would be the first opportunity we had to actually meet the potential activists who would have to carry the burden of the upcoming demonstrations. We realized that we would be subjected to intense public scrutiny and any serious mistake could be fatal to the entire operation.

The Yesha Council and the NRP gave us the cold shoulder, but at least this time their antagonism was not accompanied by a frontal attack upon us, as had occurred the previous year during the 'doubling operation'. There were two reasons for this difference. First, the Yesha Council was convinced that we would fail, and it did not wish to be accused of hampering our activities. Second, after three years in which it had blocked effective action against the Rabin government, its ability to do any real damage had become extremely limited.

We avoided any contact with the Yesha Council that would make us dependent on them, which is what had happened the previous time. We were in the process of establishing our own reputation and credibility in the eyes of the public and we expected to rise or fall on our own ability and merit. To my surprise, shortly before the assembly, one of the heads of a local council, a person with whom I had established a friendly relationship, contacted me and asked to meet with me as the official representative of Yesha. We met and, among other things, he implied that we would get the support of the Yesha Council if we met certain conditions. I politely explained that we welcomed any person or organization that wished to join us unconditionally, but we would not enter into negotiations on terms. Apparently there were voices in the Yesha Council for and against our new initiative. Later, the members who supported our move were outweighed by the opposition, and their initiative tapered off.

As the date of the convention approached, our preparations became more frenzied. Many of our neighbors in Karnei Shomron volunteered their active support, some by making calls, others by operating computers, organizing, preparing the logistic support. We divided up our lists so that each volunteer was responsible for contact with five activists. All instructions and announcements were given to each volunteer for distribution to his five activists. In addition, we obtained the telephone numbers of all those activists who had fax machines, and all correspondence was sent to them automatically by a program donated by one of our neighbors. All activity was strictly voluntary. All the participants donated their free time and their telephone lines without a murmur.

A day before the assembly, Shmuel and I went to Ariel to make the final arrangements. We were not going to leave anything to chance. The route to be followed by each registrant was checked and redesigned until it was exactly what we wanted. Every participant would pass along a number of stations at which he would fill out a registration form. These forms would be available on many stands near the entrance, so that no bottlenecks would be formed. Everyone completing a form would hand it in and receive a kit in which there were various informational handouts as well as a form that would permit contributions to be made by standing bank orders. The registration forms included a tear-off slip that our volunteer would stamp and return to the participant so that it could be used as an entrance ticket to the meeting hall. In this way we ensured that we would have information on each participant and would know who had actually attended. Ushers were stationed at all the entrances to make certain that only those who had registered could enter.

There were also stands located at various points at which there were shirts emblazoned with the slogan "*I am ready to be arrested for my Homeland – because this is our land*" on the front, and the symbol of 'Zo Artzeinu' on the back. We had invested a lot of thought in designing the motto. It included a map of Eretz Yisrael, a menorah (for both the Zionist and Jewish association) and the words 'Zo Artzeinu'. I did not trace any borders on the map, in order to circumvent arguments on that controversial issue. We were a small group seeking a broad consensus and maximum participation, so it would serve no purpose to get involved in ideological arguments.

The evening before the meeting, we assembled all the volunteers in the local air raid shelter. I presented a short review of what we were trying to achieve and Shmuel dealt with the pragmatic details and the assignments of each individual. Women carried out a large share of the work. My former personal secretary, Leah Kahanowitz, took over the role of secretary of the movement. Ayala Grosser, a talented computer specialist, dealt with organization, management and communication with the various communities.

Our neighbors' children worked till late at night folding handouts and preparing the kits. At this point I began to worry that the General Security Services (GSS) or the police might raid us, confiscate all our material and arrest us, even before the convention took place. We had made no secret of our intentions, so it was obvious that the security services knew what we were planning, when, and where. It was logical that they would try to stop us even before we got started.

In retrospect, it appears that the Rabin government had fallen victim to its own fabrications, and did not believe that these 'propellers' could possibly do any serious damage. The government was convinced that, at the most, a mere 2 percent of the population was represented by 'Zo Artzeinu' and very few would actively participate or support demonstrations. They were so convinced that they did not bother to seriously follow our activities and there apparently were no undercover agents at the first assembly, which dealt with the blocking of the roads. I am convinced of this because undercover agents were present at all of our later meetings. However, at this early stage we were not sure what to expect, so we took precautions. The cartons containing the kits were hidden at a neighbor's house, and the next day we brought them to the meeting place only after we ascertained that the coast was clear and that they had not prepared 'a royal welcome' on the way to Ariel.

That was the only time we took such preventive action, since civil disobedience, as we understood it, meant that all our actions were in the open. However, at this critical beginning point we could not take chances, since the entire campaign would grind to a halt if the convention did not take place as planned. Once the public became aware of our existence and activities, there was no longer any need for such circumspection, although the attorney general, Michael Ben Yair, saw to it that the newspapers carried banner headlines saying that he intended opening an investigation of our activities on suspicion of sedition. Much later, our homes were indeed searched by the police, and much of our material was confiscated, but despite the fact that all our assemblies were flooded with police detectives, we totally ignored their presence.

We began receiving some indication that people were planning to attend, but we had no real way of estimating or predicting. I asked Shmuel what he thought and his laconic answer was "Either the place will be overflowing – or no one will be there." On Friday morning we arrived at the designated place. Shmuel was there before me, making final arrangements and assignments. A trickle of people began to arrive, many of whom seemed to be there out of curiosity. Then, the place began to fill up rapidly. Within a short time, the first piles of shirts were sold out and the handouts had to be replenished. Despite the growing crowd and pressure, everything remained orderly and quiet, a rather exceptional situation. It was obvious that the arrangements made an impression on the participants. They entered the main auditorium, took their seats and began reading the distributed material.

This was the first time that we met many of the activists, and they also had an opportunity to become acquainted with each other. The majority came from the large cities and towns; few were from the settlements over the Green Line. New faces, religious and secular, rabbis, professors, pensioners, farmers, grandparents and young people, a solid cross-section of the population. It is appalling how the media were later to stigmatize this charming group in devastating terms. We knew a number of these people from our previous activities and we respected their opinions. Among them were Prof. Pinchas Heiman of Ra'anana and other academicians from the Weizmann Institute and Jerusalem. The auditorium was soon completely filled and the overflow crowd reached into the corridors. We kept a tight schedule. We did not adorn the stage with well-known personalities, because we wanted this assembly to have the single goal of planning concrete action. This crowd was tired of speeches from politicians and others who were capable of fancy slogans and speeches but very short on action. Shmuel, acting as master of ceremonies, made a few opening remarks and was followed by Rabbi Benny Elon, who presented a short *dvar torah*. Rabbi Elon also sat at the head table on the stage with us. I was actually the only scheduled speaker.

To a round of applause, Shmuel introduced me as the Chairman of 'Zo Artzeinu'. Up to that point, we had never discussed official positions nor made appointments. Suddenly, before the large audience, I was appointed chairman of an undefined organization. I got up to speak. Although I was nervous and tense, I managed to project an image of confidence and self-assurance.

I presented a short review of the position in which we found ourselves. I said: "This time, in contrast to all the previous times, we are going to be really successful. I am happy to see all these wonderful people who came here today. I am also just as pleased to note those that did not come." This was greeted with looks of puzzlement, so I explained. "Do you see any Members of Knesset here? Council Heads? Politicians looking to make the headlines? Those of you who came did so because you feel the pain of the terrible political situation that we are in and are ready to sacrifice personal convenience in an attempt to save what remains to be saved."

This was exactly what this audience wanted to hear. People had given up on the established organizations and parties and no longer expected that salvation would come from their direction. But since people naturally seek leadership, we had to shoulder responsibility and create an independent base of authority. From the very first, it was important to me to emphasize our being totally independent and free of any connection with any established group. If this key message remained obscure and it could be presumed that the source of authority lay with the Yesha Council or one of the political bodies on the Right, we might indeed have scored a degree of legitimatization in the short term, but very soon the whole project would blow up in our faces, as happened the first time around. My very first remarks were therefore quite succinct, and risked raising the ire of members of the audience, which might lead to the convention's veering from its stated goal.

I took this calculated risk, and was proved right. Later, shortly before the start of the actual campaign, certain groups on the political Right and in the Yesha Council did indeed come out against us – but to no avail. The vast majority of the public paid them no heed, and carried out our plans to perfection.

After my introductory words, I turned to the details of the planned protest. Sipping occasionally from a glass of water, I explained the purpose of the demonstration, and what each person was expected to do. I described various possible scenarios and how they should be handled. I took out the contents of the kit and explained each item. The audience paid close attention and I could see many of them taking notes (with the pencils that we had provided in the kits). I gradually became more relaxed and spoke as though I were sitting with a few friends, rather than on a stage in front of a thousand people. The performance was more like a learned discourse in a university course before attentive and conscientious students than the launching of a serious step in a campaign of civil disobedience.

When I finished, Shmuel arose and made a few humorous remarks at my expense. "Luckily, Moshe ran out of water, otherwise he would keep talking and we would not make it home in time for Shabbat!" The audience responded with laughter that served also to break some of the seriousness and tension. It was clear that we were on the right track. Obviously, the next step was to field questions, but we were wary of doing so. Too many meetings have gone out of control because of questions that turn into speeches, disagreements among the audience, shouting, and all kinds of reactions that could undo the whole effort, turning an effective, purposeful assembly into a tiring symposium. We could not afford to take such a risk, but neither could we conclude the convention on a 'dictatorial' note.

We had foreseen this eventuality and had hit upon a novel technique, which proved quite successful.

"We have been traveling around the country for two weeks", declared Shmuel. "I think we have heard every possible question, so we will do the following. We will present and respond to the ten most frequently asked questions. Others can be asked after the formal adjournment." With this, Shmuel motioned to Ayala Grosser, who joined us on the stage. Ayala presented the questions alternately to Shmuel and me, and we responded. It was extremely successful. I would note further that Ayala's appearance together with us added to the effect. Here was a housewife and mother who took time off from her Shabbat preparations to be involved in our program. It added a touch of ordinariness and helped to dispel the image of 'Zo Artzeinu' as a bunch of reckless radicals.

Just as we were finishing, Professor Pinchas Heiman of Bar-Ilan University suddenly rose and asked for permission to say a few words. Professor Heiman, a dignified individual who, unlike most Israelis, always maintains a formal dress code, turned to face the audience rather than those of us on the stage. "I have met Moshe and Shmuel on several occasions and I was not quite sure what to make of them. To me, this assembly was a test. I now know that they are serious and reliable, and I pledge to do all within my power in Ra'anana to see to it that this program succeeds."

We could not have wished for this meeting to end on a better note. We closed with the singing of *Hatikva* and *Ani Ma'amin*. We left the stage, only to be surrounded by a crowd that wanted more information, or desired to offer suggestions, to shake our hands and congratulate us and wish us success. I was really tired and wanted to rush home to unwind from all the tension and excitement. But the crowd stayed around for a long time. I finally managed to break away and got home.

Shmuel had arrived home before me and was already planning the next stage.

Our first exposure to the public had been an unqualified success, far beyond all our expectations. By the onset of the Sabbath that evening we already knew that a large number of the attendees had made contributions and signed standing bank orders that would cover the costs of the convention and even give us the means to keep going. The audience had included people who were ready to participate in any kind of protest activity, as well as many persons who had already engaged in all sorts of activities and who had come to the assembly to see who we were and how serious and dependable we were. The latter, many of whom came from communities in Yesha, were known to be activists, although they were not part of the established leadership.

One of these was Dan Tor from Ofra. Dan, a husky imposing figure introduced himself to me at the end of the convention. He had waited quietly while I spoke with the many people who had gathered around me after the formal part of the meeting was over. When I finally broke free and started toward the entrance, he stopped me.

"I don't believe that there is any organization which has shown the leadership potential that I saw here today," he said. "I identify with everything you said today. But you are making one major mistake. You are trying to give the impression that you are a well-oiled machine that can press rapidly forward. That is simply not true, and if you don't set up some kind of infrastructure you will, perhaps, make several impressive protest demonstrations, but then you will fall flat on your faces!"

Dan suggested that he work with us and for a while he did so. However, for various reasons he was unable to continue. But his point was well taken. After several protest demonstrations, and after we had been beaten by the police and besmirched by the media, the initial enthusiasm of the people to function within the framework of 'Zo Artzeinu' waned. And the lack of an institutionalized organization behind us seriously impaired our ability to carry on the struggle.

I was not particularly happy about being placed in a leadership position. I had really hoped simply to get the ball rolling, but expected others to pick up the challenge and lead on. I preferred to be jailed for a certain period after the first operation, and leave it to others with leadership potential to take over. I had hoped that the initial successes would give people a feeling of confidence and the concept of non-violent protest would take root, so that I would not have to continue to push the idea and worry about all the details. I had hoped that people would continue to fill the intersections, to squat in the streets, to fill the jails, in short, to become a troublesome element that the Rabin government could not ignore, and which would force a change in the government's policies or the holding of new elections.

I had hoped that a determined local leadership would arise in all sites where the first demonstration would be held, and that additional activists who had previously stayed on the sidelines would come forth to join them, and that I would be relieved of the necessity for total involvement.

In retrospect, I now realize how naive I had been. I did not realize, as I now do, that people need to be led. That is, they naturally look for leadership, for a father figure. An indication of this is the father-worship that reached unbelievable heights after the Rabin assassination. My aspiration to return to my normal life after the first demonstrations was based on wishful thinking rather than on logical assessment.

★ ★

'Zo Artzeinu' had become a visible threat to the legitimacy of the government of Israel. As 'Zo Artzeinu' prepared for the first big operation, the government turned to what it considered to be a tried and true solution – the intercession of the Yesha Council. The Council had proven in the past, willingly or otherwise, to be a tool in the hands of the authorities. Rabin had always treated the Council with scorn, and knew that he had nothing to fear from it. The Council, composed of the elected leadership of the individual communities of which it was composed, was administratively strapped and cumbersome and, worse, ideologically confused. The budget for the Council was provided by the Ministry of the Interior, that is, the Rabin government, so the members, like puppies, were kept on a short leash. That is, they could bark and look hostile and make a commotion in order to impress the frustrated public that they were acting on its behalf, but all this only within the range and manner acceptable to the government.

Rabin, who held the end of the leash in his hand, had avoided meeting with the members of the Council for almost two years (since November 1993). Meeting with him was a privilege that could be won only upon proof of proper behavior or by providing some *quid pro quo*. Suddenly, with the appearance of 'Zo Artzeinu' on the scene, he changed tactics. The Council was invited to meet with him. The appointed time, interestingly enough, was Tuesday, August 8, at 5:30 p.m., the precise moment when our demonstration was scheduled to begin.

Rabin was sending a very clear message to the Council. "I am ready to meet with you but you had better prove to me that you really have the power and authority that you claim." He expected the Council to use its power and influence to neutralize our efforts, in order to maintain a semblance of leadership. He was not aware of how deep the split was between the two bodies. As far as he was concerned, we were all the same. Various elements in the settler establishment did indeed try to neutralize our activity, but without success. 'Zo Artzeinu's' independent capabilities were demonstrated in the clearest fashion.

At that wretched meeting between Rabin and the heads of the Yesha Council, the first reports began to arrive from the intersections throughout the country. The weakness of the Council and its uselessness as a government tool became apparent.

According to reports, the surprising magnitude of the demonstrations prompted several government ministers to comment that several more such demonstrations would cause the government to fall. It became clear that 'Zo Artzeinu' must be stopped in its tracks, democratic principles notwithstanding. Nothing must stand in the way of preserving government power.

In the week and a half that remained before the planned demonstration, we resumed preparations. Those who had participated in the assembly became our enthusiastic ambassadors throughout the country. We were flooded with telephone calls and requests for the kits, and we could hardly keep up with the demand. In order to prevent any misunderstanding, we produced a simple accompanying cassette explaining the contents. I stood in our yard in front of the camera on a terribly hot afternoon and repeated all that I had said in Ariel. Unfortunately, it transpired that the camera had not been working properly, and I had to undertake the whole effort a second time.

We continued to travel throughout the country. On the Sunday after the Ariel assembly, I went to Kfar Chabad to meet the local leadership in the central synagogue. Our contact was Rabbi Meislish, a modest but highly active person, with a graying beard and a mischievous twinkle in his eyes. After the evening services, Rabbi Meislish arose and addressed the crowded room. He ended his moving words with the reading of a chapter of Psalms. It was an emotional experience for all present.

I was somewhat hesitant. My family had *Chabad* roots and many of my family were *Chabad Hassidim*. On the other hand, there was also a branch of my family that was left wing. I had been raised and educated in the spirit of Religious Zionism but I was not a *Hassid*. That is, I was not a Hassid in the sense of unquestionable acceptance of the leadership of a *rebbe*, nor did I dress accordingly. However, like many other non-Hassidim, I was an admirer of the Lubavitcher Rebbe, the head of the movement.

And now, I found myself the center of attention, speaking in a room that brought back pleasant memories of my childhood. I do not remember exactly what I said, but it apparently made an impression, because the Chabad Hassidim became major performers in the drama that was to follow. As I left (quite drained), someone suggested that I meet Rabbi Menachem Brod. Rabbi Brod is a young and brilliant person, the editor of *Sichat HaShavua*, a brochure which is distributed every Shabbat in hundreds of synagogues throughout the country. Rabbi Brod and I met for a short time and he later interviewed me. I explained in detail what we were planning, and earned an unexpected dividend: This unplanned interview was reported in his brochure and widely distributed on the Shabbat before the demonstration, and thus made a major contribution to our success.

The weekly Chabad publication was not the only one that we used to disseminate our message. Two days before the date of the demonstration, I had an interview with Zvi Singer of *Yediot Acharonot,* at which I provided him with a copy of the entire kit. We assumed that the newspaper would not be able to withstand the temptation to publish it, or parts of it, in the paper on the day before the demonstration. And they did not disappoint us. Thus, people who had heard of the upcoming demonstration and wanted to participate but did not know the details could find them on the second page of the newspaper on the afternoon before it was to take place. It could not have been better.

We continued to rush from one meeting to the next, with groups and individuals, and as the set day approached we felt that we had done all we could, and that there was nothing left to be done except to pray for success. One of the indications that our message had gotten through came as the result of a chance encounter with Elyakim HaEtzni, the activist lawyer from Kiryat Arba.

At that time, at various localities, there had begun local initiatives of various kinds to create facts on the ground, without any connection to the program of 'Zo Artzeinu'. One of the most prominent took place at Giv'at HaDagan in Efrat, south of Jerusalem. Nadia Matar and her associates from 'Women in Green' had established the beginnings of a settlement. Actually, they had occupied a hill that legally belonged to the community and upon which it was planned to build homes. In Beit-El, the inhabitants had occupied Givat HaArtiss and tried to create an extension of their settlement. All of these attempts had been promptly squelched by the government, to the accompaniment of much publicity.

As veterans of the 'doubling operation', we knew that they were maneuvering themselves into a vulnerable situation. They were concentrating all their efforts at one point and, when defeated, they would become discouraged and quit. The army could calmly concentrate its forces, choose the appropriate time, and eject them out without much effort. Furthermore, it was the Yesha Council that took responsibility for all of these local actions, and this in itself assured their failure.

One evening before our demonstration, I went to Beit-El to meet with the protesters on Giv'at HaArtis. As I descended the hill, I met Elyakim HaEtzni, who had been one of the founders of the Yesha Council but had remained faithful to his principles and did not blindly follow their dictates. He was one of those who had been opposed to the independent activities of 'Zo Artzeinu', but now he was visibly impressed. "How did you manage it?" he asked. "Everywhere I go, people are looking forward to 'Super Tuesday', the day of the really big happenings." I explained how things had worked out and went on my way. Elyakim, a lawyer, had been one of the first persons to advocate using the democratic tool known as non-violent civil disobedience. He had been at first skeptical about our chances of success but when we actually pulled it off, he became one of our most enthusiastic and articulate supporters. Finally, someone had put into action what Elyakim had been preaching for so long. The fact that it was not an organization with which he was associated meant nothing. He was above petty considerations. He was to become a major participant in our work. He participated actively in all our meetings, was a much-valued adviser when we were planning strategy, and eventually provided us with sorely needed legal advice.

The increasing interest shown by the media worked to our advantage, as their growing coverage made more people aware of our plans. The newspaper correspondents and broadcasters competed with each other in ridiculing our ephemeral band of protesters that was threatening a nationwide traffic blockage. Their attitude was not based simply upon their traditionally leftist political views, but upon a realistic, objective evaluation of the likelihood of success for such a threat, in view of the failures of previous confrontations over the previous three years. No one took us seriously, and their sarcasm was reinforced by the recommendation by Asaf Hefetz, head of the national police, that drivers should make it their business to travel along the roads at the designated hour since the police would easily handle the situation.

In a sense, the media and the authorities reinforced each other's thinking. Each derided our attempts, to the point where the field was left wide open to us.

The success of our road-blocking operation caused a complete turnabout. They were all nonplused by the meteoric success of a professional, well-oiled movement. The media began to describe us as a well organized, tightly disciplined, menacing underground movement, and the police sent overwhelming forces to every intersection likely to be the focal point for a demonstration.

When I arrived in Jerusalem for a small protest demonstration and found that the police who had been sent to confront us included units from as far north as Acre, I realized that someone at the top of the hierarchy had lost his wits. In an interview in a local newspaper, one highly placed officer stated that our success was due to 'modern technology and hi tech computers'. I didn't know whether to laugh or cry!

The inability of the media to understand what was really happening was brought home to me in an amusing interview that took place in the garden of my home. Itai Angel, a correspondent from TV Channel 2, who usually covered foreign affairs, immediately asked me to point out to him the underground headquarters from which we directed our movement. "Where are all the telephones and fax machines? Where are all the operational charts, diagrams, maps? Where do you keep all this hidden? Where are the assistants who pore over the plans and maps?" he asked.

I stared at him in amusement. By coincidence, Leah Kochanowitz arrived at that moment. Leah had been secretary of my firm before we started 'Zo Artzeinu' and continued with us in our protest efforts. "Here," I said. "Here is 'Zo Artzeinu'. Leah and I."

Itai gave me an incredulous look. "Come on. Where is the whole setup that you employed to bring the whole country to a halt? You don't expect me to believe that this is it." "It sure is," I responded. "We have no organization, no membership, no membership cards. Nothing."

Itai is an intelligent person, and he grasped the enormity of the difference between his preconception before he arrived for the interview and the reality that he now became aware of. He burst out in laughter, and ceased his attempts to discover the whereabouts of our 'headquarters'.

★ ★

On the day before the protest, we held our first press conference in Beit Agron in Jerusalem. Shmuel, Rabbi Elon and I faced the reporters and answered questions. The media interest brought many newsmen, who tried to draw out as many details as possible about 'Zo Artzeinu' and its plans. As expected, the questioners were quite hostile. Our relationship with the Yesha Council was brought up a number of times in different ways. We studiously avoided criticizing the Yesha Council or its members. Our attitude toward the law was another topic that was raised. One of the questions that stands out in my memory was posed by Gil Litman, the radio Second Program's correspondent in the 'territories'.

"How many intersections do you think you will block?"

"Your guess is as good as mine," I answered. "We have done everything we could, but at this point, there is no possible way to estimate what will happen tomorrow."

Although this answer did not satisfy the press, it did reflect the true situation. We had done everything that time and ability would allow, but we had no idea what the response would be. The big unknown was the degree of commitment to be expected of our supportive public. After all, this was not a matter of mustering armed units by command, and we had no idea whether our supporters would indeed take to the streets. Our contact with the public had been indirect. We did not assign specific individuals to the various junctions, nor had we determined precisely what function each individual would perform and where he would be placed. We had made people aware of a master plan, we had arranged assemblies and parlor meetings, and had used the media as best as possible. The previous three years did not provide justification for optimism. After all, we were trying to inculcate a new conception that called for violating conventional behavior and overcoming the inherent reluctance and fear in every honest citizen of direct confrontation with the forces of law and order. We knew that there were many who identified themselves with our cause, but there is a huge gap between sympathy and the willingness to clash with the authorities. We were afraid that the most committed would come to the intersections, shout militant slogans, and then disperse at the first prospect of police action. It was to be the first operation of its kind, and we simply did not know how it would turn out.

After the press conference, we drove to Tel Aviv for a meeting with the key activists in a small room in the Holiday Inn. It was already late and the campaign was due to take place the following day. Several dozen heads of district headquarters were present, and we wanted to neutralize any possible last-minute hesitations and inject a feeling of mutual support among our men.

"No one can know exactly what role he will play in the drama of history. We are all conscious of the calamity that this government has brought upon us, and know that so far we have not succeeded in doing much to prevent it. Now we have created a new tool. If you implement it properly, well and good; if you shy away from concrete action, you will not be able to claim that you did everything you could. And bear in mind: the plan depends on everyone's full participation. If someone withdraws, he will in effect be removing a brick from the wall we are trying to erect.

"Are there any questions?"

I was extremely pleased that all the questions were about practical measures: what should we do if there are many police when we arrive; are there lawyers ready to assist those arrested; how does one actually go about blocking an intersection, etc. I answered all the questions, and in response to the last one, I responded, "Like this!", and simply sat down on the speakers' platform, to the accompaniment of laughter and applause. We shook hands and adjourned the meeting.

As we were gathering our papers to leave, Shmuel exclaimed smilingly: "You know, I think that this is really going to happen!" His words bolstered my guarded optimism. I arrived home late in need of a good night's sleep. To my chagrin, Tzippy greeted me with the news that my father and other family members had been calling to talk me out of going ahead, of the dangers I was facing. They tried to discourage me. Things had reached such a state that the next morning I drove to Ashdod to visit with my father and try to calm and convince him that the danger was not all that terrible.

On the morning of the great day, I still found time to stop over in Rehovot and visit Kobi, a close friend and foreman of the private business that I ran for many years. I had reached the conclusion that, in view of my public activities, I could not keep the business going, certainly not if I would have to spend time in jail and in courts. My business was not such that I could sell it within a short time, so the only possible solution was to close it down and lose all income, or hand it over in an orderly fashion to someone who could keep it in operation. Kobi would be the only person who could undertake that.

I explained matters to Kobi, and suggested that he either take over the business or look for work elsewhere. Kobi was in shock when I presented him with these options. He had no inclination to become an independent businessman, but he had no desire to lose his place of employment. I transferred ownership of the company vehicle to him, handed him the files of the clients and a letter with power of attorney to act in the name of the firm. I asked for no monetary obligation in return.

"Look," I said. "I have no time for negotiations.... Take it over and good luck. If it works out and you make money, pay me what you think is fair."

Kobi, besides being a responsible employee, was also an old family friend. He had been aware of my intentions to devote my time to protest, but I don't think he realized how serious I really was. He expressed his sorrow about my leaving and told me that he was sure that the protest movement would fail.

He escorted me to the bus chartered by the Rehovot activists that was to take us to the Vradim intersection. We parted and I entered the bus for the trip to the unknown.

A Country at a Standstill –
"Rabin, go to the President"

Chapter 8

"I would like to begin my testimony with a short story about something that occurred about half a year ago," I said to the three judges, when it finally became the turn of the defense in our sedition trial.

The original charges against us were served against the three heads of 'Zo Artzeinu': Moshe Feiglin, Shmuel Sackett, and Rabbi Benny Elon. As suspect number one, my testimony was the one that opened the defense. Rabbi Benny Elon had meanwhile been elected to the Knesset, as a representative of the *Moledet* (Homeland) Party, and the prosecution froze the judicial processes against him.

Over the last few months, we had listened patiently to the senior police officers who had taken the stand one after another – and brazenly lied. The worst of them was the most senior of all, the commander of the operational branch of the Jerusalem police department, Deputy Superintendent David Krausa, who described the demonstrations of 'Zo Artzeinu' as the most violent demonstrations that he had ever experienced. The truth is that the demonstrators of 'Zo Artzeinu' came to the demonstrations with their hands demonstratively tied above their heads – which did not spare them from the violence of the police. But before presenting our version of the events, we had politely and quietly sat through the long months in which the prosecution developed its case. The prosecution made every effort to portray us to the three judges as dangerous characters, inciters and firebrands, who had even instigated the murder of Yitzchak Rabin. The McCarthyism that flourished in those days, the wild media onslaught, the cross-examination of rabbis, and the weighing and castigation of every word of the right-wing leaders, fit the prosecution's line perfectly. Sentence fragments that had been quoted in newspaper interviews were brought as evidence to the court. Selected passages taken out of context from personal letters that had been taken from my home were read off and no effort was spared to make the most of the dismal public atmosphere in the wake of the Rabin assassination.

When the prosecution had concluded its presentation, everyone waited in anticipation of what I would have to say. I was not represented by a lawyer and so I could speak freely as long as my statements were relevant to the subject.

★ ★

The judges nodded their agreement, and I began my story.

"Half a year ago, I traveled to the United States to raise money to cover the expenses of this trial. As I approached the automatic doors, from where you go to the bus taking you to your airplane, the doors closed just before I passed through, and I was left to wait for the next bus. An airport stewardess keeping watch at the exit identified me and said:

" 'I recognize you. You're the man who brought the entire country to a halt.'

"I immediately realized that here was someone who did not identify with my world outlook; she appeared to be a typical radical, and I had no idea what she could want of me.

" 'Yes, it was me, ' I said with a faint smile and a presentiment of the cold shower that I was about to be subjected to before the doors opened and saved me.

" 'I want you to know one thing,' said the stewardess, 'I am leftist – very leftist! And the same holds true of all my friends! But when you did what you did, **I realized there was a problem.**

"'So long as life continued to flow placidly in its regular course, I thought you were only 2% of the population. That is what Rabin declared. But when I couldn't get out of my house, when it affected me – I suddenly grasped that there is half a nation, maybe more, which thinks otherwise. The next day', she continued, 'I spoke with all my friends and they all felt exactly the same.'

"I parted from the stewardess, feeling greatly elated. Suddenly she and her friends had finally realized that it was possible that the king was naked. For three years the Right had demonstrated in every possible way, but these people couldn't absorb our message, and continued to cheer the king's new clothes – until 'Zo Artzeinu' came along and, like the small child in the tale, opened their eyes."

It was not unintentionally that I chose to start my testimony with this particular story. It was important for me to cause the judges to carefully rethink the essential nature of 'Zo Artzeinu's' activities. Public relations and public opinion are not simply a matter of salon gatherings and friendly chat, and frequently concrete action can be more effective than a thousand words. Many of our activists had feared that the actions of 'Zo Artzeinu' would only antagonize the general public and cause us to be hated, but I did not share this apprehension. "Our aim is not for us to be loved", I said again and again. "Our goal is that they should respect us and listen to our message." Of course we were fiercely attacked by the left wing, but none of us had aimed our public relations efforts at them in any case. "Why does everyone root for the Maccabee Tel-Aviv soccer team?" I would ask. "Because they're nicer or more moral? People support them because they're determined and victorious." It is not true that public opinion tends to the side of the underdog or the just; it favors the one who proves to be determined and persistent.

A resolute, earnest and undaunted person is someone whom it is worth listening to – in which case he gets a chance to convince.

In any case, debates of this sort had already died out in that period, when it became clear that being 'nice and restrained' in demonstrations does not achieve a thing, and that the image of the wronged crying out for help did not gain us any sympathy in the public. The main question now was not whether to carry out a new type of demonstration, but whether it would succeed[1].

All of our planned activity was based entirely on a subjective, hypothesized reading of the feelings of the general public. A short time before the demonstration my friend, Elyakim HaEtzni, told me: "Maybe you will find four people crazy enough to go out with you and block an intersection. I certainly hope you succeed, but I am afraid that you are simply fantasizing. The masses are tired, resigned, and spoiled, and no one will bother to join you." My assessments were different. I sensed the accumulation of general frustration, and I believed that a brave leadership would be able to drag the masses along with it.

What actually followed was total success for our program, beyond all expectations. My intuitive reading of the public's mood, feelings and readiness to go out to battle was accurate. All we did was to instill self-confidence in the hearts of the activists, to set the date and the standards and rules of the demonstration, and to display leadership. The rest was done by the members of the various town headquarters, who had already spent many days and nights in demonstrations without end and who were just waiting for an opportunity like this. Even local leaders who had been initially wary of antagonizing public opinion joined the preparations at this stage.

Every town headquarters had its own unique quality. In the north, the HaMovil junction was blocked for traffic by people from Kfar Yehoshua and farmers from the surrounding villages. In the center, the residents of Kfar Habad blocked highway No.1 leading from Tel Aviv to Jerusalem. The Ra'anana junction was blocked by a large group of the city's inhabitants, led by Prof. Heiman of Bar Ilan University. The Ashdod junction was blocked by religious Kibbutznikim from the area. Even in cities further away, such as Safed, Kiryat Mal'achi, and Arad, the country stood still during those hours.

---

[1] The general acknowledgment that being the underdog endows one with moral superiority did not necessarily apply to Zo Artzeinu, despite our experiences. Actually, Zo Artzeinu was struggling to maintain Jewish values, and these do not invest the underdog with such an aura. (See *The Cringing Revolt*, by Gadi Taub.)

Thus, on that day and at that hour, 78 central intersections were blocked all over the country. All of Israel stood still for a number of hours, and it became obvious that this was not the work of just 'two percent' or merely 'propellers', as Rabin had labeled the settlers.

Dr. Mozi Finkel gave testimony in our trial:

"Who are you?" I asked.

'Mozi' described dryly and in great detail a life story of volunteering and constant work for the public good.

"I grew up on the Carmel, the Ri'ali school, Scouts, parachutist unit of Nachal, volunteer in Yerocham, the Technion – hydraulic engineering, moved for ideological reasons to the Yokne'am development village, the Yom Kippur War and the protest afterward, participated in a mission of the Foreign Ministry providing help to African countries suffering from drought, worked in the framework of the United Nations, ..."

"Enough?" asked Mozi with a smile.

Mozi related how the northern group had arrived at the decision to join the operation, and then went on to describe the protest itself.

"Very prominent professors from the Technion joined the demonstration. We came to the Tishbi junction, cleverly evading the police who were waiting for us at the nearby intersection.

"At the appointed time, we blocked the intersection. There weren't any police there. They were waiting for us at the Megido junction. There wasn't any violence at the intersection, and to this day I am still exhilarated by the recollection that from all the hundreds of cars that were stuck in the intersection, crowds just came out and joined us...

"The crowd stood there along a distance of many kilometers in a very pleasant and supportive atmosphere...

"When the police came, we gave them water.

"A long time passed before order replaced the chaos. We finished with a handshake with the police.

"We went home with a feeling of satisfaction that we had been able to impress the public with our demonstration..."

Senior Police official: "They'd better stop these dangerous escapades -- before there's bloodshed!"
A COUNTRY AT A COMPLETE STANDSTILL

Rightist demonstrators blocked 80 intersections throughout the country. Thousands of drivers were stuck in traffic jams. 130 demonstrators arrested.

Yediot Acharonot, August 9, 1995

The government's response turned hysterical. With the government's legitimacy undermined and demoralization suddenly spread far and wide, fear grew amongst the country's leaders.

Authority – any authority – is based on the basic, natural human wish to obey. 'Flocking together' is a natural human impulse that is the basis for the government's rule, and when the sheep declare themselves free and disperse in every direction, the shepherds panic.

Ministers voiced open concern that the continuation of the intersection blocking would lead to the government's fall and replacement, and this brought a harsher response from the government. An amazing number of forces were allocated to deal with every event of 'Zo Artzeinu', even when it was a matter of the smallest local event. An inordinate degree of violence was employed at clear instructions from the top leadership and on such a broad scale that it could not have been merely a local 'deviation'.

But even more than the policemen's violence, the post-Zionist élite's existential need – to close ranks and defend itself against the public challenge that was endangering it – was felt when the Judicial Branch was quickly swept into a political collaboration with the Executive Branch, and this in clear violation of Israeli law.

It might be hard to believe, but the following story exemplifies this critical point.

As mentioned, I had participated in our first operation, by blocking the Gan HaVradim junction between Rehovot and Rishon le Zion. Hundreds of arrested protesters were led that night from this intersection to the Rishon police station nearby. The registration formalities were long and tiring, and it was only about midnight that the last of the detained protesters were recorded. Several hours passed before the higher police ranks realized that the 'big fish' responsible for the party that night was amongst those arrested by the Rishon police. I was taken for a thorough interrogation, but I refused to cooperate with the investigators. According to the guidelines that we had set earlier, I told them that "this is a political inquiry, and I have nothing to say".

For the Israeli government it was very important that the next morning I should be seen on all the television screens being led to the courthouse. It was important for them to subject me to a quick and extremely strict trial, so that the public should learn the price of my actions. By the late night hours, all the protesters were released, except for the 'big fish'. One of the protesters at Rishon was Dr. Moshe Peretz, who asked me, "Do you think that we should agree to our release as long as they don't release you as well?"

I didn't see any special purpose to be achieved by continuing to have our people held in jail, and I encouraged them to return home. "Even if I remain alone under arrest, it won't bother me. Today's work is finished and I don't see any reason why you should stay," I answered Moshe.

An officer from the Rishon police approached and explained that they intended to release all the protesters, but they were doing so in small groups to prevent disturbances. I didn't give much thought to what he said, though his explanation seemed strange. Why was he taking the trouble to explain their intention to me? When the last of the protesters was released, they explained that I was to remain at the police station, and it was then that I understood that truth and falsehood are of equal moral value where the police are concerned. Much later, I saw the report that Abraham Aden, the police ombudsman had published during the 80s, in which he described the 'Culture of Lies', as he called it, which was prevalent amongst the police. I was led along side streets to the Rehovot police station (such was the fear of rioting due to my arrest – in the middle of the night...), and already the next morning I was led into the Rehovot Magistrates' Court. I assumed they were bringing me for an extension of my detention. No one explained anything to me. My only experience in events of this kind was the arrest in Tiberias after the 'Doubling Operation', where we were indeed brought before the local court for an extension of our detention and afterwards released until our trial began, about two years later.

Now, at the Rehovot Court, I assumed that I was being led for an extension of my detention, although I wondered why it was so soon. The fact is that the police could have held me another day and a half before such an extension was requested – and only ten hours had passed. It did not cross my mind that I was going to be put on trial that very morning. Israeli law does not permit bringing a person to trial less than 48 hours after his arrest, and in special circumstances, such as a security risk, it is possible to bring him to trial after 24 hours. I was brought to trial in less than ten hours. I was brought into the court through the back door, and only after some time did I realize that I was in a courthouse and not in a police station.

I sat on a bench in a rear room of the courthouse, when into the room came the lawyer Dr. Haim Misgav.

"You are about to face trial," Dr. Misgav explained. "Your friend Shmuel contacted me yesterday and I will represent you. You will certainly not admit to anything," he continued.

At this point, I interrupted him and thanked him politely for coming. "I am very thankful for your having taken the trouble," I said, "but I am not interested in representation. I will represent myself."

Dr. Misgav tried to convince me, but I stood firm. I explained that this was not an ordinary case, since I wanted to provide an example of civil discontentment, and that was why it was important for me to sit in jail. In the end, Dr. Misgav acquiesced, but followed after me into the courtroom.

When the words "The Court is now in session" were announced, Judge Avital Beit Ner entered the court.

The courtroom was filled with reporters from all the media. Apparently there was great public interest to see what would be done to the man who had so suddenly sprung up in the Israeli scene and totally disrupted the normal flow of daily life. The appearance of the lawyer Dr. Haim Misgav also aroused interest, since a lawyer of his stature promised an interesting trial.

Before the trial started, Dr. Misgav suddenly got to his feet and informed the judge that I was forgoing legal representation. Nevertheless, he asked and obtained the judge's permission to say a few words at the start of the trial and at its conclusion. During a brief recess, I asked him to go out and quote to the reporters, in my name, the following statement by Thomas Jefferson: "When the government is evil, jail is the honest man's refuge." Dr. Misgav did so, and the quote made headlines the next morning.

The trial began.

The judge turned to me, explained what I was charged with, and asked me if I pleaded guilty. The charges included 'raising fear among the public'. This phrase seemed ludicrous to me. "I did not raise fear among the public. I raised hope," I told the judge. She chose not to enter into an argument and began asking me a series of dry questions, leaving no work for the prosecution.

"Were you at the Gan Vradim junction yesterday at 5:30 p.m.?" she asked.

"Yes," I answered.

"Did you take part in the demonstration there?"

"Yes."

"Did you block the intersection?"

"Yes."

"Did you hear the officer call over the loudspeaker for the public to disperse?"

"No," I said, shrugging my shoulders. "But I assume that if he had to do so, he performed his job faithfully."

An uneasy feeling took hold of those present in the courtroom. It was clear that the suspect was not trying at all to defend himself, and was not playing according to the rules of the game. The fact that the entire trial was being held in clear violation of several basic rights of every suspect and accused person, and in violation of the law itself, did not prevent the judge from continuing this farce.[1] In this way, the court itself behaved as a law-breaker who wants 'to raise fear among the public', fear of identifying with and participating in the 'terrible deeds' of the accused.

THE DAY AFTER ROAD BLOCKING, LEADER OF OPERATION TRIED AND CONVICTED

Moshe Feiglin, one of the heads of 'Zo Artzeinu', was sentenced to a suspended six-month term of imprisonment and fined 10,000 shekels for illegal assembly and participation in disturbances and confrontations. The State Attorney's Office is drawing up dozens of additional charge sheets which will soon be presented against rightist demonstrators.

...The Police yesterday warned that in the event of similar demonstrations in the future they will have no alternative but to apply more severe measures to disperse violators, apparently referring to the use of powerful water cannons and tear gas.

Ma'ariv, August 10, 1995

---

[1] A person may not be brought to trial without allowing him a minimum period in which to prepare for it, to peruse the evidence to be brought against him, to select a defense lawyer of his own choosing, to bring witnesses, etc. Denying these procedures to the accused is tantamount to turning a trial into a farce. And this is precisely why the law stipulates that there must be a minimum period between arrest and bringing to trial. However, this trial in Rehovot was not meant to pursue justice; it was meant to achieve media coverage while the effect of yesterday's demonstration had not yet worn off in the memory of TV viewers.

The entire 'trial' from its beginning until the verdict was read did not take longer than half an hour. I was found guilty, and since I had no criminal history, the sentence was ('only') a suspended term of imprisonment of six months and a fine of $3000. The sentence was much harsher than what was customary in cases of this kind.

When I left the courthouse, reporters converged on me from every side, and only then did I realize what impression the 'Zo Artzeinu' movement had made, since I was cut off from the media from the moment I was arrested. I showed the photographers the verdict, and told them, "I intend to frame this verdict and place it in a very prominent place in my living room, and in fifteen years, when my son asks me, 'Abba, what did you do in those terrible days to change the situation?' I will point to this verdict."

Declarations of this kind are not heard frequently in our country, and my words, which were publicized prominently, made a great impression. I did not let the verdict of suspended imprisonment change my plans for the future, and did not abstain from joining further demonstrations that I organized, and for which I was ready to accept full responsibility.

I did not know at the time about the law requiring 48 hours before a trial, but I believe that even if I had known, I would not have invoked it in order to delay the proceedings against me.

However, the judge certainly knew the law. Undoubtedly, the Prime Minister did not pick up the phone to *demand* that the judge go ahead. Things don't work that way.

But when the 'natives' defiantly raised their heads, the leftist judicial élite instinctively came to the defense of the leftist political élite. It was done naturally, and Judge Beit Nir herself probably did not realize the significance of the issue.

As this chapter was being written, two years after the event, it became known that when the police brought to trial an Arab who was employed without a security check in Rishon le Zion – before that very judge – in less than 48 hours from the time he was arrested, the judge fulminated against the police. (Arabs from the west bank of the Jordan River are allowed to work only with security clearance, to prevent unmonitored entrance by potential terrorists.) Judge Beit Nir even fined the police for bringing that Arab to trial too hastily. In that particular case, she knew perfectly well how to defend individual rights.

And that Arab later went ahead and perpetrated a suicide bombing in the 'Apropo' coffeehouse in Tel Aviv, killing three women and orphaning a six-month-old girl.

★ ★

As soon as I came home, we began to plan our next move. We did not want to lose the momentum. The government was hit hard. We had established ourselves as a factor to be taken into account in Israeli public relations and the public anticipated further steps. My house became a beehive of activity. The phone rang ceaselessly. People suddenly found relief and a vent for their feelings in the image of that young vibrant movement which had succeeded overnight in restoring some of their self-esteem. The warm anonymity that had sheltered us before our first operation dissolved, and we found ourselves in the spotlight. However, we did not have the organizational setup required in order to function vis-a-vis such a large public, nor did we want this. I wanted to preserve the popular nature of the movement; I did not change my home phone numbers, continued to work at home, and answered all the phone calls. Eventually we added another phone line so that the kids could also converse freely with their friends.

Tzippy suffered greatly from this exposure. She held tight to the little privacy she was able to maintain, and set a couple of hard and fast rules to cope with the situation: No reporters to be allowed into the house, no phone calls to be answered after eleven at night. I had to come up with various excuses for the reporters whom I would host in the garden: the air conditioning was not working, the house was being cleaned right now, etc. The effort paid off, and despite the storm raging outside, Tzippy was able to continue to manage a normal household as much as possible.

Whereas before the operation, the media's attitude wavered between scorn and a demonstrative display of disinterest, now the situation changed, and reporters surrounded us and wrote, photographed, and broadcast. We had no way of processing all this material, and certainly no way to respond to it. Tales were woven about us, the media, as is customary, inflated our dimensions, and the level of expectations of the public, which was faithful to the Land, soared heavenward, as did the fear of the government and the police. The realization that we had to continue pressing the government, and the many expectations from us, all these were channeled towards me, and created a heavy feeling of pressure and responsibility. I regretted that Judge Beit Nir had not left me in prison – to rest a bit.

I often find myself thinking about that stage and, with hindsight, conclude that if we had navigated differently, we could have achieved more. At that point, we had tremendous public support, we had instilled a new vigorous spirit, and we could easily have organized large public protests at short notice, had I not insisted on the sacrosanct/foolish principle of not asking for a permit, as another expression of disobedience. We could have initiated simultaneous demonstrations of hundreds of thousands of people in all the large city centers. We could have marched through the cities, organized strikes in different sectors, and found ways to give expression to widespread protest by sectors that were later afraid to join us in view of anticipated police violence.

Licensed protests were proven to be irrelevant in the previous three years and had we undertaken them, we would have returned to square one as simple 'propellers'. But by now we had proved that we could do much more. In contrast to the Yesha Council, we were treated at this point as a serious factor that was certainly able to 'bite', and it was clear we had a stick as well as a carrot. It would have been wisest to tread the fine path between these two extremes, but this is wisdom attained by experience. At the time, the persistent humiliation by the government, the repulsion from the Right wing establishments and from politics in general, the public pressure, and a measure of foolhardiness – all militated at that time against sound judgment.

It was important for me to develop the issue of civil discontent. I looked for ways to convert the theory of non-violent civil disobedience into reality. Elyakim HaEtzni, who had preached this issue for years, came to me and suggested that we engage in sit-in protests at the entrance to governmental offices. I liked the idea and integrated it in my plans, but I had already formed at the time a more popular and appealing idea. I thought of the famous march that Dr. Martin Luther King had led to Washington, D.C. I wanted to cook up something of that sort here in Israel.

I started to formulate the idea and draw up operational plans. Many good people now joined the inner activist core. The most outstanding of them were Dr. Nitza Kahane and her sister Tamar Hakun from Jerusalem, Julie Turnberg from Tel Aviv, Michael Fou'ah from Mitzpe Netufa in the Galilee, and a good many others to whom I regrettably do wrong in not mentioning them by name. A private helicopter pilot called me and enthusiastically offered his services, which I indeed made use of later on. Michael Fou'ah, who is a profound thinker and is gifted with excellent communication skills, took upon himself the job of spokesman. When I came up with the plan of a 'March to Jerusalem', Michael added the slogan: "Prime Minister Rabin, Go to the President [to offer your resignation]."

The plan was to gather activists from all over the country, who would arrive simultaneously at designated points along Highway #1 from Tel Aviv to Jerusalem. All of them would then march along the shoulders of the road and when reaching Jerusalem, they would mark the sidewalks to show Rabin the way to the President's residence.

The operational plan underwent several revisions, and the final version was presented to the activists in a convention that was convened in Beit Orot in Jerusalem.

The heads of the various town headquarters contacted me, and I divided marching segments of equal distance among them. It was clear to me that all the telephones in my house were being continuously eavesdropped, as were the telephones of the activists with whom I was in contact. But I ignored this and even used this fact to pass on messages to the police. I had no doubt that the police chiefs understood, just as the thousands of demonstrators who participated understood, that there was no intention to block the highway but only to march along its edges.

The persons in charge were informed at precisely what point along Highway #1 it was legally possible, upon reaching it by bus, to stop the bus and let the participants get off, and at the close of the march, to get the people back on the bus. The intention was that at about 12:30 p.m. there would be a long line of demonstrators carrying signs "Rabin – Go to the President" for the entire length of the highway. The operation went into action as planned on the 28th of *Menachem Av*, 5755 – August 24, 1995.

This time the police took no chances. The high command was fully aware of the pressure being placed on the government, and needed no explicit instructions in order to understand that the law must not, in any way, serve as a barrier preventing the police from stopping the demonstration.

Thus did the Israeli Police turn into a law-breaking body. The buses that the demonstrators had hired to take them to the demonstration were stopped by the police before they even set out, and the demonstrators were not allowed to get off the buses for hours. This was in effect a mass arrest of thousands of citizens all over the country, without arrest orders and without fulfillment of any legal condition for arrest. Whoever tried to get off the bus was beaten harshly and was immediately charged, of course, with assaulting a policeman. Among the buses that were stopped were quite a few innocent tour buses of tourists who were traveling to Jerusalem without any link to the said demonstration, but if the occupants looked religious, the police took no risk and treated them the same.

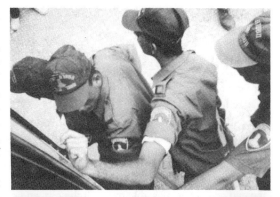

Israeli law does not permit this kind of arrest or detention. None of the policemen who stopped the buses and imprisoned their occupants for long hours had any warrant for arrest. None of the travelers on the bus was interrogated, and for all practical purposes, there was a mass denial of freedom from citizens, some of whom were suspected of intentions to demonstrate against the government. It is easy to imagine how such an outrageous conduct would have been treated, if it had been directed against leftist demonstrators. After all, we had no intention of blocking Highway #1, but rather to march along its edges, but the police preferred to assume otherwise and to act in an illegal and violent way.

That day, I used the services of Yossi, the helicopter man, intending to hover above the line of marchers, and join the marchers in the city. The use of the helicopter was actually meant to provide another pinch in the buttocks of the arrogant Rabin government, and add to the marchers' morale. Here the people are marching in multitudes towards Jerusalem and their leaders are even using sophisticated stratagems.

This gimmick indeed helped raise the morale of the abused people in the buses and made the headlines that day. During the flight, the news department of Channel 7 called me on my cellular phone. Our flying toy had no doors and because of the noise of the rotor, I couldn't hear the interviewer. I simply waited until he finished his question and then called on the demonstrators to make every effort to come to the city's entrance, and continue from there on foot to the President's residence as planned.

The scene I saw that afternoon, while hovering above the besieged buses all along the highway, was not particularly encouraging. I feared that the operation was a failure. But it turned out that I was wrong. It was the behavior of the police that spurred the demonstrators to continue, and even though the highway march was not carried out, in the end everyone was able to reach the city and carry out the second part of the plan.

Meanwhile, a police helicopter was sent to intercept the 'Zo Artzeinu' helicopter. It was a most ridiculous scene. In the helicopter in which I sat there was barely place for two people. I sat shoulder to shoulder with the pilot, without doors, and every small wind moved this toy off course. I did not intend to have an 'air engagement'... and I asked the pilot to land. We landed in the Latrun army base area, and the police helicopter continued to keep a watchful eye from above, until large police forces arrived and led me to my arrest in the Beit Shemesh police station, and from there to the jail in the Russian Compound of Jerusalem

The Beit Shemesh police chief had a hard time trying to record in the police register the precise reason for the arrest. It was hard to charge me with assaulting a police officer or in blocking a roadway. He kept flipping the pages of the police manual, and after searching desperately for at least an hour (!), finally found a reason that could perhaps fit the case.

★ ★

Demonstrators who resided in the capital and did not undergo the hardships of the day were the first to start the march within Jerusalem, while tracing footsteps on the paths leading to the President's residence. Rabbi Benny Elon gathered one such group and marched with it along Sderot HaNasi. When their passage was blocked by the police,

they all raised their arms and continued marching until they were arrested. Benny was led to his arrest in the Russian Compound and that evening we met in the same cell. All the time, more and more people streamed into Jerusalem from every direction and marched towards the President's residence.

In the end, all the people who were detained in the buses managed to arrive in Jerusalem, and joined those who marched in the city. The march along Highway #1 did not take place, but in Jerusalem there was a huge stream of people from all directions heading towards the President's residence.

It was one of the most quiet, spontaneous, and elegant protests that Israel ever knew. No centralized assembly, no expensive stage and sound amplification systems, no organized bussing – the nation came in masses to Jerusalem with the most legitimate demand that could possibly be made in a democratic country, and did so in a very impressive and restrained manner.

The demonstrators were totally quiet and raised no voices. Women pushed baby carriages; there was no blocking of any roadways, and certainly no violent act of any sort. The event could have ended quietly, but as it later became clear, when we pieced together the behavior of the police with the buses and their behavior in Jerusalem, a strategic decision had been taken to create fear among anyone who intended to go out and demonstrate with 'Zo Artzeinu', regardless of the manner in which he did so.

The police were brutal. The policemen's behavior, which was witnessed all over the place, could only have been the result of explicit guidelines from the higher command. Officers of the Special Patrol Unit beat the marchers mercilessly, their violent behavior stunning those who came and who later gave testimony in court. Mrs. Tzvia Zinger from Psagot testified that a mounted policeman had brutally whipped a young woman. Mrs. Maya Avinun who had come all the way from Nahariya to participate in the march related how she was severely beaten by policemen, who subsequently prevented her from being evacuated for medical treatment. Boris Chechkis, an

engineer from Haifa, told how he was punched squarely in the face by the Special
Patrol Unit Commander Efi Chavivian when he dared to ask him a question.

MK (Member of Knesset) Ron
Nachman, who was present in the
area, testified:

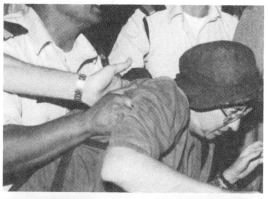

"I saw policemen standing with
whips on the sidewalk and
shoving a woman with two
babies in her carriage. And I saw
that more people were marching
on the sidewalk and the
policemen were shoving them. I
am not talking about the street –
but about the sidewalk. I said to
the officer, 'Sir, I demand to
know why you are pushing that
woman,' but he didn't answer. I
told him, 'Don't you see that she
is wheeling her babies?' and he
still didn't answer. I told him: 'I
am a member of the Knesset and
if you won't answer, I'll file a
complaint against you.' But in
fact I couldn't, because he had no
identification tag. Most of them
didn't – that was the policy.

"I turned to the officer who held the loudspeaker.
I told him: 'I am MK Ron Nahman and I demand
to know the law you are basing yourselves upon
when giving orders to push people who are
walking on the sidewalk – not the street, I
emphasize!' He told me: 'I don't have to justify
my behavior to you. I have my orders.'

On the right, District Commander Aryeh
Amit. On the left, David Krausa.

"I asked him who gave the orders, and he said: 'I don't have to tell you.'

"I said to him: 'Sir, are these orders from the Regional Commander? From the Police
Minister? From the Prime Minister?' He didn't answer.

"...I went to speak to Aryeh Amit, the Regional Commander, who stood on the sidewalk and commanded the forces. I turned to him; he did not want to answer me and began to walk away. I ran after him like a small child, a Member of Knesset running after a police commander. I called to him; he did not want to answer.

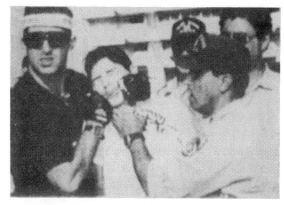

Ma'ariv, August 24, 1995

"I saw the cavalry striking people on the sidewalks with their whips, from there all the way to the office of the Prime Minister. I saw this with my own eyes.

"My eight-and-a half-year-old daughter ran to me, clung to my hand and told me she was terribly afraid of the horses and the police.

"I called up Eitan Haber, Rabin's assistant. I talked with all the levels of command.

"I tell you unequivocally that this [police violence] was a strategic decision of the Israeli government which was frightened by the intensity of the demonstrations, and did not know how to deal with such matters. That is why they employed the army, the police, and even the border patrol."

A demonstrator and a mounted policeman at the demonstration this week near Binyanei HaOoma.
Ma'ariv, August 8, 1995

★★

Despite the hardships that the demonstrators underwent, many of them did reach the demonstration's destination – the area of the President's residence.

The following is part of the testimony of the most prominent prosecution witness, the chief of the operational branch of the Jerusalem Police, Deputy Superintendent David Krausa (testimony on April 17, 1996):

"At 17:30 thousands of people arrived heading in the general direction of the President's residence, with the intention of arriving at the residence itself. Wherever demonstrators were seen, a proclamation was made requesting them to quietly disperse, and when they failed to comply, we evacuated them, using reasonable force."

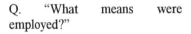
Reasonable force ...

Q. "What means were employed?"

A. "In this case, policemen were employed, and they used their hands. After which, mounted policemen and *maktazim* were called in a number of places."

Q. "What are 'maktazim'?"

A. "Pressure hoses for spraying water."

Q. "How many policemen were employed that day?"

A. "To the best of my recollection, over 1500, close to 1800 policemen."

In the evening, a spontaneous demonstration formed opposite the Russian Compound calling for our release. Two policemen rushed into my cell, gave me a loudspeaker, and asked me to request the demonstrators to disperse. It was already night, the operation had succeeded beyond all expectations, and I felt that the time had come to call it a day. I turned to the demonstrators, thanked them and asked them to disperse. The people agreed, turned back and began to disperse. I turned to return to the jail area, when at that moment, police of the Special Patrol Unit ran out towards the demonstrators, whose backs were turned towards us and who did not see the approaching danger. The bullies beat the demonstrators, and it was only after a long time that the police allowed the ambulances to evacuate the injured who remained lying on the street.

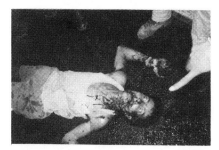 

Reasonable force ...

I was stunned. I felt that I had been manipulated for the execution of a violent exercise. Suddenly, I noticed at my side a very prominent police chief, a red-haired bulldog-faced man who, I later understood, was the chief of the operational branch responsible for that action. "I'll decide how they will disperse," hissed Krausa. I knew that I had to repress my feelings. I was very close to breaking all the rules that I had set for myself, and so I hurriedly departed from the area and returned to my cell.

The testimony of Yisrael Orange regarding that event:

"...Thirty men with boxing gloves ran towards the people and started to beat everyone – men, women, and children, who fell to the ground. I saw them kicking a woman who fell upon her baby inside the carriage – and they continued striking her.

"Everyone began to disappear. I saw how seven policemen, among them Revivo, the Deputy Commander of the Special Patrol Unit, dragged a boy, who I now know to be Bramson, knocked him to the ground, and while he's flat on his back, started kicking him. That is, everyone is kicking him, seven policemen together, like this, boom, boom, giving it to him on his chest, stepping on his chest. He is lying there half-fainted and they are stepping on his chest, hitting him on his head...

"The policemen are bending down. That is, it's not enough that they have used their feet, they are also bending down and delivering blows with their hands, at his head, his chest, his feet – and this is not one policeman. We are talking about seven policemen... I saw that he was beginning to turn blue... I told them that I am a paramedic and that I want to pass through ... I called an ambulance... I returned to the boy... I saw that he was scarcely breathing...

"Whèn he returned to his senses somewhat, I turned to Revivo. I told him, 'Sir, this is a Jew just like you... How could you do this to him?' He told me, 'Stop right there..'. He ran towards me with seven people and threw me to the ground. I told him, 'Take me, take me...' but he first had to hit me... Now they were kicking and striking me, for some two minutes, 120 seconds – maybe 300...

"I tell them, 'Enough, enough, I can't take it anymore, arrest me..'. I wanted them to stop... They dragged me like this, with my head on the floor, into this waiting room in the Russian Compound...

"I am not a man who cries. I am 23, but then, when I called to Revivo, 'How are you doing this?' – I cried. I was extremely upset...

"An investigator called Gabi Bareket entered.

"So Gabi Bareket enters and gives me what was left of my broken eyeglasses...

"...And then after 20 minutes of being pleasant ... he asks me..

'Why did you assault the policemen... (?!)'

"I explained to him that there was no such thing – quite the contrary.

"Suddenly Dudu Revivo comes in, lifts me up, and punches me once, twice, three times, all in the presence of Bareket...

"Kicks me. Knocks me to the floor...

"The other officer, the investigator, sees and doesn't interfere...

"He leaves – Gabi continues to investigate...

"Again Dudu comes in, this time with another policeman – I think they call him Ram Condrovesky, he is very tall, enters with motorcycle gloves...

"They both grab hold of me, together, one, two, lift me, and strike me.

"Gabi didn't feel comfortable by now... so he left the room.

"I told Revivo, 'Enough, enough...' . Then he tells me – 'Next time you call "Revivo", you'll return home in a body bag...'

"They lift me – and together bang my head against the doorpost...

"They did so twice or three times, until I passed out...

"I have X-rays of the place where my head was cracked...

"The next day they brought me to be remanded in custody before Judge Yoram Noam.

"He was so shocked that he ordered my immediate release and the opening of an investigation against Revivo.

"After that, no one summoned me to testify, or asked me anything. No one was interested in what I had to say. Three months later I received a letter informing me that the investigation [concerning the police brutality] was closed for lack of evidence...

"I wrote a letter to the Officer Investigation Department. I told them: 'How come that they didn't ask me? I have what to say. There were many witnesses. Riki Sarit was there, and witnessed what was taking place. Many people saw this...' Then they send me a second letter, repeating that due to lack of evidence the file has been closed, and they are unwilling to re-open it..."[1]

When I was released during the late night hours from the Russian Compound, a demonstrator approached me, and gave me a cellular phone. "Call *Arutz* 7," he said. "They are having a talk show and callers are talking about the events of the day." I called. With a bit of trepidation, they included me among the speakers. "Just don't get us into trouble," the secretary at the radio station told me. (*Arutz* 7, being an independent, unlicensed news station broadcasting from outside Israel's territorial limits, was subject to several attempts to close it down. The efforts of Education Minister Shulamit Aloni to close down the only station that served as the voice of the Faithful to the Land of Israel created the fear that there would be those who would use my words as justification for closing the station.)

---

[1] In an attempt to rid themselves of Yisrael Orange's insistent demands to investigate the matter, the police took a step quite usual in such circumstances: The police entered a charge against him of criminal conduct for 'attacking a policeman'. After a full year and a half and a string of false testimonies, Judge Yitzchak Shim'oni reached the following conclusions. Case 451/96: Court decision: "A thorough appraisal of the testimony of both parties leaves one with the irrepressible feeling that were it not for the violent conduct of the police in dispersing the demonstration and the blows rained on the accused and on others and the complaints which were addressed to the Officer Investigation Department, this charge sheet would never have been presented. The impression one gets is that it was that behavior which led to the charge sheet against the accused and not any violations on his part, as claimed."

While I was waiting for my turn, I could hear those who were speaking before me – people from all over the country who participated in the demonstration, and were still stunned over the treatment at the buses and the violence of the police. Several of them described the Police Special Patrol Unit as 'Nazis'.

I went on the air, and invalidated any comparison of this kind, and did the most that I could to calm the listeners.

"Take photographs," I told the listeners. "Don't curse – guard your tongues. And don't worry – the day will come when we will bring them, and mainly those who sent them, to judgment in court, in a legal, orderly way. What is happening here justifies setting up a state inquiry commission more than any other commission ever called into existence in the State of Israel. They are acting this way because they are hysterical. In the end they will fall. We are in the right and that is why we can afford to be patient. We will still be on the receiving end of their blows in the near future, but in the end, they will fall and will have to account for their actions. They will be investigated and judged for their illegal meetings with terror organizations, for selling the national assets for a pottage of lentils, for abandoning the residents of the country to become victims of terrorist organizations. They will be investigated and judged for establishing an army of saboteurs in the heart of the land, and for having armed them with Israeli weapons. They will be investigated on suspicion of treason, breaking the public trust, paying bribes on an enormous scale for political objectives, and now, for using the branches of government in a violent and illegal way against their political opponents.

"What you must do now is just to take photos, and grind your teeth. Take pictures and document everything, because this inquiry commission will one day be convened, and those responsible will be called to judgment.

"Today is Thursday," I finished. "Soon it will be Shabbat. Return home, rest well, and restore your energies, because the battle is not yet over."

The broadcast calmed the atmosphere and gave hope. I was perhaps able to calm the deep feeling of frustration resulting from the unwarranted brutality. Instead of screaming – take a picture, and certainly don't raise a fist to fight back.

I believed in what I was broadcasting as far as the facts were concerned, but in the matter of the inquiry commission, I knew that I was fibbing. The thoughts were expressed in order to calm the public and bring some hope, but I knew quite well that even after a change in the administration, no investigative committee would be formed. I entertained no false hope that 'Bibi' Netanyahu would behave any better than Menachem Begin. Even though Netanyahu himself spoke in those days of an inquiry commission for the Oslo crimes, it was perfectly clear to me that the Israeli right wing was not capable of investigating and certainly not of judging the perpetual masters of the land, the leftist elites.

The operation was a success. Again, 'Zo Artzeinu' proved itself able to act on a nationwide scale – despite police preparations (and in fact, very much thanks to them), and despite the ceaseless shadowing and sheer brutality. Almost all the participants finally had made it to the capital and many of them were able, despite everything, to demonstrate opposite the President's residence.

Jerusalem was covered with the slogans "Rabin – Go the President". A combination of police over-reaction and media luck turned what at first seemed a total failure into a very successful protest. The protest earned broad media coverage, my helicopter became the day's perfect gimmick, and the general impression was 2:0 in favor of 'Zo Artzeinu'. But what had happened was merely an omen of what lay ahead.

It became clear that the rules of the democratic game become nullified as soon as the leftist government meets an effective protest. The regime, concerned over its public image, learned that it was possible to brazenly break the law, make thousands of illegal arrests, and encourage violent police behavior. During this time the media kept a discreet silence and was in cynical collaboration with the various police investigation systems and, sometimes, even the judicial branch. There, once again, there was a repetition of police brutality, and after the final round of vicious blows, the participants scattered and returned to their homes.

Complaints to the Department for Policemen Investigation were actually complaints to the cat that guarded the cream, and a complaint to the court systems required the inner strength that people no longer had after demonstrations of this kind. Very rarely was justice done in the end (even in the case of Yisrael Orange or in the judgment of our own sedition trial, where the judges explicitly noted the vile behavior of the police, it was only to fulfill an obligation. A real rectification was never undertaken and none of the bullies has paid for his deeds.).

The police went out of their way to break cameras and destroy evidence. When complaints against them for various offenses were filed, counter-complaints were suddenly and 'surprisingly' opened against those complaining – and who has the time, the money, and the strength to cope with organized systems and their legal departments. A few were persistent and even scored convictions. Ephrayim Havivian, commander of the Special Patrol Unit, was tried and convicted, as was his deputy Dudu Revivo, but surprisingly they both remained in their positions, and were meted out nothing more than symbolic punishments.

One determined citizen who took the trouble to sue the district commander, Aryeh Amit, scored a verdict of a heavy personal fine on the commander. Under heavy pressure, the judge changed the personal verdict and contented himself with payment of the fine by the police. As a rule, all the accused officers remained in office, and were even promoted to more advanced positions.

Their brutality proved to be effective. The police achieved its goal, and the demonstrators were afraid to return to the streets. From here on, it was clear to every activist that participating in the 'Zo Artzeinu' activities meant vicious blows, false court charges, and involvement with a hostile judicial system. Not many were willing to continue to cope under such conditions, and I, as head of the movement, was not flexible enough to quickly grasp the new situation that had been created and to change tactics.

A few days later, newspaper headlines announced that the State Attorney's Office was considering charging 'Zo Artzeinu' with 'sedition'.

> THE RIGHT: THE DAY INTERIM AGREEMENT IS SIGNED WILL BE DECLARED DAY OF NATIONAL MOURNING
> **ATTORNEY-GENERAL: 'ZO ARTZEINU' WILL BE TRIED FOR SEDITION**
> *Yediot Acharonot*, August 29, 1995

I had no idea what the legal meaning of the charges meant, and I didn't delve into the matter. I only knew that never before had such a charge been brought against an opposition group acting against the government, except when it was on the basis of racist incitement. Michael Ben-Yair, a close friend and ideological partner of Yitzchak Rabin, mobilized the judicial system for a political battle, making use of a law from the pre-state mandatory era which had never before been applied in the history of the State. It was obvious that the government was under pressure, and the democratic character of the country was not the most important thing in the eyes of those who were in control of the government and the courts.

Still, I did not at first understand why the State Attorney's Office had to go and make headlines, for they were only disgracing themselves. However, I realized very quickly that the public in general does not distinguish between being accused and being convicted. For Ben-Yair and the State Attorney's Office, it was important to target the government's opposition as lawbreakers, the actual court case being of secondary importance. Ben-Yair was interested in the headlines more than in the actual charge-sheet against us, and as far as he was concerned, he had achieved his goal. Two years would go by before the trial would end, millions of dollars would be invested by the government in searches, investigations, preparing the file, and the trial itself. But all this was a cover for the immediate goal that was achieved in making these headlines – demonization of the heads of the successful movement that was able to wage an effective struggle against the government. The poor investigators did not know what they were supposed to be looking for, but the real goal was to see us in the news reports, going in and out of endless hearings, in the role of outRight villains.

At that stage, the political system had recruited not only the police and the army, but also the State Attorney's Office and the judicial systems. Ben-Yair did not really intend to charge us with 'sedition' – after all he was a lawyer and knew well the effect of such a charge upon the democratic image of the State of Israel.

Only after the murder of Rabin would the investigation suddenly come alive. The harsh media incitement cleared the ground, and the indictment was presented to the Magistrates' Court in Jerusalem.

Not before it was leaked (of course) to all the media.

'Paris' or 'Tiananmen'

If at the start, before blocking the roads, we were like a ticking bomb whose potential energy could not be accurately assessed – a little David approaching Goliath with his slingshot – now, after two successful nationwide operations, we were considered a serious threat. It was obvious that it would not be long before another operation would take place, and baseless rumors about us circulated in the media.

I was already aware that a direct confrontation with the violent arms of the government would crush our remaining strength and public readiness to continue with demonstrations; nevertheless, I made no change in our tactics. It was sort of an entrenchment in our positions, and obstinacy, which had indeed brought us this far, but was now becoming an impediment. The psychological pressure was great; expectations soared. I refused to deviate from the principle I had set for myself not to request a police permit, and above all – I tried to do battle relying exclusively on principles rather than sagacity.

We decided on a mass demonstration in front of the home of the Prime Minister in Jerusalem. The designated area was to be Paris Square, and the intention was to stream there from all over the country and squat on the road opposite his residence.

A short time beforehand, activists all across the land were to honk their car horns for two minutes, to reproduce the effect of the Memorial Day sounding of the sirens – memorializing the hundreds of victims who had been killed since the Oslo Accords were signed.

The implication was evident: Channeling all the demonstrators to one specific place would enable the police to organize themselves properly and employ terror against us. Running counter to the simple logic which would have militated against such an action stood a naive faith: the wholehearted dedication and self-sacrifice of thousands of people arriving with the clear knowledge that they would be the object of vicious beatings, people who would demonstrate total passivity – such devotion simply had to win in the end.

That's how it was with Luther King in the USA... wasn't it?

As we had done before previous operations, we planned to hold an orderly convention, in which a clear operational plan would be distributed. This time the Jerusalem Beit Orot did not suffice. With our typical *chutzpa*, we decided the venue should be the Binyanei HaOoma, the main convention center of Jerusalem, the most imposing national center we could think of. Shmuel went to check out available dates, cost, etc.

We were afraid that in view of the general climate in those days the management would be hesitant about renting us a hall. Our anxiety proved to be justified, but on other grounds. The management would not believe that we were seriously thinking of ordering a hall with a capacity of 2500 places at one week's notice. Organizers of events on such a scale normally make their reservations a year in advance. But in light of our previous experience, we were filled with self-confidence and had faith in our success.

There was one difficult problem. Channel 7, which was operating under the constant threat of closure by the Minister of Communications, Shulamit Aloni, could not afford to support us openly, and therefore refused to publicize the event. Of course all the other means of communication were closed off to us. We had to resort to the old tried and true method: billboard notices, and mentioning the event in every media interview. In those days I became quite expert in sandwiching in such messages in the course of being interviewed by newspaper correspondents. We rented the large hall and got to work, which we completed within five days with great success.

All the extra-parliamentary protest movements had been invited to participate in the proceedings. The hall was jam-packed. For lack of seats, many had to stand in the aisles.

Among the speakers were Elyakim HaEtzni, Nadya Matar, Prof. Israel Hanukoglu of the 'Organization of Professors for a Strong Israel', colonel (res.) Moshe Leshem, and many others.

While the hall was filling up, a correspondent from the *Davar Rishon* newspaper turned to me with the question.

"You don't think that you have failed?"

I failed to get what he was driving at. "What have we failed in?" I asked. "The hall is filling up."

"Yes, indeed," he replied, "but they are all religious people."

His observation was not all that exact, but basically he was right – most of the crowd were religious. The answer that came from my lips expressed my entire world outlook.

"We have not failed," I asserted. "The hall is full, but **you** have failed."

"Why us?"

"Because you have failed to come," I explained.

This answer said it all. We are entering history, we are no longer just being appended. Success or failure will no longer be a function of "Did we succeed in mobilizing you", but rather to what degree we managed with our own resources to affect developments. The feeling of being an 'appendage' had been so deeply ingrained in us that at various demonstrations of the Right, there were cases where protesters had removed their *kippot*, or had worn hats, in an attempt to create the impression that the proportion of secular participants was greater than it actually was. This sense of inferiority naturally radiated out into the surroundings, so that the question posed by the correspondent of *Davar Rishon*, despite its provocation, was based on a genuine public feeling. His perception was that the protester was a rightist / settler / crocheted-kippa wearer, who was doing his best to have an effect on history. He did not entertain the possibility that these were people who felt themselves genuine Israelis, an essential alternative to what was happening outside the hall. Would he have dared pose a similar question at a convention of 'Peace Now': "Haven't you failed? After all, you have not succeeded in rallying the religious?!"

My response was actually the essence of the difference between 'Zo Artzeinu' and the other protest movements. The activists who had joined 'Zo Artzeinu' did so with an invigorated feeling of liberation. The entrenched settler establishment became aware of the difference and attacked from the right, while the Left establishment became aware of the danger and attacked from the left – and how!

The participants in the convention left it in high spirits. The size of the gathering and the enthusiasm displayed impacted on every member. One woman, who asked why we should provide the police an opportunity to beat us once again, received a straightforward answer from me, namely, that our strength lies in the passivity that we would exhibit. Towards the close of the meeting, we distributed posters with a photograph of a Jerusalem policeman in the act of brutally mishandling a youngster, and suggested that they be posted up all over the country. In this lies our strength, we explained. We, the people, do not wish and do not intend to defend ourselves with force, but a policeman who behaves brutally will find his photograph prominently exhibited everywhere and will be ashamed to show himself.

Our working assumption had always been that among those attending our conferences there would always be a significant number of detectives and General Security Service agents.

At that time there was perfect synchronization between the security élites, the heads of the GSS, the IDF and the police, and the leftist government. This is not the place to delve into the roots of this phenomenon, but it was evident that thousands of settler telephones were bugged; countless relevant jokes circulated among the faith-keeping public at that period. Many residents would routinely lift the receiver of their telephones with the greeting, "Shalom to all Listeners", instead of the customary "Hello".

We were aware that the convention hall was infested with detectives with tape recorders. When, shortly after, our trial began, a member of the national police unit for the investigation of crimes, a detective named Karni, took the stand and described how he had discreetly taped the speakers at our convention. The taped material had been transcribed and was presented as evidence in the trial. We had not recorded the talks at the convention; the Israeli police had done the job for us, and presented us with the finished product as part of the testimony.

The guidelines for the demonstration opposite the residence of the Prime Minister in Paris Square demanded an even greater degree of passivity than heretofore. We knew that we were leading the public towards a most violent suppression, and that the only weapon at our disposal was the police's sensitivity to public opinion. To that end, it was most important to cleave to the principles of nonviolent civil disobedience to the most unsparing and extreme degree.

The representatives of the media were told the precise place where the demonstration was slated to take place, and the participants were told to come to the rally with their hands tied above their heads. I also advised those who thought themselves up to it to blindfold themselves. This was greeted with some mutterings, but the assembled members accepted my recommendations, gathered up the distributed materials and dispersed.

That very night, the poster of the vicious policeman was posted up everywhere, and his identity was revealed. It was a concerted attempt to exert psychological pressure on the police to refrain from the application of violent force, an attempt that did not bear fruit.

The police on their part also engaged in psychological warfare, with the cooperation of the media, in an attempt to discourage the public from taking part in the demonstration. In interviews granted by the Police Commander and senior police officers, a clear threat was articulated that great force would be used. The means for crowd dispersal were broadly displayed; the TV channels broadcast from the offices of the Police High Command, and the police even announced the code name of its planned operation for the following day:

'Devil's Dance'.

★ ★

The demonstration in Paris Square was planned for Wednesday, 18th of Elul, 5755 (September 13, 1995). As with all our demonstrations, we tried to hatch up a unique

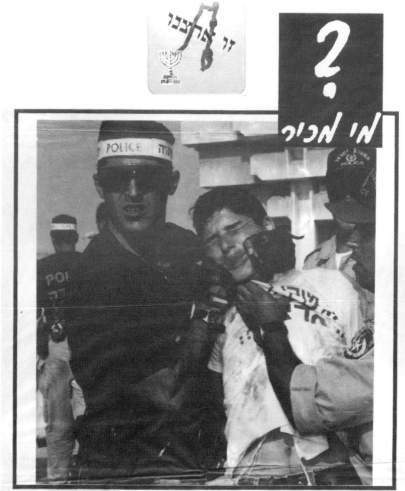

Who can identify him?

A POLICE THUG WITH BRASS KNUCKLES ATTACKS YOUTH LOYAL TO HIS PEOPLE AND HOMELAND

Anyone with information regarding the identity of this hooligan is requested to fax 'Zo Artzeinu'

gimmick for the media. It was important for us to display creativity and a sense of humor. The first demonstration had not required anything remarkably distinctive. The blockage of the road was in itself a revolutionary innovation on the Israeli scene – in its nation-wide character, as in the implementation of civil disobedience. In the second demonstration, we undertook the tracing of footsteps along the paths leading to the President's residence, to show Rabin the exact route to be followed. The use of the helicopter and the march that was to have taken place along the Jerusalem highway were also an interesting novelty, which lent the demonstration the flavor of a special 'happening'.

What we were going to do this time? Would this be still another straightforward demonstration in Paris Square in Jerusalem? We hit on the following:

Situated near Paris Square is the well-known Kings' Hotel. We decided to rent a room on a lower floor, with a suitable balcony facing the square, and sneak in a powerful amplifier device. We would then seal the entrance to that room from inside, enabling us to address the demonstrators above the heads of the police with a fiery, inspiring speech, without fear of interruption. The idea was to deliver our message directly (somewhat Mussolini-like...) to the media, and to encourage the demonstrators lying on the road below. Shmuel wanted me to undertake the role of speaker, because he had no faith in his ability to express himself well in Hebrew and preferred to be with the demonstrators below. I could not agree. I knew it was going to be rough down below, and I couldn't send the public off 'to battle' while staying out of it myself. Reluctantly, Shmuel accepted the responsibility. I sat down and wrote out the speech, and Shmuel perspired a whole night committing the text to memory.

I arranged to meet Rina Matzli'ach, correspondent of the Second TV Channel, at the entrance to Jerusalem, an hour before the demonstration. The media folk knew that Zo Artzeinu would not put on a 'simple' show and they anticipated some surprises, but I had a problem of how to convey our plans to the press – but not to the police. I was aware of police surveillance over our every step and move and did not want to reveal our little gimmick, so I took precautions. Our meeting was held in Channel Two's hired car. "Just tell me where to position our camera," pleaded Matzli'ach. I explained our plan, and rode off to the center of town.

Across from Beit Agron I met Shoshana Chilkiyahu. Shoshana, a war widow and a celebrity among Jerusalem's veteran citizens, drove her car up Hillel Street, and I joined her. It was time for the simultaneous honking, and, to my great pleasure, all the cars driving along that street stopped, their passengers got out and stood at attention, while the drivers honked continuously for two minutes. The din was deafening.

When we reached King George Street, our way was blocked. I got out and continued on foot. Many demonstrators were streaming in the direction of Paris Square carrying 'Zo Artzeinu' placards, while many others marched with their hands tied demonstratively above their heads. Some had taken the trouble to come equipped with their gas masks, for use in the event the police carried out their threat to use tear gas.

On the way, I met Michael Fou'ah, carrying a placard with tied hands. We marched along together down King George Street. To our right was Heichal Shlomo (the building of the Chief Rabbinate), and up ahead I saw the Kings' Hotel, which overlooks Paris Square. The closer we came, the greater the noise and tumult. The street was alternately blocked off and then re-opened, at times in order to facilitate the streaming in of huge police forces from every side, at times because of the demonstrators who succeeded in squatting on the road for a few minutes.

The number of policemen on duty was astounding. It seemed as if the entire Israeli police force was on hand, shoulder to shoulder. Throughout Jerusalem and the roads leading to it, ring after ring of police barriers had been put up, and whoever looked like a potential demonstrator was immediately arrested. The fact that thousands did, nonetheless, manage to find their way to the square was in itself quite surprising. (In a private conversation I had with a senior police officer a year later, he vividly described the fear of the unknown that had gripped the police in the face of this new phenomenon in the theater of Israeli demonstrations, and the hysterical reaction to every event associated with Zo Artzeinu.) Four ranks of policemen standing one next to the other cut off movement from the sidewalks to the streets, preventing attempts to break through to the heart of the road. I found myself among several hundred protesters on the pavement pressed tightly between the wall of policemen and the wall of the Kings' Hotel. The group seemed like a leaderless flock. I took charge, and shouted to them to watch me and do as I did. I lifted my arms, which were demonstratively tied together, high above my head, and called upon them to do likewise. When I assured myself that the crowd had recovered from its confusion and

was beginning to act in a unified manner, I turned around to face the police and began striding in the direction of the road. The crowd behind me followed, but there was no chance of making any headway. The police greatly outnumbered us, and we were immediately shoved back. A few more attempts, and I found myself lifted up high by a group of policemen and taken to the police van.

Police Officer: If you don't leave this area, I'll arrest you.
Shmuel: Excuse me, Officer. What does my shirt proclaim?
("I'm ready to be arrested for the sake of my country!")

As I was being carried aloft by the police past the Kings' Hotel corner, I glanced up at the balcony from which Shmuel was to have broadcast his speech to the nation. I expected to see Shmuel loudly delivering his oration, and policemen beginning to climb up to the balcony in an attempt to silence him. Instead I saw Shmuel with his back to the crowds, bent over the loudspeakers, trying to re-attach the wires. It transpired that Shmuel had indeed followed the plan, had positioned himself in the selected hotel room with the microphones, and had connected all the systems properly, but when he began his talk, the equipment failed to function. After a few vain attempts to 'revive' the system, he gave up and went down to the square to join the demonstrators.

Until my arrest, the conduct of the police was relatively restrained, but then the leash was loosened and matters took a violent turn. The police made wide use of horses, water cannon spouting colored water, lashes and horsewhips. The first targets were those who carried cameras.

"Your name, please?" asked Judge Cohen.

"Menachem Bloch," answered the witness.

"Please answer Mr. Feiglin's questions."

Q. "What is your occupation, Mr. Bloch?"

A. "I am now retired, but until two years ago I was a teacher of English at Bar-Ilan University."

Q. "Please tell the court what took place at Paris Square."

A. "Let me first explain that I attended the convention of 'Zo Artzeinu' in Binyanei HaOoma in Jerusalem, where I saw a photograph distributed to the members showing a policeman brutally mishandling a youngster who had participated in one of our demonstrations. I was greatly upset by the sight, and impressed with the rapidity with which the cruel police officer was soon identified by name. I then decided that when participating in any future demonstration, I would see to it that I had my camera with me, so that I could lodge a proper complaint.

"Like thousands of others, I stood on the sidewalk at the demonstration area. I had come to give expression to my identification with the protest."

Q. "You stood on the pavement?"

A. "Certainly. I didn't budge from the sidewalk. There were young protesters who tried to cross into the road, and when they were dispersed, they fled into the courtyards of the various buildings, with the police in hot pursuit. I saw the policemen entering the large courtyard near where I was standing and beginning to deliver blows. I took out my camera and began filming. Suddenly policemen swarmed around me. I turned and began to run, behind a large crowd of others. I felt the blows raining down on my back, and it seemed they were trying to make me fall, at the same time that they were pulling at my camera. I had tied the strap around my neck, and held the camera in my

hand, and I felt several attempts to wrench it out of my hands. Somehow I managed to escape the blows, but I continued running. I said to myself, Menachem, that's enough for one day. Enough. At the age of seventy, you have finally, for the first time in your life, suffered physical blows, and from the Israeli police, no less. OK. Enough. Now for home.

"I turned off the main street, and found myself confronted by a group of six policemen. One burly policeman approached, glowered at me threateningly, and said: 'You come from there, eh?'

"I understood that he was angling for justification to beat me up; after all, it was certainly obvious where I had come from. And my 'Zo Artzeinu' shirt, asking to be arrested..., certainly did not hide my affiliation. I realized that I had to respond as unprovocatively as possible.

"I said simply: 'And now I wish to go home.'

"Another policeman came up from behind me, grabbed me by the collar of my shirt, and pushed me on my way."

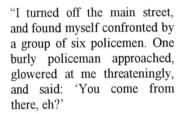

"Thank you, Mr. Bloch. No further questions."

The purpose of the dispersal was not to clear the intersection for traffic but to punish the public for participating in the demonstration.

People who were simply standing on the pavements or even further away from the curb, in the courtyards of buildings, were mercilessly beaten up. The most shocking incident of all involved a weakling of a girl who was standing not even on the sidewalk but under the pillars of the first floor of an apartment building. The mounted police went up into that area; the girl was grabbed by her hand and dragged along the street.

"Your name, please."

"Michal Melamed."

Michal briefly described seeing her sister seized by a mounted policeman and dragged down the street.

The prosecutor, Advocate Abarbenel, tried to trip her up in his cross-examination.

Advocate Abarbenel (prosecutor): "Your sister, what's her name?"

A. "Miriam."

Q. "How old is she?"

A. "She is now twenty-six."

Q. "Now twenty-six. A mounted policeman lifted her up on his horse and began galloping while she's on the horse?"

A. "No. She wasn't on the horse. She was being dragged along. He grabbed her by her wrists with one hand and galloped off with her dragging along."

Q. "And this was under the building above the supermarket?"

A. "No. It was on the plaza of the building which is above the supermarket."

Q. "What does that mean?"

A. "There is a large square at the entrance to the building."

Q. "I understand. That means that it was right under the building?"

A. "Yes."

The mounted police entered the courtyards of the buildings and trampled everyone in their way. Michael Fou'ah, who was in charge of one of the groups, was hit with a club on his head and his face was covered with blood.

עימות אלים בירושלים: המשטרה נגד "זו ארצנו"

VIOLENT CONFRONTATION IN JERUSALEM: POLICE vs 'ZO ARTZEINU'

Two demonstrators and 11 policemen injured in violent 'Zo Artzeinu' demonstration in Paris Square in Jerusalem; leader of movement and 21 protesters arrested; police used horses and water cannons; the settlers made use of a radio station; in photo: one of the demonstrators being arrested; see page 2 for full report

Ma'ariv, September 14, 1995

The stream of water sprayed by the water cannon struck, by mischance, the traffic-lights post in the square and felled it, which shows just how much of a blow it can deliver to a human being. An elderly lady who stood alone at a corner of the square was attacked by two horsemen who subjected her to a violent beating with their clubs, and left her lying in a puddle of colored water in the center of the road.

This scene was caught in the lens of the camera of Channel One, and was even screened in the evening news program. Chaim Yavin (the anchorman) refrained from posing any hard questions regarding the filmed incident.[1]

Instead, the broadcasters again and again emphasized the prevalence of violence at the demonstration without specifying who was implementing it.

We were the ones who suffered terrible beatings – while the media and the police accused us of being violent. The daily *Yediot Acharonot* outdid itself when it carried a report, the following day, under a huge headline, quoting 'senior police sources', of the suspicion that 'Zo Artzeinu' was activating units for beating up policemen (?!). The symbiosis between the police and the politically mobilized media negated the democratic basis of the state and the possibility for civil disobedience. Rabin's Israel was not a true democracy, and therefore civil dissent could not be tolerated.

We had believed that tied hands held aloft in front of television cameras would prevent physical violence and enable us, despite everything, to move the wheels of non-violent, passive civil disobedience forward.

We were mistaken, terribly mistaken.

The prosecution in our sedition trial admitted that civil disobedience had always advanced the countries in which it had taken place to a higher moral plane and to a more benign regime. However, the prosecution argued, the activity of 'Zo Artzeinu' could not be

---

[1] This phenomenon, in which violence manifested by the establishment is taken as proof of the victim's guilt, has been thoroughly described by the well-known psychologist Piaget.

considered a valid case of civil disobedience in its positive democratic sense, because civil disobedience is typically called for only in unsavory regimes.

When I stood up to present my defense summation, I referred to this argument and

said: "I find it strange that the prosecution has tried to argue a point that has absolutely no basis in history. Is the United States of Martin Luther King an example of an unsavory regime? Is England, against which Ghandi struggled, an unsavory regime? Is the France of the students' revolt an unsavory regime? It's true," I added, "that there was an attempt to carry out civil disobedience in a totalitarian regime; there were Chinese students who tried to do so in Tiananmen Square, and to everyone's surprise, they succeeded. For several weeks it seemed to the outside world that it was indeed possible to carry out such action in a totalitarian state. But when the period of grace came to an end, the chains of the Chinese army's tanks crushed the students in the square. Thus ended the idea that civil disobedience could take place in non-democratic countries.

"In Israel as well, an attempt at civil disobedience took place in a certain square. It was known as Paris Square. The demonstrators at Paris Square were under the impression that they lived in a true democracy, a state in which such means would be tolerated.

"Israel is certainly not a dictatorship, but, apparently, neither is it a true democracy. You, honorable judges, must now decide where Israeli democracy is headed[1] – towards 'Paris' or 'Tiananmen'."

After the demonstration, I was led to detention in the Russian Compound, where I went on a hunger strike. The following morning, I was transferred to the Petach Tikvah police station (to this day I do not know why to Petach Tikvah – perhaps to distance me from 'turbulent' Jerusalem), and was brought before the judge for an

---

[1] Earlier, Shmuel had described in his testimony the stark contrast between the description of what had happened in the United States and what had taken place here in Israel, and discomfited the judges, as detailed later, on page 235.

extension of my arrest. The judge sent me home under house arrest for a week, stipulating that my phone was to be disconnected.

I suddenly found myself busy mopping the floors and paying some attention to other domestic duties. I jokingly explained to the many visitors who dropped by that the judge had sentenced me to perform 'community service' under Tzippy's supervision.

Our phone line was not disconnected. The police investigators and the GSS preferred that I continue making use of it, since I was listened in to all the time. It reached the point where once a telephone conversation was interrupted by one of the senior investigators of the national police department for the investigation of crimes, a genial fellow named Ofer Gamliel, who had something to say...

A car assigned to detectives was often parked opposite our home. Although we made efforts to downplay the discomfort with humor, and affected ignorance of what was taking place, it was really impossible to free ourselves from the Orwellian feeling created by 'big brother' spying from every side. The mail we received was always opened, and I still keep as mementos invitations to parties addressed to my children which passed through censorship...

The invasion of our privacy was especially hard on Tzippy. We learned that the GSS had the means to install listening devices in our home, and perhaps even viewing devices, and probably made use of them. These devices are tiny and almost undetectable. The listening range is very short, which is why the detectives spent so many hours in the parked car. This Bolshevik-like behavior proved to me once again the nature of the regime against which we were campaigning. The government's weakness, their alienation from the people among whom they dwell, and their sliding into utilization of totalitarian tools in order to subdue a legitimate opposition struggle – reinforced my basic hypothesis, even if at a most unpleasant cost.

At a certain stage, I had the impression that the GSS had severed its contact with us and left our case exclusively in the hands of the police. Apparently they realized that we were a political movement, certainly not an underground body that posed a danger to anyone. The detectives of the national police department for the investigation of crimes had to continue their surveillance because they had received orders from the attorney-general, Michael Ben-Yair, to gather material in preparation for the possibility of presenting a charge-sheet of a unique nature, an indictment for 'sedition'.

We were in the midst of the Ten Days of Repentance, and every day a quorum came to our home for the morning prayers and *Selichot*. On the last day of house arrest, a company of Special Patrol Unit policemen and two carloads of detectives arrived. The detectives invaded my home and several others, gathered and made off with all written and printed material, and escorted me together with Shmuel and other residents to

Petach Tikvah, for interrogation in the offices of the national department for investigation of crimes.

★ ★

The demonstration in Paris Square was the last of the large-scale activities of 'Zo Artzeinu'. The buds of civil disobedience had been viciously cut down, and we found ourselves in a new situation. The media, which at first had displayed a degree of professional interest in the western phenomenon novel on the Israeli scene, quickly aligned themselves with the 'politically correct' Rabin stance and began to vilify us as violent people. Most of the public was very supportive, but it was clear that large-scale operations would no longer succeed. Nonetheless, we tried to find a way to enlist the masses in civil disobedience in their own homes, without exposing them to the harsh treatment of the violent arms of the authorities.

Michael Fou'ah made a very original proposal. One of the engineers of the electric company had told him that if a specific number of house-owners were to turn on their electricity and then turn it off simultaneously, it would cause nationwide electricity cut. This suited our purposes admirably. Instead of going forth to block roads and getting beaten in the process, we would stay put at home and 'block' electricity from entering our homes. We distributed a page of instructions to our activists for the operation, to be known as 'Protesting by Lights'.

The evening TV news program 'Mabat' began on the day of the operation with a broadcast from atop the roofs of Jerusalem, in anticipation of the results.

Detailed instructions for the 'Protesting by Lights' Campaign

The 'Protesting by Lights' operation failed. We learned from sources inside the electric company that the effect of the operation was indeed felt, but the company had readied itself for this contingency, the sudden drop in pressure was backed up sufficiently, and there was no need to disrupt the current.

That put paid to the idea of civil disobedience, and all that was left for us to do was to exploit our reputation and leadership and organizational ability for limited and annoying operations, in order to try and maintain at least something of the spirit of struggle on a low flame, until once again there would be an opportune time to renew the struggle on a more serious level.

The government of Israel had managed to clear the stage of that widespread public protest which had succeeded in shattering the 'propeller' image, but the pressure of dissent was still there, and continued to expand. The empty stage necessarily beckoned to actors of an entirely different sort, actors who have no place in the center of the playing field of a democracy where everyone plays and has the right to play – while the lunatics are left in the shade.

★ ★

I was greatly perturbed by the label of 'violent activists' that had successfully been stuck on us, and I sought a way to water it down. I decided to rely on humor. We searched for a gimmick that would express protest and simultaneously arouse gales of laughter at the regime's expense – even from those who do not see eye to eye with us.

It was the holiday season. The Intermediate Days of the holiday of Succot were approaching, and we felt it important to carry out a successful action in order to maintain the momentum of the struggle.

A group of new immigrants from France, who had gained experience during the students' protests in Paris against France's involvement in Algeria, joined up with 'Zo Artzeinu' and came with the following proposal:

Under the slogan 'Rabin is leading us like sheep to the slaughter', a flock of sheep, draped with 'Zo Artzeinu' shirts, should be let loose to wander through the center of Jerusalem – and let the Police Special Patrol Unit cope with them instead of with human protesters. The sight would be hilarious, quite apart from the fact that it would be quite clear to viewers at home which side the harmless sheep represent.

We started preparations immediately. We had never before functioned clandestinely. On the contrary, I made sure to act always in an open manner, and not allow myself to fall into the trap of excessive secrecy. I knew that our home telephone was being bugged 24 hours of the day (most probably to this very day), and that every document published would find its way to the police without delay. I therefore followed the opposite course. Every paper I wrote, I immediately distributed widely, thus preserving my identity as a free person, while the 'shadows' about me continued to chase the wind.

But with operations of this kind, strict secrecy had to be maintained if we were not to be thwarted.

To bring a flock of sheep to the center of the capital, to clothe them in the movement's shirts, to bring demonstrators and newspapermen to the designated area, and all this under the very noses of the detectives – this was certainly no simple escapade.

Tamar Chakun, who very conscientiously orchestrated our activities in Jerusalem, was given a simple assignment: to set up two protest vigils on King George Street across from the Mashbir square, bearing signs proclaiming, 'Rabin is leading us like sheep to the slaughter'. On our fax network (to which at least ten policemen and GSS detectives were subscribers...) we informed our people that there would not be any blocking of roads by the protesters, nor any other illegal action – and we stood by our word. I indicated to Tamar that there would be certain additional stages to the demonstration, and Tamar understood, performed her part, and refrained from asking superfluous questions.

I notified the newsmen of the vigil opposite the Mashbir square. A protest vigil on the pavement was a very common sight in those days; were it not an action undertaken by 'Zo Artzeinu', no reporter would have come to cover the event. "Apart from the vigil, what else is planned?" they wanted to know. "It will be interesting," I said laconically. Apparently we had a 'good reputation' among the journalists, who did not want to miss out on 'something interesting', and they showed up in droves.

The police sensed that something was brewing, but were hard put to place their finger on it. Large police forces were concentrated in Jerusalem and its environs. It later transpired that the police had anticipated another road-blocking operation. A sympathetic farmer from one of the southern moshavim loaned us a flock of sheep that morning. We were very apprehensive that the police had already put two and two together and had somehow, by piecing together snatches of information gleaned by listening in to telephone conversations and our slogans, figured out what we were up to.

For that reason, we wanted to transport the sheep in a closed truck, but that didn't work out, and the sheep were taken to Jerusalem in an open trailer.

We met our farmer at a secluded rendezvous on the outskirts of Jerusalem, first making sure that we were not being followed. We set to work energetically clothing the poor sheep in our movement's shirts. Meanwhile the protest demonstration was already forming in the center of town. The sheep were brought into the city under the searching eyes of thousands of policemen who had been put on alert that morning. Apparently the police were on the lookout for organized groups of crocheted-kippa-wearing youth carrying Israeli flags, and they didn't associate sheep with a forthcoming 'Zo Artzeinu' demonstration.

We arrived with the sheep right up to the corner behind the Mashbir building, from which a narrow path and staircase lead up to the square and King George Street.

Shmuel saw to the sheep, and I found my way to the demonstrators and newsmen. I was under great strain. I was afraid that at any moment the police might violently disperse the protest vigil, or discover the flock of sheep getting ready under their noses. Shmuel kept calm and saw to all the details, as usual.

I was besieged by the reporters, who, as usual, were short on patience. "Is this what you brought us here for?" I asked them to be patient: "Those who wait will not be disappointed." And, sure enough, within minutes the flock of sheep began to spread out into the center of the road, led by an energetic activist named Rivka Matityahu.

Yediot Acharonot, October 13, 1995

It took the astounded policemen a few minutes to realize what we had cooked up and to begin corralling the poor sheep, which kept evading them, scampering back and forth from the sidewalk to the road.

I was left alone. All the photographers delightedly rushed to film the sight, and from our point of view the results were perfect. The scene was extremely funny: dozens of grim-looking policemen, the tumult of walkie-talkies and confused orders, around a flock of sheep declaring their readiness to be arrested for the sake of the homeland, searching for some grass to nibble in the center of King George Street.

All the newscasts that day began with this story, and the whole country rocked with laughter, both the Right and the Left, and our violent image was somewhat scaled down.

We ended the demonstration at the moment we felt that our objective had been reached and that otherwise it might explode into a violent confrontation. The sheep were returned to the *moshav*, and we went off to the gathering organized by Professor Hillel Weiss, which was taking place not far from there, in Heichal Shlomo.

A population census was about to begin at about that time. It provided us with yet another opportunity to display our lack of faith in the establishment, by refusing to cooperate – a step that borders on a minor misdemeanor.

We decided to call upon the public not to take part in the census, which was due to start in a month's time. As usual, we had a problem with communicating this recommendation to the public at large. We had no advertising budget, and apart from faxes and telephone calls, there was little we could do. We again had to resort to worming our way into hostile media broadcasts and sandwiching in a report concerning this boycott in the various interviews.

Another action was due to take place earlier. On Saturday night, the Prime Minister was to address an international economic conference in Binyanei HaUma. We decided on a step that in democratic countries is popular among national protest movements: we would sneak in among the guests to the convention, handcuff ourselves to the seats, and interrupt the Prime Minister's speech with shouts of protest against the disaster he was bringing upon us. The object was to express our dissent in an international forum, to embarrass the Prime Minister, and to undermine his position and the legitimacy of his actions. Rabin had a very weak personality. His volatile temperament worked against him, and he would very quickly lose control of himself. We hoped that this is precisely what would happen in full view of the delegates assembled from all over the world – and that is indeed what happened.[1]

---

[1] I recollect that a few days earlier I had seen on the evening TV newscast 'Mabat' how demonstrators for environmental control (the Green party) had 'attacked' a British minister. They threw on him a can of red paint. The minister was all spattered with the paint but remained unruffled – and even Chaim Yavin treated the incident humorously. We, in contrast, did not dare to initiate physical contact of any sort with the Prime Minister, for we knew how such a step would be interpreted. On the other hand, we viewed creating a disturbance during his appearance before the audience as an acceptable move – which is how it is viewed in normal democracies. A few days before Rabin's assassination, I called upon the public to lie down before the Prime Minister's limousine. Ben-Yair seized upon my words as if he had found a treasure, and in the charge-sheet drawn up against me, this call was interpreted as incitement to murder...

For fear of eavesdropping, we sat on the pavement of a cafe in Ra'anana, and planned our steps. We carefully weighed all the details: how to implement the boycott of the census, and how to carry out the demonstration during Rabin's talk in Binyanei HaOoma. We realized that anyone causing a disturbance would be immediately ejected from the hall, and that this would happen no matter how many of our supporters had infiltrated. We decided to act in pairs. Eight pairs of demonstrators, attired most elegantly, would purchase tickets and enter the hall as bona fide participants.

Before that, all sorts of ideas, some quite bizarre, were raised in the course of our deliberations in the Ra'anana cafe. Someone suggested releasing scores of mice in the convention hall; the women in the audience would climb up on their chairs, confusion would reign, and the Prime Minister's speech would come to an inglorious end. Someone else proposed the use of stink bombs at the start of his address.

I invalidated all such proposals because of one fear: too great a commotion might lead to general hysteria in the hall, a mad rush for the emergency exits and physical harm to the participants. It was necessary to decide upon a way of disrupting his address without frightening the audience or causing them to get up and leave.

We thus decided to make do with the following plan: Our men would enter and seat themselves in various places throughout the hall.

Each pair would be equipped with handcuffs and a small klaxon used to scare away rapists.

As soon as the Prime Minister began his talk, the pairs would proceed to chain themselves to the base of their seats with the aid of their handcuffs, and the first pair would begin the show. A minute's blast with the horn until the small gas container was depleted and then loud cries of condemnation of the political process. Security guards would of course fall upon the chained pair and it would take about ten minutes to file away the handcuffs and escort them out of the hall; another five minutes till the audience calmed down and the Prime Minister renewed his talk. Then the second pair would do likewise – and so on. That evening the Prime Minister would no longer think of finishing the talk as planned, and the guests would return to their respective countries as ambassadors carrying an unambiguous message – the people of Israel do not at all see eye to eye with their government, as it has tried to claim.

Shmuel, as usual, undertook responsibility for the technical aspects: selection and coordination of the people who would carry out the plan, and purchase of the necessary 'commodities'. I assumed responsibility for the census boycott and publicizing this step. We were still in the midst of our deliberations when the mobile phone rang. It was the editors of the TV 'Popolitika' program, inviting me to participate in a discussion on the subject of violence (as a representative of the violent elements, of course...) which was to be held that very evening.

I had often been invited to take part in that program. I sometimes agreed, and at other times, refused. The moderator, Dan Margalit, I personally liked. He was a leftist, like all the others in the media, but at least he admitted it, and journalistic professionalism took precedence over his personal views; I sometimes sensed that he was trying somewhat to balance the obvious orientation of that cannibalistic show.

I fully understood the objective of the program's editors: to portray me as violent, and to induce me to make provocative declarations that would be defined as violent. I had never been invited to enumerate and detail the complaints that led hundreds of thousands to take to the streets. Such information was carefully sifted out in the Israeli media and discreetly hidden from the eyes of the public or presented in a ludicrous light. I was invited so that I could be pilloried. This was effected in various ways. Once I was invited following the murder of an Arab of Halchul (as the representative of the murderers...), when the GSS argued that the crime had been committed by residents of Kiryat Arba. On my way to the TV station I learned that the perpetrators were actually Arab killers, and I succeeded in turning tables completely – on the live program. On another occasion I was invited against the background of a general discussion of the rising tension in the streets.

I was always presented as one who was responsible for the problem, not as one who was trying to cope with it. One of the stock techniques was to confront the interviewee with a short TV segment that apparently contradicted his claims, and ask him to respond. The interviewee finding himself in a live program and obligated to deal with the 'truth' that was just revealed normally loses his balance. On one such occasion, I explained again and again that 'Zo Artzeinu' protesters never acted violently in their demonstrations. Dan Margalit cut me short, saying, "Let's have a look at this incident." I already guessed what was waiting for me. "No doubt they have fished up an episode showing a numskull delivering a punch at someone, and now I will have to prove that 'I don't have a sister'...,"[1] I said to myself.

The incident was screened, and we saw a bearded fellow trying to approach Rabin, shouting something at him. The demonstrator was, of course, intercepted about thirty meters away from the Prime Minister and arrested. This was the most 'violent' clip that the editors of the program managed to dig up from their archives after three full years of intensive demonstrations by the Faithful to the Land against the leftist government. Of course I immediately tried to point out how ridiculous this supposed accusation was, but when I later viewed a recording of the program, I saw that the camera had shifted away from me, that someone else was now the focus of the

---

[1] A reference to the situation in which one's reputation is sullied by remarks pertaining to one's sister – when one simply does not have a sister.

program, letting the viewer believe that he had indeed been shown a violent attack but that he had simply missed out on something in the screening.

The general public is not aware of the destructive power of the media. Few people understand the power of this tool, or the manipulative manner in which it can be exploited. Whoever wields the authority to stage-manage and edit the programs effectively controls the reality screened to the TV viewers, so that they absorb what is screened as the gospel truth.

For me, therefore, accepting an invitation to appear on a TV program meant starting out from an inferior position.

It would therefore seem the height of foolishness to participate in such programs, and, in general, to cooperate with the media. Indeed, many people on the Right do not agree, as a matter of principle, to being interviewed.

I could not afford such a luxury. I had to take advantage of every possible means of reaching the public, so that our activities should be known to all, so that our activists should be aroused, and so that the public should learn that we had indeed acted. I therefore agreed to appear on the program, in full knowledge of what lay in store. In those days I was interviewed quite often, and generally managed to root out the sting and to expose the media's method – and to exploit the media for my own purposes. Matters got to the point where I began to note that the newsmen shied away from interviewing me live, and to this day I made every effort to appear only on live programs.

The TV office sent a taxi from Jerusalem to pick me up and bring me to the 'Popolitika' studio. Shmuel clearly delineated the limits of my performance. "Listen," he said, "I don't care what else you do or 'babble' there. The one matter you must dwell on is the boycott of the census. Otherwise, it will all be a waste of time. I want you to take along a census form and rip it up before the cameras. I, on my part, will see to it that everything ticks in Binyanei HaOoma during Rabin's address, but you must make sure that all the people of Israel see you tearing up that form."

We laughed over this division of functions. I accepted the terms and rode up to Jerusalem. On my way, I had plenty of time to contemplate probable developments. After all, I could not simply take out a census form from my pocket and tear it up. This had to relate to something said during the interview. I tried to guess the nature of the question that would be posed to me, so that I could be ready to tie the answer to tearing the form to shreds. I was still engrossed in such speculations when the taxi drew up before the gates of the TV headquarters.

The subject regarding which I had been invited was the usual one: violence. After presenting the subject, and exchanging views with a number of leftists concerning the terrible violence manifested by the Right, Dan Margalit turned to me, asking: "Nu, what have you got to say to all this? After all, you people of 'Zo Artzeinu' are the main factors in this violence."

"Nonsense," I answered.

"What do you mean by that?" Dan said.

"Non - sense," I enunciated slowly.

"OK, explain yourself," Dan responded, doing his best to get the ball rolling.

"We are totally opposed to any form of violent action," I replied. "Yes, we are ready to violate the law openly and pay the price, but we will never be violent."

I had laid Margalit a trap. It was clear that journalistic curiosity on the one hand, and the hope, on the other hand, that a further response would get me hopelessly entangled would spur him to ask me for an example of such a non-violent violation of the law.

My words were calculated to draw from Dan Margalit the inevitable request, "Give us an example."

"I will indeed give you an example," I slowly replied, without any interruption from the rest of the panel. "Boycotting the population census is an illegal act. We do not have faith in this government's reliability, on its maintaining the secrecy of the details that this questionnaire calls for, and will not be included in a census taken by this government. Yesterday I received the census form; you can now observe what I am doing to it."

I produced the census form and tore it up before the cameras.

Margalit suddenly realized that I was using him, instead of the other way around, and I discerned his anger. Throughout the remainder of the program he did not permit me to say another word, and even a year and a half later, when I was again invited to participate in this program, he reminded me of this incident.

Thus, by devious manipulations, we succeeded somewhat in exploiting the tendentious Israeli media.

★★

Now it was Shmuel's turn to fulfill his assignment. The men were already paired off for their role in Binyanei HaOoma. Shmuel was to meet them on Saturday night with the handcuffs and the klaxons. He was to buy eight klaxons and sixteen pairs of steel handcuffs. On Friday, having finished his day's work in the postal service, he set off on his shopping. He encountered no difficulty in buying the klaxons, but he did have a problem with getting sixteen sets of handcuffs.

Shmuel went into a sports and weapons shop, and innocently asked for sixteen sets of handcuffs.

"Have you got a security agent's identification card?" the proprietor inquired suspiciously.

"No," Shmuel answered.

"Sorry. In that case, I can't sell you any."

Shmuel spent a few hours in Tel Aviv trying to locate a store that would sell him the metal handcuffs, but to no avail. His tales of needing them for his kids, for their games of cops and robbers, fell on deaf ears. Each of the stores demanded the proper credentials.

The planned action was due to take place the following evening, and the handcuffs were indispensable for its execution. It then transpired that this New Yorker was familiar with certain facts of life that I had no inkling of. In great embarrassment, his garment fringes (*Tzitzit)* flapping in the wind, with a red face and hardly remembering the little Hebrew he knew, he went straight into one of those seedy shops that provide implements for improving relations between males and females, and with lowered eyes said to the proprietor: "I need sixteen sets of steel handcuffs."

The shop-owner, without a word, turned to the shelf, and produced sixteen shiny sets.

"This is for political demonstrators," Shmuel muttered in confusion, while counting out the cash.

"Yes, yes, that's what they all say," the owner said indifferently, turning to the next customer.

The operation in Binyanei HaOoma was carried out as planned. The GSS knew of the plan, apparently by crosschecking what they had garnered from snatches of telephone talks, and apparently knew even the exact number of 'Zo Artzeinu' people in the hall (this became clear from the voices overheard on the police walkie-talkies). But the guards at the entrances did not know precisely who among the guests entering the hall were suspects, and our pairs succeeded in infiltrating. A few were identified and caught, and their handcuffs were confiscated, but five couples nevertheless succeeded in carrying out their task to perfection. It was clear that the organizers of the convention had been forewarned. At the beginning of his address, Rabin turned to the audience and very theatrically explained that he wished "to see the faces of the guests", whereupon all the lights in the hall came on enabling the security agents to scan all the rows.

Two minutes into Rabin's speech the first pair began their performance. The readiness of the security forces shortened the response time and the pair's removal took no more than ten minutes. At this point Rabin still maintained his composure, and nonchalantly observed what was taking place. Two minutes after he resumed from where he had left off, there was a repeat performance, this time from a different quarter of the huge hall. This time Rabin's face turned red, the veins of his neck looked as if about to burst, and he began to rant unintelligible epithets about 'Kahanists' or something similar.

American or European presidents with democratic backgrounds are accustomed to incidents of this nature and accept them as a feature of the culture of a free country. The hippies of the sixties and seventies, the Green activists of the eighties and nineties, had all created much more embarrassing situations for leaders of free nations, but the son of Red Rosa could not accept this form of expression, for true democracy had never coursed in his veins. I do not know how the lecture ended, because all the demonstrators spent the rest of the night locked up in the jail of the Russian Compound. One thing is clear: Rabin lost control of himself, as expected. Had he given the matter a little thought, he could have invited the audience to observe the live demonstration of 'Israeli freedom of expression' under his rule by calmly sitting down on a corner of the stage and allowing himself and the audience to 'enjoy' the performance. By doing so, he would have defused the demonstrators' actions and raised his own esteem in the eyes of the public. But we had not the slightest fear that the redhead from Kaduri would react in such a way. Had we been dealing with a person like Yossi Beilin, I would not have taken this gamble.

The operation in Binyanei HaOoma taught me an important lesson in matters pertaining to demonstrations and the media.

Even if one has brought preparations for an operation to perfection, and also seen to all the media aspects, as we had done, there was still the dominant factor needed to ensure success – pure luck. This operation had indeed come off very well, but that night the first rains fell and an Egged bus winding its way down from Jerusalem towards Jericho slipped at one of the turns of the road and plunged into the depths, many of the passengers meeting a tragic death. The next morning's newspapers all dealt with the accident, and our publicity stunt received no media attention.

The protest activities initiated by 'Zo Artzeinu' and other bodies made their mark, and the Rabin government's prestige continued to drop. Despite the media's support of the government's policy, the widespread open protests worked upon the general public, and public opinion surveys showed Rabin grievously behind the opposition's candidate. At great cost, the party in power organized an event, well staged and well covered by the media, which was to prove that the Left had wide general support, and that the Right was committed to violence. I did not then fathom what violence they were referring to in their slogans – I, who had always been in the eye of the storm, was aware only of government violence... Today I understand what lay behind the change in the slogan of the gathering from 'A Peace Rally' to 'Peace, Yes! – Violence, No!'. A week after our caper in Binyanei HaOoma, a huge gathering in support of the government took place in Kikar Malchei Israel. Dozens of buses streamed in from kibbutzim and Arab towns, filling the square to capacity. The big lie played up by TV as if the whole public was with Rabin angered many activists, who contacted me and asked for my opinion as to what should be done during this mass rally.

Indeed a few dozen right-wing demonstrators showed up at the site. I was totally opposed to their presence.

My intuition told me that an attempt would be made during the rally to stigmatize the entire Right as violent. The rally's slogan, 'Yes to peace, No to violence', appeared questionable to me, smacking of a propaganda ruse, and I preferred not to have rightists in the area.

"This is their show," I said. "A government that has to organize rallies in support of itself displays great weakness. Any rightist demonstrator appearing at the site will be playing straight into their hands. Leave them alone; they are collapsing."

And so they indeed were – until a young fellow from Herzliah, shockingly imperturbable, killed the Prime Minister in cold blood, overturning everything. The vile murder completely turned the tables, wiping out all perceptible chances of replacing the Left. Yigal Amir had killed Rabin the man, but in doing so had given the best imaginable boost to the policy he had been leading. Now there would no longer be even in the slightest opposition to the political moves ahead. The majority of the public, shocked to the core, now veered in the direction of support for the Labor Party. Amir had saved the Left. There is no greater lie than to assert that Netanyahu won the elections that took place about a year later thanks to Yigal Amir. Netanyahu won in spite of Yigal Amir.

Rabin was killed, and there began a campaign of incitement never heretofore witnessed in the country – against anyone who was tainted with loyalty to the Land of Israel. People waiting for a haircut were arrested in broad daylight for having cracked a joke. Kippa-wearing soldiers were ejected from cars waiting to give soldiers a lift, and many people generally felt uneasy about walking about with *kippot* on their heads. Violence and acts of vandalism against religious Jews spread everywhere. A rigid McCarthyism, concentrated in a small country, in which everyone knew everyone, pervaded every corner. The goddess of the media was Rabin's widow, who blamed the head of the opposition, Benjamin Netanyahu, for the murder. Rabin's blood drips from Netanyahu's fingers, she declared. Everyone who did not identify with Rabin's policy (not to mention anyone who actively rejected it) became an active accomplice in the murder.

People were arrested, rabbis stood in line for investigation by the national unit for the investigation of crime, and even Bar Ilan University found itself under crossfire, and felt it necessary to expel students who had expressed themselves very forcefully against the late Prime Minister (one of whom, Yitzchak Newman, of blessed memory, a recent immigrant to Israel, could not cope with the pressure and committed suicide).

The public fearfully retreated into their homes. The chapter of street protests had come to a close. The sewer manholes were opened and a flood of venom not witnessed since the days of the 'Season' (when the Haganah hunted down members of the Underground and handed them over to the British mandatory authorities) burst forth. People identified with the Faithful to the Land movements feared for their physical safety. Drivers of cars with stickers denouncing the Oslo Accords were arrested and sometimes beaten. There was no longer any chance of continuing to struggle at that time against the looming catastrophe and the relinquishment of the land into the hands of the Palestine Authority. Within a brief period, Shimon Peres, now Prime Minister, handed over to Arafat seven towns and wide areas in Samaria, and supplied the terrorist army with Israeli automatic weapons, without public opposition. Within less than one year, the PLO soldiers made use of those arms – to shoot, from the areas placed under their control, at IDF soldiers, killing sixteen of them.

The Rabin Assassination

Chapter 10

The individuals gathered in my small attic office looked as though they had come from another planet. Long beards, large skullcaps and penetrating eyes. They were Motti Karpel and his friends from Bat Ayin, who appeared at my home on Saturday night, November 4, 1995, having asked to speak with me on a certain matter. I was glad to receive them.

Motti explained the purpose of the meeting.

"Until now we have been involved in protest demonstrations against the government, but it is now apparent that, to meet the challenges, the national camp has no choice but to create an alternative leadership, an alternative to both the Right and the Left."

Motti's words did not surprise me. I had never seen myself as part of the so-called Right, nor any other camp for that matter. Ostensibly, I had carried out important work on behalf of Netanyahu and the Likud. I had brought large crowds out to demonstrate against the government – and what more could a parliamentary opposition expect? The dream of every opposition leader is the creation of tremendous public agitation capable of toppling the government and causing it to fall into the hands of the opposition like ripe fruit.

I assume there will be those to whom this will come as a surprise, but the fact of the matter is that I had never spoken with 'Bibi'. I never tried to initiate a meeting, nor did he ever receive any letter from me prior to his election. As a matter of fact, I had not initiated any contact with any Knesset members of the political Right. After my bitter experience with the 'Doubling Operation', the political Right, like all other rightist bodies, became irrelevant in my eyes. 'Zo Artzeinu' was able to bring tens of thousands into the streets and, after three years of vilification by the Prime Minister, the veteran Likud voters were able to savor a degree of gratification. The 'propellers' could relax in front of their television sets and enjoy the sight of the government being discomfited by the public. The Likud was indeed their political home but it was 'Zo Artzeinu' that straightened their posture. Netanyahu was careful to keep his positions hazy and let the Faithful to Eretz Yisrael pull his chestnuts out of the fire.

It is therefore not surprising that when the newspaper *Ma'ariv* published its list of the one hundred most important men of the year, the leaders of the Left were in the top positions while Bibi appeared on the list as number 49. (I found myself in eighth place!) The media as well as most of the public did not differentiate between 'Zo

Artzeinu' and the parties of the Right. In the eyes of the public, if you were against the Left and not a *haredi* (ultra-orthodox), then the only slot you fitted in was that of the Right. Activists of 'Zo Artzeinu' were sure that I was in close contact with Netanyahu and the Likud. Left-wing politicians demanded an investigation of monies transferred to 'Zo Artzeinu' from the Likud, while, in actuality, we never received a cent from the Likud or any other establishment body. The Left could not grasp the fact that the protesters covered their own expenses, were not bussed to the various demonstrations by the Histadrut, nor attracted by artistic performances to come and participate in the demonstrations.

One morning my phone rang and I recognized the voice of the editor of a well-known periodical. He got right to the point:

"I have a budget of one hundred thousand dollars to run a campaign on your behalf in the Likud primaries."

Up to then, several parties had wanted to embellish their electoral lists with my name and I had always refused, but this particular offer was the most serious and attractive. The Likud was shortly to choose its electoral list, which, aside from Yitzchak Mordechai, comprised the same anemic mediocrities who had been unable to block the Oslo tragedy. The image of the 'little guy' who had discomfited the government, backed by an adequate budget, would probably have led to one of the top spots on the list and a promising political career, not to mention the fact that it would also have rescued me from further legal procedures in the trial for sedition that was already under way at that time.

I respectfully and patiently explained to my interlocutor that I could consider neither the Right nor the religious in general, nor the Likud in particular, to be a serious alternative to the Israeli Left, and consequently I had no interest in joining any existing political party.

Motti did not have to go into long explanations, since I was more than receptive. I was fully aware that blocking intersections was not the solution to the problem but merely an attempt to stabilize the situation until a fundamental solution was found. Now that the public was afraid to demonstrate in the streets and the protest movement had been stifled, it was necessary to begin seriously weighing the alternative. It was natural for Motti and his friends to turn to me to promote the idea, and I was happy that they had taken the initiative. We sat around mooting ideas for a while when suddenly we learned that someone who did not believe in long-term solutions had found his own solution...

The agitated voice of Tzippy, who was watching television while folding the laundry, cut us short. "Come! Come quickly!" she shouted.

"What happened?"

"Rabin was shot!"

"What!?"

We crowded around our old TV set. We were totally shocked and bewildered; no one knew what to think or what to say. It was obvious that it was necessary to let the dust settle before assessing this entirely new and unforeseen reality. The assassination would obviously be followed by mass arrests of right-wingers, and no one would differentiate between 'Zo Artzeinu' and other factors.

That very evening, everyone associated with opposition to the Rabin government was to be singled out as an accomplice in the assassination. Even Netanyahu would not be able to 'tiptoe between the raindrops' since, from the outset, Rabin's widow declared him a murderer with blood on his hands. All the more so anyone who had really been active in the struggle against the leftist government; he would be automatically condemned as being covered with the blood of the victim...

The political exploitation of the assassination was beyond imagination. The concept of 'incitement' as the cause of the murder was disseminated with a vengeance by all the media, and no one proved able to withstand its force.

The discussion we had begun that evening was no longer pertinent, as it was obvious that we had now entered a very difficult transitional period. I bade my company farewell, released to the press a statement vehemently condemning the assassination, and prepared a small package containing my *tefillin*, toothbrush and several basic items. I then sat down to await the knock on the door by the police, a knock that, to my surprise, did not come.

I could not fall asleep the whole night. The murder of a Prime Minister of the Jewish State was an impossible act, beyond imagination. For some reason, I had thought that this could never happen. Something was destroyed that evening, when Israeli society lost its innocence in the chilling smile of a psychopath.

The disagreement that I had had with the Prime Minister, the awful danger that I felt his policies were leading to, did not dull my sorrow. But I had no way to express this sorrow. The Rabin family, in their blind hate, and the Israeli Left, in its cynical exploitation of the murder, turned the national mourning into an affirmation of Rabin's national policies. Expressions of sorrow by someone who had disagreed with Rabin were taken to mean admission of indirect responsibility for his murder and acceptance of his course of action.

By associating disagreement with Rabin's policies with responsibility for his death, the Rabin family saw to it that the late Prime Minister served as a representative of the Left rather than as the head of a government representing the entire nation. By doing so, they prevented a large part of the people (who were not prepared to accept responsibility for his murder...) from participating sincerely in the mourning. They thus dishonored his memory.

In the summer of 1995, the Rabin-led Labor Party was in dire straits. The Oslo 2 agreement was confirmed in the Knesset by a razor-edge majority of one vote (after MK Alex Goldfarb was bribed with a new Mitsubishi car) and the possibility that the government would fall was quite real. The general feeling was that the government was forcing its policies on the people. The opinion polls were predicting a disaster for the government in the upcoming elections. Rabin had lost the great advantage he had over Netanyahu. Opposition leader Netanyahu now held a commanding twenty-five percent lead in the polls.

On October 30 (four days before the assassination), public relations experts of the Left convened in preparation for the 1996 elections. Aryeh Rottenberg, who had led the previous successful Labor Party campaign, described how (in 1981) Shimon Peres had used a shocking tactic to save the day for the Labor Party, at a time when its situation was as dismal as it was now.

That election was held right after the successful attack (which Peres opposed) on the Iraqi nuclear reactor, when the popularity of the Likud soared.

Peres was aware that he was extremely unpopular among the voters. He was booed everywhere he went. Peres adopted a brilliant tactic (which says something about his character). He exploited the undisciplined, wild behavior of a marginal group of Likud voters for the good of the Labor Party. He deliberately went to areas where he knew that he would be bombarded with rotten vegetables, knowing that the television cameras would gleefully record the unbridled attacks upon him. He knew that most people were repelled by this offensive behavior and would, in response, give their vote to Labor. Repeated screening of the rude conduct of his political opponents helped sway many voters to the Labor camp.

Rottenberg: "Peres's tactic was brilliant. He skillfully encouraged violence against himself. He knew that it would serve his purposes."

Question from the audience: "Does that mean that there actually may be provocations to violence?"

Rottenberg: "I think that in 1981 much of the violence was contrived. In 1996, too, the campaign will be highly charged and there may be attempts to divert the campaign by such tactics..." [1]

As mentioned, in the summer of 1995, the Labor Party was facing disaster. All the well-rehearsed and orchestrated peace rallies, under the direction of Eitan Haber, head of the Prime Minister's office, and the broadcast handshakes with terrorists, had been replaced by the painful public awakening to the real ramifications of the Rabin policies in the form of unprecedented waves of terror. The number of peaceful citizens blown up while riding buses, Jews stabbed in the back, or simply victims of hit-and-run 'accidents' and similar terrorist actions were worse than in the days of the *fedayin* (murderous infiltrators) of the 1950's. Arafat incited these outrages, explicitly preaching *jihad* (holy war) and labeling terrorists who were killed as *shahidim,* martyrs. The

A BLACK MARCH
Gregory Abramov was murdered on Aliya Street in south Tel Aviv. Joshua Weisbrod was stoned to death in a refugee camp at Rafiach. Simcha Levi was stabbed to death with a knife. And we are not at all through with the list of victims. We bought pistols, we armed ourselves with clubs -- but the killing does not let up. Below are the 15 individuals who were murdered in the month of March alone. Rabin, what do you intend to do about it?
Ma'ariv, March 31, 1993

hand that shook the hand of Rabin was and has remained the most stained with Jewish blood since the days of the Third Reich[2], and the public began to open their eyes.

---

[1] *Nekuda,* issue no. 190.
[2] I have been corrected by someone who pointed out to me that Stalin killed off more... He was right.

The huge demonstrations, unprecedented in Israel, eroded the confidence of the public, even amongst the wavering citizens, in the government. It became apparent that a large proportion of the population felt that the government had erred and that many were willing to go forth into the streets and pay the price of their opposition. It became impossible for the government and the media to ignore the waves of protests, since the blocked intersections were only too visible. The government could no longer claim that a minuscule fringe of a mere two percent of the people were forcing their position on the general public, since it became obvious, now that the whole country had been jammed, that a large percentage, perhaps the majority of the public, were opposed to the 'peace process'.

Weizman: Our acute domestic dissension must not lead to attacks

Prime Minister's Office worried about wave of violence against Rabin and Ministers
Ma'ariv

The undermining of the public's confidence in the nation's leadership gained momentum. The Labor Party was moving headlong towards its downfall, and alarm bells rang loud and clear among the party old-timers. It was obvious that 'creative thinking' was needed to save the situation. The rabbit pulled out of the hat was the tried-and-true tactic: to paint the Right as radical and violent. The attention of the public was diverted from the main controversial issues to the 'real problem'. All the media were recruited[1] to paint a picture of a violent political Right threatening the foundations of the state.

The truth of the matter is that there simply was no such violence. Although the voters of the Likud are mainly from the middle and lower classes of Israeli society with a manner of expression that is sometimes crude, lacking in refinements of articulation, that is a far cry from blatant violence. True, a small number of radical Right groups advocating violence did make an appearance (Ayal, David's

GSS fears extremist violence against Rabin and senior officials
Yediot Acharonot

---

[1] When I speak of their being 'recruited', I do not wish to imply that the editors realized the nature of the political exercise in which they were playing a role. But it is clear that the Labor Party had no problem in conveying to the left-leaning, sympathetic media the line it was advocating.

Sword, etc.) and were dutifully given wide coverage in the media. But it eventually turned out that they were all hatched by the General Security Services chief *provocateur* Avishai Raviv. There were also various aberrant 'gurus' calling themselves rabbis who declared, as it became known later, that shedding Rabin's blood was permissible. These eccentric personalities were generally totally unknown before the assassination. As one involved in the protest movement, I had never heard of any of them, and there was certainly no support for them by legitimate spiritual leaders. (Later in this chapter, I will quote some of the prominent spokesmen for the intellectual and political Left, and it will be clear that there is no basis at all for comparison between the incitement led by the Left establishment and the radical statements from the fringes of the Right).

The government decided to hold a mass rally in order to convey two messages:

1. The people are with us, no matter whether 'the people' are thousands of Histadrut workers bused in to the rally in organized transportation, thousands of Arabs bussed in from their villages, kibbutzniks who will not have their salaries deducted for absence from work while at the rally, and, finally, unreflecting youth enticed into coming by the free appearance of their singing idol Aviv Gefen.

2. The Right encourages violence.

The name of the rally was changed from 'Rally for Peace' to 'Peace, Yes – Violence, No'.

All the speakers focused on this issue, and it was the central theme of the Prime Minister's speech as well.

Nothing could have been a more appropriate preface to what was about to happen than Rabin's speech, which was concerned only with the danger of violence, violence that was about to bring him down. Singers enthralled the crowd with songs of peace and love. Rabin even cut his own speech short to allow Aviv Gefen to jump on stage and provide his youthful fans with justification for their attendance.

The area was packed with well wishers, and the funds and apparatus of the Histadrut and the kibbutzim had been well invested in the successful staging of the event.

In reality the whole affair was a political rally signaling distress.

Were it not for the bullets shot at Rabin's back by the dark-skinned, kippa-wearing assassin, it is highly doubtful that the rally would have basically affected the dismal situation of the Labor Party. TV viewers saw tens of thousands of 'spontaneous' supporters of the government's policies[1]. But the average Israeli was not particularly impressed by this one-time public expression of support for the government, and became absorbed in the plot of the Australian movie *Crocodile Dundee*, which was being shown at the same time. The following morning the situation would have remained the same, and the collapse of the Labor Party would have gone forward at the same rate as before.

But the movie was suddenly interrupted by a dramatic announcement, and from that moment nothing would be the same again.

Rabin was assassinated by a person of the Right. The proof that 'the Right was violent' was there for everyone to see. No one paid any more attention to the Oslo process and its dangers, and indeed the polls showed Peres, the new head of the Labor party, with an extraordinary, unbelievable lead of eighty percent over Netanyahu.

The 'Conspiracy Theory' took off. There were unsubstantiated rumors that Yigal Amir had been sent by political elements to commit the act. Reality is sometimes more surprising than fiction, but such a mad theory cannot be reasonably accepted without irrefutable evidence. Yigal Amir, Golani veteran, law student, uninhibited and frighteningly cool-headed individualist, probably a psychopath, committed his crime out of totally independent motivation, killing Rabin on his own initiative. At the same time, from amidst the waves of incitement and suspicion, astonishing facts began to surface, which indicated that Amir's plans and intentions were well known to the authorities.

Could anyone have imagined that this time Peres would not have to go to rallies and be bombarded with rotten vegetables as in 1981? It was known that this time there would be "a little Yemenite who is out to murder the Prime Minister"[2], who is under surveillance and control, and will do the dirty work of directing attention away from the controversial, existential issues towards the subject of 'violence' in a most convincing way. After all, he actually intends to kill Rabin.

"All the élites in Israel are joined together under the umbrella of the Labor Party."
Daniel Ben-Simon, *A Different Land* (pub.
by Aryeh Nir)

★

---

[1] Nobody openly queried how it came about that a regime in a democratic country had to organize a mass public demonstration of support for itself, in the fashion of totalitarian regimes which are notorious for staging public demonstrations of this sort.

[2] From the report of the Commission of Inquiry.

"A scene from the theater of the absurd: In a cafe in Rehovot, Prime Minister Moshe Sharett, Isar Har'el, the head of the Mossad, and their spouses, meet to plan strategy on how to respond to what Sharett describes as the enmity expressed by the newspapers *LaMerchav* (Achdut HaAvodah) and *HaBoker* (General Zionists).

"The head of the Mossad freed several of his operatives from all their other assignments and ordered them to probe in old files... (of members of the opposition at that time – *my note*)."
Tom Segev, *The Seventh Million* (Keter
Pub.), page 274

★

"I am not a wrathful prophet but rather someone who sees things clearly, as I have tried to show in this long and winding essay which is focused on the existential danger to Israel embodied in the '**ideological lawbreaking' of the extreme Israeli Right.** "

> Carmi Gillon, head of the General Security Services during the Rabin administration; from his M.A. thesis, Haifa University, January 1990.

★

"I disapprove of Shimon Peres absolutely and unequivocally, and I consider his rise to prominence a cancerous, moral corruption. I shall sit in mourning for the State of Israel if I see him become a Minister in the Government..."

> Moshe Sharett, *Personal Diary*,
> Vol. V, p. 2301

★

Is it conceivable that Labor Party leaders shared their distress at the findings of the polls in the summer of 1995 with the other élites "under the umbrella of the Labor Party", for example, with the GSS...?

★ ★

About a year before the rally, two brothers, Eitan and Yehoyada Kahalani were imprisoned by the Jewish department of the GSS under suspicion of planning to kill Arabs. In order to get a conviction, the GSS used very doubtful methods. They saw to it that the weapons of the two brothers, without their knowledge, malfunctioned, and they were allowed to continue to take the actions of which they were suspected, that is, to actually attempt to kill an innocent Arab. Apparently, the GSS felt confident enough that it was not endangering anyone's life in order to get a conviction. The stratagem worked and the intended victim escaped unharmed.

Is it possible that someone believed that he had control of Yigal Amir's actions just as he had had in the Kahalani case, but instead of pulling the strings, found that he was being dragged along?

The GSS had had prior leads about the Kahalani brothers that brought about their capture. The GSS also had information about Yigal Amir. The GSS agent, Avishai Raviv, whose sizzling and effervescent reports to his superiors led to his being nicknamed 'Champagne' (as described by journalist Amnon Abramovitch after Raviv was exposed by Rabbi Benny Elon), posed as a close friend of Yigal Amir. He heard of his plans to assassinate Rabin, was photographed with him as he brandished the gun that later was used for the murder, and even encouraged Amir to do the deed[1].

Shortly after the Left took over the government (in 1992), Avishai Raviv began to appear in Rightist circles. He found himself a niche in the students' organization of Bar Ilan University and immediately became prominent as one of the most radical, always appearing at trouble spots brandishing an automatic weapon. He always drove an elegant car and had several apartments. No one could figure out how the young student could afford all those luxuries.

Raviv set up several fictitious organizations with names reflecting death and violence with religious overtones. 'Sword of David', *Ayal* (Organization of Fighting Jews), *Dov* (Suppression of Traitors) and other imaginative organizations in which he was actually the only member. He established himself at several addresses in Hebron, and, exploiting three befuddled youths who fell into his net and a fat government budget, began to fulfill the mission to which he had been assigned by his GSS handlers: to portray the settlers as violent and unworthy of recognition as *bona fide* Israeli citizens, and heating up the already overcharged public atmosphere. (Incidentally, Raviv was not the only such agent; in the 'Zo Artzeinu' demonstrations we identified a number of provocateurs, and even exposed them at our trial.)

The Achilles heel of the Oslo process was, and still is, the Jewish settlements. The dynamics of the process would lead to the uprooting and destruction of the settlements, which would be impossible to implement because of the broad public sympathy and support for the settlers. The settlers also represented the clearest ideological opposition to the policies of the Left. It was therefore necessary to besmirch them and in doing so defame the entire Right in the eyes of the general public, in an attempt to win the votes of the center.

---

[1] From the evidence given before the Shamgar Commission.

Raviv was extremely successful in the performance of his task. He would make his way through Hebron, wearing a skullcap and carrying an Uzzi submachine gun, overturning Arab vendor stalls, and always making sure that his belligerent activities were recorded by the television cameras that inevitably were on the spot when he went on his rampages.

Raviv did not restrict himself to the (legitimate) activities of a planted agent whose role was to ferret out and thus neutralize the really dangerous fringe elements, as flypaper is used to attract moths and flies to their extermination. On the contrary, he acted as an initiator of criminal actions while seeing to it that he received enough media coverage to ensure that his activities would be portrayed as the norm among the settlers.

"Avishai engaged me in private conversations and told me several times: 'Benny, Yitzchak Rabin must be put out of the way.' 'But how?' (the boy asked Raviv). 'Even if it requires committing suicide' (answered Raviv)."

> *Yediot Acharonot*, October 31, 1997;
> interview with a former member of the Eyal
> Organization.

An analysis of Raviv's activities shows clearly that his mission was not to catch criminals (it is questionable whether he ever fulfilled such a function) but rather to damage the reputation of those who opposed the government. Raviv staged initiation ceremonies for all sorts of fictitious Jewish extremist 'underground' organizations, always with television cameras present to record the event. In at least one instance, the staging was done with the active assistance and cooperation of Eitan Oren, the correspondent of the official state first TV channel. This occurred one night when Raviv brought the three befuddled young fellows whom he had recruited to the old cemetery in Givatayim, to the grave of Yair Stern, the leader of the Lehi underground organization during the British Mandate. Here he staged an initiation ceremony to a nonexistent organization dedicated to vengeance.

The correspondent for television Channel 1, Eitan Oren, presented the make-believe initiation as authentic. I actually believed it myself and did not know how I would manage to deal with such a mortifying phenomenon when asked to do so by the media.

With his head covered with a stocking, Raviv was televised simulating combat against the IDF in a built-up area. Because of the fair end-of-summer weather at the time and the general alienation of the state from those who lived over the Green Line, it was easy for Raviv to find several youngsters to participate in the sham. The weapons and the military-like planning created the impression of a real underground organization. The newspaper correspondents, either innocently or willfully, spread the story. Needless to say, people like Yossi Sarid, Darawshe, and other politicians of the Left eagerly jumped on this bandwagon.

It was 'obvious' that the Right was violent and would not hesitate to shoot even IDF soldiers. By means of the bogus organizations that he created, Raviv took responsibility for every act of violence perpetrated among the Arabs, thus stigmatizing the entire settler movement. Surprisingly... Raviv was never arrested. When an Arab in the village of Halhoul was murdered by his own brother, the GSS, before the truth surfaced, quickly spread the rumor that the crime had been perpetrated by Jews. Ayal, of course, took credit for the act, further proof that the settlers would stop at nothing, not even murder!

There were many other provocateurs in addition to Raviv. At our trial for insurrection, a video clip of one of our demonstrations, taken by the police, was screened. The film showed that **all** the demonstrators were totally passive, with the single exception of one participant who attacked the police and tried to get others to do likewise.

Izzie Katz appeared as a witness for the defense. He identified the violent protester as someone who had appeared at a public meeting (in Beit Orot) that was held in preparation for the demonstration. At that meeting, Shmuel Sackett identified the fellow as a GSS agent and asked him to leave. When he refused, Shmuel and I physically ejected him. This provocateur did not give up and did indeed participate in the demonstration in order to do the job for which he had been sent by the GSS.

When the murder in Halhoul became known, I was immediately invited to the television program *Popolitika* (as representative of the murderers, of course). Luckily, on the way to the program I received a telephone call from a friend in Kiryat Arba who told me what had really happened. When I announced on the program that the murder had been committed by Arabs, I was attacked by Amnon Danker, who asked scornfully, "How do you know?" Two days later everyone in Israel already knew the truth, but the GSS continued with its lies. Environment Minister Yossi Sarid demanded that the government "cut out the Jewish cancer in Hebron!" All the while the government knew the truth but continued to spread the lie in order to justify evacuation of Jews from Hebron, City of Our Fathers.

It is thus evident that the GSS worked in close cooperation with Prime Minister and Defense Minister Yitzchak Rabin. The purpose of these efforts against the Jewish settlers was to provide a cover-up for the real goal – to further the political aims of the Leftist government.

★ ★

יודיעות אחרונות

"יהודים רצחו הערבי בחלחול"

Jews murdered Arab of Halhul

So surmise the GSS investigators. Five men in army uniform, equipped with an Uzzi and an M-16, entered the village, identified themselves as soldiers, beat the male residents, handcuffed them, and carried out searches in their homes. When they saw Salmein Zamara (24) approaching them wielding a club ...

Yediot Acharonot, September 10, 1995

Avishai Raviv was an intimate friend of Yigal Amir. He was aware of Amir's plans, spurred him on, and knew what he was planning to do at Malchei Yisrael Square.

Raviv was at the Square when Amir shot Rabin in the back. He was ready for what was going to occur and he immediately went into action as planned.

★★

The cries "He's shooting blanks!" that were heard simultaneously with the sounds of the shots were reported in the media before they were denied. Those responsible for the scenario were unable to maintain the required secrecy in the moments of pressure and crisis following the shooting, and the plot began to unravel. Three minutes after the shooting, when no one yet

"אבישי רביב הסית את עמיר לרצוח את רבין"

Avishai Raviv incited Amir to murder Rabin

"You just talk. Let's see if you are a man." So said Avishai Raviv to Yigal Amir, according to the testimony of students of the 'Lehava Women's Academy' in Kedumim, when Amir told Raviv of his intention of doing away with Yitzchak Rabin. The principal of the school, Sarah Eliash, heard this testimony from several of her students the day after the murder...

knew what had actually happened and whether Rabin had been injured, the newsmen's beepers began to ring. The uniform message that appeared on the beeper screens was:

"This time we missed – but next time we will succeed." This message was signed by the fictitious organization created by Avishai Raviv, Ayal.

This was widely reported that evening.

Why did Raviv mistakenly think that "this time we missed"?

Was this hasty announcement prepared before the assassination?

Perhaps the bullets in Amir's gun were actually supposed to be blanks?

Perhaps Rabin was actually supposed to survive the shooting, thus allowing the government to achieve an electoral bonanza – a failed assassination attempt on live television, which fortunately ended with "this time we missed".

שטה ועוד לא לגמרי תופסת. כשאני רואה את
הארון וחושבת על זה שהוא שם. זה עדיין בכל
זאת 47 שנות חיים משותפים, לא מעכלים אותם
בהרף עין כזה, ואפילו לא אחרי 30 שעות".
– מה הרגע האחרון שאת זוכרת?
"זה הרגע הנורא, שירדנו במדרגות. הוא ירד
לפני מוקף במאבטחים שלו. בדרך כלל, הם
מקיפים אותו, ולכן גם אף פעם לא חשבנו שיכול
לקרות כזה דבר נורא, ואני אחריהם לפתאום
נשמעו היריות והוא נפל על הרצפה מיד, וסולם
נופלים עליה, ולי אומרים זה לא אמיתי, זה לא
אמיתי. דוחפים אותי לאוטו אחך ומריצים אותי
משם כמו באמבולנס, עם צפצופים ושידעתי
והגענו עד מחסום השב"כ. ואני כל הזמן שאלתי
איפה יצחק. אם זה לא אמיתי, אז איפה יצחק.
אנתנו לא יודעים, כשנרע נגיד. מה קרה? אנחנו
עוד לא יודעים, כשנרע, נגיד לך.
"וככה עוברים רגעים ארוכים ואני יושבת לב.

An interview with Leah Rabin, in which she describes the fateful moments as they descended the rear steps. "...Suddenly shots were heard, and he immediately fell to the ground, and they were all on top of him, and they said to me: 'It's not for real, it's not for real...'"

Raviv was unaware that the planned scenario had gone awry and that the Prime Minister had indeed been killed.

He continued to play his role – "This time we missed – but next time we will succeed."

★★

The disclosure by Rabbi Elon and the leftist journalist Amnon Rabinovitch that Avishai Raviv was a GSS agent should have set off alarm bells. But the Left, with its connections in the media, could not forgo the opportunities he provided for accusing the Faithful to Eretz Israel of all kinds of evil motives and intentions. The facts that almost demolished the theory were quickly swept under the mat, and the media campaign of incitement went on full blast. Abramovitch frankly admitted publicly that he had erred when he fulfilled his professional duty as a journalist by exposing Raviv, since by doing so he had provided the Right with a potent weapon.

The national television channel continued to show the phony swearing-in ceremony again and again, even after it was proved to be completely fabricated, and the propagandists of the Left persisted in making repeated use of this TV clip.

One and a half years after the assassination, Michael Karpin produced a propaganda film (funded by David Moshowitz, a leftist) which was screened on Channel Two, and which accused the entire Right camp of the murder. This video naturally included the Raviv staged performances, without letting the viewers know that he was a GSS agent and that what they were viewing was a complete fake.

A large number of theories were circulated after the assassination, some of which are quite plausible. One investigator invested one and a half years of diligent research and drew conclusions ever more astounding than what I have recorded here.

In the two years since the assassination I have received bits of information as well as various documents concerning the assassination, information and documentation that are truly staggering. I did not seek this information nor do I consider it to be of prime importance. However, because of my anti-government activities, many people thought that I was the proper address for this information. I was sorely tempted to publish in this book all the information I now have. But I have learned that the public, like a small child, cannot absorb too many overwhelming facts at one time, no matter how true. The rope by which a public can be pulled toward historical truth is quite fine and if it is pulled too hard, it will tear and no one will continue to listen. If I were to publish all that is known to me, this whole book would be rejected as a work filled with conjectures. Apart from that, as I noted already, I do not believe that the conspiracy issue is all that important ...

I decided, therefore, to include only data that is generally broadly known, and to restrict myself to raising questions and arousing doubts. I realize that there are items of information that are still missing, and that my conclusions regarding what took place suffer from lack of all the pertinent information and from much inaccuracy. At the same time, I know of no scenario that can point the way to a more logical solution to the puzzle. I think that only future historians will be able to fill in all the missing gaps. Suffice it to say that several factors played a role in this drama; that the simple theory, 'incitement – Amir – assassination – and no more', is patently not the whole story. Too many agencies and individuals were involved, including especially the GSS and the government, for this story to be so complete and simple.

The facts have already been reported in the state controlled media and are undeniable. The pressing questions that were raised have been quickly silenced. Anyone who raised questions was accused of attempting to brush off responsibility. When Michael

Karpin[1] was asked why he did not mention in his film that Raviv was a GSS agent, he ingenuously answered: "Because the Right exploits this issue to deny responsibility for the murder."

ה"אובזרבר" הבריטי, המסתמך על גורמים ביטחוניים ומקורות ישראלים

השב"כ תיכנן התנקשות מבוימת ברבין
ויגאל עמיר ניצל את התכנית

★ התוכנית נרקמה כדי לתרגל ולבחון את סידורי השמירה על רבין ולהקנות לו תמיכה פוליטית בציבור ★ אנשי השב"כ, שידעו על התוכנית, לא קלטו שמדובר בהתנקשות אמיתית. אחד מהם צעק "כדורי סרק" וניסה להעלים את אקדחו של עמיר ★ העיתון הבריטי חושף גם קטעים מהדו"ח הסודי של ועדת החקירה בעניין פעילותו של סוכן השב"כ אבישי רביב להכפשת מפלגות הימין ★ ראש "המוסד" החדש, דני יתום, היה קשור לפרשה. "ויש רואים בקידומו ניסיון לקנות את שתיקתו" ★ מקור המקורב לועדת שמגר: "זו וטרגייט גרסה המהדורה ישראלית; שערורית ענק העוסק בפוליטיזציה של שירותי הביטחון הישראליים" ★

(המשך בעמוד 7)

א. בן אהרן

[Hebrew article body text in multiple columns]

THE (BRITISH) OBSERVER REPORTS, BASED ON ISRAELI SECURITY SOURCES:

GSS planned staged assassination of Rabin -- Yigal Amir took advantage of it

The idea behind the plan was to drill and test the procedures for guarding Rabin, and to garner political support among the public. The GSS agents, who were aware of the plan, did not grasp that a real assassination had just taken place. One of them shouted, "Dummy bullets," and tried to conceal Amir's pistol. The British newspaper also reveals sections of the secret report of the Inquiry Commission relating to the activities of the GSS agent Avishai Raviv towards besmirching the good name of the parties of the Right. The newly-appointed head of the Mossad, Dani Yotam, was involved in this affair, and "there are observers who believe that his appointment was an attempt to buy his silence". A source close to the Shamgar Commission: "This is an Israeli version of (Nixon's) Watergate; a monstrous scandal involving the politicizing of the Israeli Security Services."

Yated Ne'eman, April 2, 1996

---

[1] On Channel 1 (May, 1997), in the program 'Media File', hosted by Ram Evron.

Leftist journalists have made no attempt to hide their political leanings, which explains why none of them has ever made a real effort to get at the truth about Rabin's assassination. As noted, Amnon Abramovitch, who exposed Avishai Raviv, even admitted that he would have hidden the truth about Raviv if he had foreseen the uses to which the Right would put it. So speaks an authentic senior representative of the 'free press', 'the watchdog of Israeli democracy', which is bound to bring the unadulterated facts to the public's attention, thus enabling them to form their own opinions.

Is it true that incitement led to the murder? That is the essential question. All the perplexities and all the unexplained technical questions concerning the assassination do not alter the basic fact that Yigal Amir admitted that he had planned and carried out the murder of Yitzchak Rabin. Even if someone should prove that Amir shot blanks and was only a tool in the hands of others, it would not detract an iota from the force of the Left's argument. Yigal Amir was indeed a member of the Right camp, a kippa-wearer, and a dangerous extremist, who committed his deed at a time of severe conflict with the Prime Minister. Clearly, had the general climate been tranquil, this young law student would not have been moved to this action. It would appear, then, that the accusation of the Left, that the incitement in the air was a major cause of the murder, was justified. It follows, therefore, that since incitement was a major cause, anyone who contributed to that incitement was an accomplice to the murder, no matter to what degree the GSS was involved in the tragedy.

"The anti-government demonstrations and incitement became more acrimonious and, in the end, someone decided that the Prime Minister deserved to be removed violently from the scene."[1]

This apparently obvious and simplistic conclusion was broadcast widely and repeatedly by the Left and its supporters in the media. The temptation to exploit the murder to place the blame on all those who were opposed to the government was clear. Apparently, this is the expression of an uncontrollable natural impulse. Nor is there anything new or strange about the behavior of the Israeli media. However, the sentence quoted above has become part of the Ministry of Education's official curriculum. Which means that the children of most of the citizens, who had expressed opposition to the Rabin administration, are taught in school that their parents shared responsibility for Rabin's murder...

---

[1] From the special file (pub. by The Center for Educational Technology, p. 25) distributed under the auspices of the Ministry of Education to all educational institutions on the second memorial day of Rabin's murder. The message: If you protested against Rabin – consider yourself an accomplice to his murder.

The internal contradiction in that statement has been repressed and has never been adequately considered. It is clear that, in the wake of all the protests and demonstrations, the legitimacy of the head of the government was undermined. That is precisely what the demonstrations were meant to do. That is exactly what the power of public protest can achieve. Public demonstrations cannot make government level decisions, but they can serve to question the decisions taken and to deny public legitimacy for the execution of such policies. Undoubtedly, it was easier for Amir to commit his deed against the background of continuous and tremendous public agitation, but it is cheap demagoguery and political cynicism to claim that the overall political climate was the cause of the murder.

The general public, which was in a state of shock after the murder, did indeed adopt that simplistic theory, and Peres's standing in the public opinion surveys soared dramatically. Had Peres not fallen into the self-made web of lies that his camp was spreading, he would have realized that, despite the efforts made by the mobilized media, the public would eventually snap out of its dejection and recover from the shock. Had he then immediately called for elections, he would have returned to office as one of the most widely supported Prime Ministers in Israel's history.[1]

Was the political incitement indeed confined exclusively to the Right? When the Left was in opposition and settlement activity flourished, the Leftists employed much more provocative terminology. The intellectual and political leadership of the Left, writers, poets, academics, Members of Knesset and heads of institutions, incited against settlers and the Right in a manner inestimably more foul than that employed against Rabin.

Some examples:

" (Gush Emunim is) a messianic cult, cloistered and cruel, a band of armed gangsters, guilty of crimes against humanity, sadists, murderers and pogromchiks, who have emerged ... from a murky nook of Judaism... from the depths of bestiality and contamination... in order to institute a rule of mad and bloodthirsty ritual."

Amos Oz, *Yediot Acharonot*, June 8, 1989

"When the decisive moment comes, we will have to use force against the settlers in Ofra and Elon Moreh. Only those who are ready to lead tanks against Ofra will be able to stop the fascistic erosion..."

Professor Zev Sternhal, *Davar*, April 15, 1988

---

[1] A majority of 80%, as shown by the polls taken shortly after the assassination, is inconceivable in democratic countries. Such a majority is always indicative of a dictatorship trying to cloak itself in democratic garb, such as Egypt or the Palestine Authority.

"I call upon you to take up arms against them...yes, to take up arms."
Professor Yeshayahu Leibovitch, *Ha'Aretz,* September 27, 1985

"There may be a situation where I will say: There is no longer any point in maintaining this society... And then, a civil war will not frighten me."
Moshe Negbi, *On Democracy and Obedience*

" The settlers live on bloodshed..."
MK Dedi Zucker, *Ha'Aretz,* April 19, 1987

"Gush Katif is an abscess that must be done away with."
MK Chagai Meron, in the Knesset, August, 1994

" (What will be the fate of the settlers who find themselves under PLO rule?)
Let them leave!"
Yitzchak Rabin, *Yediot Acharonot,* June 8, 1993

"I personally will fight even with weapons (against the settlers)."
Chaim Baram, *Kol Ha'Ir,* February 26, 1988

"Someone should assassinate Sharon."

Siman Keri'ah, # 19, page 82

"If it comes to shooting, I feel I am ready to shoot them (the settlers)."
A.P., *HaShavu'ah BaKibbutz,* August 10, 1988

"Anyone who volunteers to serve [in the IDF] in Yesha is like a member of the Nazi SS."

Professor Moshe Zimmerman

"Judeo-Nazis."

Professor Yeshayahu Leibovitch

"In the image of the Nazis."

Professor Moshe Zimmerman

"A little Nazi."

Amnon Denkar

" A cancer."

Yitzchak Rabin

"Collaborators with 'Hamas'."

                                                                    Yitzchak Rabin

                               ★ ★

"I know that many people are angry with the police and call them all kinds of names. I am not prepared to hear, Heaven forbid, the label 'Nazi' used against any Jew."

> (Moshe Feiglin, spoken in the presence of thousands of supporters in Binyanei HaOoma, Jerusalem, on September 7, 1995. These words are taken directly from the pamphlet of 'Zo Artzeinu' distributed in advance of one of its activities, material which was secretly recorded and presented by the prosecutor in our trial for sedition.)

                               ★ ★

Furthermore, coarse language and utterances such as Nazi, murderer and similar expressions that emanated from the Right were invariably from marginal, unintelligent elements, never from the leadership, political or spiritual. In the case of the Left, it was just the opposite. The leadership was in the forefront of the incitement. So it is not at all clear why the Right is always 'extremist', while the Left is, at most, just 'radical'.

This argument normally meets with a peculiar response: True! There have always been harsh, inappropriate *words*, but the bullets have only come from the right to the left, never from left to right. This argument is based on a strangely short historical memory. Essentially, it says, "history begins where it is most convenient for me!"

If the history of Right-Left violence in Israel over the hundred years of political Zionism (a period that covers the existence of these two camps) is carefully examined, it can be easily shown that the argument of the Left is without any basis whatsoever. The contrary is true.

                               ★ ★

When it seemed to the Labor-led Zionist leadership that the British authorities were beginning to question their ability to represent the Yishuv (because of the activities of the underground movements, Etzel [the Irgun] and Lehi), they did not hesitate to use extreme violence against dissidents and their families. They used tactics such as dismissals from work and expulsion of offspring from the school system, to more 'concrete' steps.

The first political murder in the Yishuv was the assassination of De Hahn, which was carried out by the Haganah on July 30, 1924.[1] It was only 'the first swallow'.

In the 30s and 40s, many members of Lehi and Etzel were kidnapped, imprisoned, tortured, and turned over to the British police. Some died under torture (by special volunteers in the Haganah), and many others did not return after being handed over to the British.

The following excerpt is taken from *The Season – Hunting for Brothers*, by Professor Yehuda Lapidot:

"In order to carry out 'the Season', 250 members of the Palmach and hundreds of others from the ranks of *HaPo'el* who were operating within the framework of the Haganah, as well as scores of others from the Intelligence Service, were recruited. They all engaged in collecting information about Etzel members, kidnapping and turning them over to the British criminal investigation department. Many were first held in jail and interrogated there, at times under torture...

"From data gathered from various sources, it appears that over 1000 Jews were handed over to the British authorities. Many belonged to the Revisionist Party but were not active in Etzel.

"On December 8, 1944, Professor Chaim Weizmann sent a secret message to the British Prime Minister reporting that the names of 500 suspects had been delivered to the British, of whom more than 250 had already been apprehended. According to the official *History of the Haganah*, the names of more than 700 individuals and institutions were provided to the British investigators and 300 persons were arrested as a result. At the same time, 50 persons were kidnapped and held in kibbutzim...

"Thirty students were expelled from their schools under suspicion of membership in Etzel."

From countless descriptions of torture and murder, I chose, as a family obligation, the story of Yedidyah Segel, of blessed memory. The description is taken from the memoirs of Rabbi Moshe HaLevi Segel, of sainted memory, who was famous as the person who sounded the shofar at the Kotel when it was forbidden by the British mandatory authorities.

"In those days, a calamity occurred in the family, caused by the hatred of fellow Jews. Yededyah, son of my uncle Yosef, of blessed memory, was kidnapped by the Haganah in Haifa. He was tortured to death. It happened on *Rosh Chodesh Shvat* 5708 (1948).

---

[1] *Who's Who in the Haganah and the Struggle*, Ephraim Talmi, pp. 151-2

The kidnappers took him to a house on Rachel Street, on the slopes of Mount Carmel, tortured him to death, and left his body on the main Haifa-Tel Aviv road...

The family published the following cry of anguish in the newspapers: 'We, the heads of the Segel family, cry out against the three-fold crime: the crime of the murder of our brother Yedidyah, of blessed memory; the crime of kidnappings and cruel investigations; and the crime of silence, indicating approval by the political and spiritual leadership of the people, which glosses over the blood of innocents and the cries of the tortured...' "

The outcry made no impact. The Yishuv was caught up in the War of Independence, which shelved all other issues, and the bereaved father carried his grief alone to his dying day.

Even after the establishment of the state, the bullets of the Left continued to cut down members of the Right. Sixteen passengers on the *Altalena*, survivors of the Holocaust who reached the shores of Israel on a ship loaded with arms for the fledgling state, were killed on the ship or after they had jumped into the sea and began swimming to the shore. Yitzchak Rabin, who participated in the killing, bragged: "We bumped them off on the ship and we bumped them off as they were swimming in the water!"[1]

It appears that the memory of the public is quite short. The time that has elapsed since the Left won the struggle for hegemony in the Zionist movement and no longer required violence for the pursuit of its goals has been long enough to wipe out general recollection of the true nature of the leftist ideology and its Bolshevik methods. All Israelis, whatever their political opinions, subconsciously believed that political murder was no longer possible in the Jewish state. Those who have grown up in Israel, a firmly established state with a stable regime, and who never personally experienced the political violence that characterized the pre-state and early state period, were incapable of conceiving such a hideous possibility in their wildest dreams. However, it seems that not only do historical events repeat themselves when conditions are ripe, but even the general reaction of surprise at their recurrence is a phenomenon that repeats itself.

The nation was in shock. This shock, reinforced by intensive and unambiguous propaganda, did not enable clear thinking and careful analysis of the event. Rabin was assassinated by a right-wing extremist. The general political climate at the time made it easier for the assassin to reach such an awful decision. But there is one question that has never been posed: How could Israel have reached such extreme polarization after 47 years during which common interests always overcame differences? Why did half

---

[1] These words were uttered by Rabin at an Independence Day celebration held at the Israeli Embassy in Washington D.C. when he was serving as Ambassador.

the population feel rejected and outcast, 'propellers' in the best case [Rabin's words] and 'collaborators with Hamas' (i.e., with their own enemy!) in the worst case [again, Rabin's words]?

The question is not why thousands went into the streets to protest. The question is, who created the distress that made going into the streets necessary?

The question is not why people expressed themselves so sharply and abusively. The question is, what brought citizens of all strata to the point where they felt they had to express themselves this way?

The question is not how the latest psychopath came into being (there are potential murderers in every society and in all fringes) but rather how the reality was created that brought this deviation to realization.

The Creator distributed the saints, mediocrities and madmen equally amongst all the opposing camps. The question is how the government managed to create a situation wherein the saints and mediocrities in the national camp became irrelevant, abandoning the field to one madman. It was the first time in the history of the State of Israel that a large segment of the population, perhaps the majority, found itself pressed to the wall and totally irrelevant to the political process in which fateful decisions were being taken. And this, not in areas, important as they are, such as the economy, society, education, and the like, but in an area that was to irreversibly shape the future of the State of Israel.

The fragile formula upon which the State was based, the twin underpinnings of Jewishness and democracy, were shattered for the first time by the Rabin government. Taking fateful, irreversible decisions on issues that are basic but controversial, on the basis of a razor-thin majority achieved with the aid of non-Jewish residents, is perhaps, strictly speaking, legal, and perhaps also democratic, but it drains the essence of the State of Israel as a Jewish State of all meaningful content.

Rabin had committed himself not to take decisions in this way, but at the fateful time he reneged on his commitment and scoffed at those who demanded that he be true to his promises.

Even if he had had a large majority endorsing his course of action, which was not the case, he should have realized that any political leader with even a modicum of democratic understanding would seek a wide consensus for such a major step. When Begin evacuated Sinai and destroyed Yamit, he had a solid majority in the Knesset and wide public backing (to my great sorrow).

The demonstrations by the Left demanding that the troops withdraw from Lebanon while Operation 'Sheleg' was still under way were very small in comparison with the demonstrations by the Right against Rabin. The famous '400,000' that 'Peace Now' claimed to have brought to Malchei Yisrael Square actually numbered no more than 30,000. The masses did not go forth into the streets, and did not risk getting beaten and arrested, and yet Begin, a true democrat, felt that he could not 'carry on business as usual'.

Even when, technically, he had full legal authority to do so.

On the other hand, Rabin, who headed a minority government (based on electoral agreements regarding surplus votes), bribery of opposition MKs, and Arab votes), viewed his opposition as nothing more than a nuisance. "You don't move me," said Rabin to half the country. All the demonstrations, protests, sit-downs, hunger strikes, assemblies, marches, tent camps of protest, all these failed to impact on the head of the government of the Israeli version of democracy. Nothing like this had ever happened before in the State of Israel.

It appears that the one who smashed the Jewish component of the formula expressed in the Declaration of Independence proclaiming Israel a Jewish and democratic state, also had to be the one to destroy the democratic component as well.

Rabin was no democrat. He pretended to be one, but his conduct was that of a dictator. He belittled and ignored the waves of legitimate protest for three years. He brutally cut down the non-violent civil disobedience that began to rise up against him when the public found it had no other means to influence the course of events.

Public pressure was brutally suppressed, the field remained abandoned, and it was only a question of time before the assassin would appear from some dark corner of the opposition camp.

In the history of Zionism, as noted, most of the bullets fired were aimed by the Left at the Right, and they achieved their objective.

The socialist camp took over the leadership of the Zionist movement without challenge, and the 'dissidents' were denied Zionist legitimization. The elimination of the *Altalena*, the execution of the 'Season', and all the other violent actions, confirmed this camp as the reigning power in the Zionist movement to this very day.

Since the episode of the *Altalena*, the nation has been calm, but it has been the calm of the victors. The Left set the norms of Zionism. With the continuous threats of war against Israel and non-recognition by the surrounding Arab nations, the historic argument over the nature of Zionism and the state had little relevance. There was no sense in arguing the merits or otherwise of 'returning' land to those who did not want peace. Moshe Dayan declared, for example, that he preferred Sharm-a-Sheikh without peace than vice versa, and in such a situation, no one had time or patience for an argument between Left and Right over basic approaches. The different camps lost their significance and ideological base. All that was left was the traditional rivalry, which did not lead to any exaggerated violence.

The debate over Eretz Yisrael that broke out after the Six Day War reawakened the old ideological rivalries and passions. But as long as the Labor Party still included an important faction on whom the Land still exerted its special pull, and the national consensus remained relatively stable, the barricade preventing the resurgence of the old violence was not breached. But when this ideological element disappeared and the Labor Party adopted a post-Zionist philosophy, they changed their approach and took to imposing the new party line on the nation (an approach that was in essence similar to that enforced by the Left in the days of 'the Season').

Thus, the old enmity resurfaced.

The Left had no reason to resort to violence since it already had achieved exclusive control over the Zionist movement. The 'establishment' was in its hands, while the Right remained faithful to Begin's philosophy of 'no war between brothers'. But Yigal Amir was not one of Begin's disciples. He also had little in common with Religious Zionism. He absorbed the negative features of all the camps: the haughty isolationism of the ultra-religious and the unrestrained fervent patriotism of the extremist fringe elements.

"Do you know the difference between a patriot and a nationalist?" a wise Jew once asked me. "A patriot is a nationalist without a sense of humor."

Ideologists without a sense of humor frighten me. Humor reins in, helping one to view reality in its proper proportions and adding the essential dimension of depth. There was no trace of this quality in Amir. The frozen smile on his face during his trial did not indicate a sense of humor or good nature. The smile was a weapon, meant to wound, not to soften.

Amir exchanged the crocheted skullcap, the trademark of Religious Zionism, for the black skullcap of isolationism, but he did not take upon himself the *haredi* discipline of obeying the sages, which accompanies that skullcap. Amir was an ideologue. He certainly did not act out of self-interest, but he freed himself of all restraints and became a dangerous bomb in an inflammable area.

Now that legitimate mass protest had been suppressed, the field was left open – for him.

The explosion was inevitable. After the assassination, Amir explained that he had been involved in all the legitimate means of opposition. Only after all else had failed did he turn to the only remaining tool of expression, the dumdum bullets.

"I went to demonstrations and I blocked intersections," said Amir. "But when nothing came of it, I decided to kill him."

It was then that I realized that had 'Zo Artzeinu' not embarked on a new kind of protest activity, which does indeed violate the strict letter of the law but stringently refrains from any sort of violent behavior, Yigal Amir would have taken the course he took many months earlier.

'Tiapiihants' – Criminal File 3996/95
(State of Israel vs. Feiglin and others)

Chapter 11

The language of the law (Article 136 of the Penal Code):
... "To incite to rebellion" includes any one of the following:

(1) **To cause hatred, scorn, or disloyalty to the State or to the authorities or the legally established court system.**

(2) **To incite or to induce the inhabitants of the country to attempt to get, in illegitimate ways, something governed by law.**

(3) **To arouse disinclination or disaffection among the inhabitants of the country.**

(4) **To create dissension and animosity between various sectors of the population.**

★ ★

We sat shoulder by shoulder, Moshe Negbi, the legal commentator of *Kol Israel* (the official state broadcasting channel), and I, facing the television cameras in Jerusalem.

That morning all the media had reported that the attorney general, Michael Ben-Yair, had decided to arraign the three leaders of 'Zo Artzeinu', Moshe Feiglin, Shmuel Sackett, and Rabbi Benny Elon, on charges of incitement to rebellion. That was the 'hot news' that day, so I wasn't surprised to be invited to the TV studio for the nightly 'New Evening' program. I *was* surprised, totally surprised, to find myself confronted, on a live program, with a prominent jurist, in a professional field in which I had no qualifications or expertise.

In the Tel Aviv studio, we were interviewed by Amnon Levi, who first turned to Moshe Negbi: "Is there any precedent for such a charge against an opposition movement? Why, is it conceivable that anyone demonstrating against the government should be charged with sedition?"

I felt I had been deceived. Here was a professional issue addressed to the jurist Negbi and I did not know how I could react to his words when my turn came.

Negbi, who was accustomed to this line of inquiry, responded: "Indeed, this is not a routine matter, but there has already been a case in which a Palestinian Arab who was accused of the same breach of the law was sentenced to a long prison term."

Negbi finished drawing his 'professional' comparison, and Amnon Levi turned to me: "*Nu*, so what do you have to say? Perhaps you too deserve a long prison incarceration?"

"I am not a jurist, and I have no intention of entering into an argument with Mr. Negbi in his professional area of specialization," I answered. "But I must point out that Negbi, who is here as an objective commentator, is far from being so, and it is important that spectators viewing this program should be aware of what is going on here. Negbi is an extreme leftist who was active in the dissident movement *Yesh Gevul* and even justified the outbreak of civil war under (what he would consider) favorable conditions. You too, Mr. Levi, are not at all objective – you have served as spokesman of (the extreme left) Mapam. If you really wish to conduct a discussion between professionals, you should invite a right-wing jurist, such as Elyakim HaEtzni. Since I am not a jurist, kindly ask me direct questions that are not of a professional nature."

My blistering counter-attack floored them. The game played by the media can be foreseen. Whenever a representative of the Eretz Israel camp finally gets a chance to express his opinions, this takes place under conditions that can only be described as blatantly unfair. Nonetheless, the spectators tend to be swayed by the false impressions created on the screen. [1]

The moderator quickly posed a direct question, as I had requested of him, and brought the interview to a rapid close.

The moment the TV lights were turned off, Moshe Negbi exploded: "That was a dirty trick," he said angrily.

---

[1] A striking example is the composition of the panel of the popular TV program 'Popolitika'. It consists of a moderator of leftist persuasion, an outright leftist, Amnon Denker, the left-winger Sheli Yachimovitch, or, alternately, the *Haredi* Rabbi Eichler, whose stand regarding relinquishment of parts of Eretz Israel does not differ from that of the first two, and last but not least, Tommy Lapid, whose opinion is determined by the degree of applause it will score with the studio audience, and which does not reflect a different approach to the Land. Side by side with a pitiable Eretz Israel spokesman who has been enticed into this lion's den, we will find other interviewees of opposing views who greatly outnumber him. In the final analysis, even should he succeed in expressing his viewpoints and making full use of the time allotted him equally with all the other participants, the final result is that he will have managed to get one-tenth of the screen time taken up in support of the opinions represented by all the other participants and the members of the panel. This technical imbalance is of less consequence than the belligerent, hostile manner in which our unfortunate representative is pilloried, since he always finds himself on the defensive, without ample time to rebut charges and explain his position.

"Look here," I responded. "I am prepared to discuss any issue with you in a forthright manner, but I am not willing to play along with the deception to which you subject the public. Why do you conceal your own position? Identify yourselves honestly, and then you can present your arguments to your heart's content."

Negbi was silent, his anger subsided a bit, and he finally admitted: "You've got something there."

We agreed to meet again and exchange views, and we parted amicably. We both had suddenly discovered somebody who did not fit the stigma associated with the other party. I felt that our brief encounter had been worthwhile if only for this reason. To my regret, there was no follow-up.

A year later, the head of the General Federation of Labor, Amir Peretz, closed down the whole country in a nationwide strike, the result of internal power struggles, causing tremendous damage, which no one could satisfactorily justify. I was quite surprised to hear the legal commentator of Kol Israel, Moshe Negbi, declare on the noontime radio broadcast: "At this very time, the leaders of 'Zo Artzeinu' are standing trial for sedition. If what they did is considered incitement to rebellion, what Peretz is now doing is the mother of all rebellions."

Perhaps that encounter between us had changed something in the approach of this person, or perhaps 'Zo Artzeinu' was no longer such a threatening force, so that it had become possible for him to relate to occurrences in a more objective manner.

The decision to investigate our activities under suspicion of 'incitement for rebellion' was publicized immediately after the blocking of the main roads. The State Attorney's Office made full use of the media in order to make its intention known.[1]

---

[1] The cynical exploitation of the media by the State Attorney's Office in order to further its positions should arouse general misgivings regarding its conduct. The State Attorney's Office is not meant to be a party in the political arena, its decisions should be strictly professional, and what should be its concern are legal considerations and its ability to substantiate the charges brought before the court. The reliance of the State Attorney's Office on leaks ("sources close to the State Attorney's Office...") to the media transform it into an interested party. This interest might be political or otherwise. During the Rabin administration, the State Attorney's Office headed by Michael Ben-Yair – like all the other élites in the country – served as an instrument in the hands of the post-Zionist government. The leaks and publicity regarding its intentions, before a charge-sheet was drawn up, and possibly even before there even was a real intention of doing so, were designed to create the impression that the leaders of 'Zo Artzeinu' were punishable lawbreakers. This meant that yet another branch of government, one which should remain apart from the political game, was being put to political use. The system of 'justice' joined, without any inhibitions, the other élites and branches of the administration which were exploited for political aims. A factor which is presumably above suspicion – the State

In reality, a charge sheet against us was not drawn up, and apparently there was no intention of doing so. The investigative setup, the prosecution and the justice system were quickly mobilized for a campaign against the new phenomenon. Yet I know that they did not really intend to place us on trial, because the investigators of the national unit for investigation of criminal activity, after prolonged investigation over many weeks, informed us, before Rabin's assassination, that the inquiry was over. Suddenly, after the murder, the investigation was re-opened, and took on new directions. Someone had obviously decided to exploit the public outrage over the assassination

---

Attorney's Office and the system of justice – had now joined forces with the police, the general security service, and the media.

An indictment against an individual, which is publicized in all the media, creates the impression of that individual's guilt in the eyes of the man in the street.

In view of the fact that the State Attorney's Office normally deals with cases with which it is not directly involved, the average individual justifiably assumes that there are reasonable grounds for its bringing charges. Apart from that, the average citizen has a basic faith in the arms of government. Man is a social animal; he requires a shepherd, and naturally has faith in him. This accounts for the fact that the state attorney can see to it that an individual is already considered to be convicted in the eyes of the public, long before an official decision has been taken by the courts. In our case, the State Attorney's Office had gone one step further, publicizing merely its general intention, without presenting charges.

Its vast power, beyond critical control, has inevitably become a destructive power. Zo Artzeinu was not the only target. Michael Ben-Yair decided to present a strange charge-sheet against the person who, thanks to the change in government in 1996, became his boss. The new Minister of Justice, Ya'acov Ne'eman, who attempted to alter the character of the State Attorney's Office somewhat, found himself on the seat of the accused, and bitterly resigned his post. Ne'eman, not like the accused 'Zo Artzeinu', knew how to grapple with the system, and in the end was completely vindicated.

But Ben-Yair had achieved his purpose. The person who replaced Ne'eman as Minister of Justice, Tzachi HaNegbi, was an inexperienced opportunist who had barely finished his law studies and never actively engaged in the practice of law. He quickly understood where the source of authority in the justice system lay, and was not anxious to look for trouble in the course of his career. Thus the State Attorney's Office acquired a rubber stamp in the form of Tzachi HaNegbi. The Ayala Chason affair, in which the justice system intervened in the decision of the prime minister to appoint an attorney-general who was not acceptable to it, was another instance of the blatant political use which the system employed to preserve its own interests. However, at this stage the public had already grasped the guiding principle behind all the maneuvering, and the public image of the prime minister not only was not damaged, but actually rose in the eyes of the public that had voted for him. The relentless use of this unchecked power, just like the unchecked use of medication, drained the state attorney, and to a great extent, the Supreme Court, of much of the public confidence which they had previously enjoyed. Thus, ironically, the justice system punished itself, by losing a great measure of national legitimacy – the basis of its power.

'Zo Artzeinu' did not 'profit' from this development, since in its time the State Attorney's Office still enjoyed overwhelming public confidence. The general public had not yet crystallized a clear stand regarding 'Zo Artzeinu', and the headlines appearing in the press quoting 'neutral' sources in the State Attorney's Office helped the man in the street adopt a position favorable to the government's.

and direct part of it at the leaders of 'Zo Artzeinu'. Indeed, if one examines the final wording of the charge sheet, one sees that the charge of sedition was merely a cover for the accusation of being responsible for Rabin's assassination.

Demonstrations and severe infringements of the law within the context of public protest are a routine matter in the State of Israel. Many before us had demonstrated and blocked highways (generally in a violent and severe manner, without the restrictions that we undertook to observe), but charge sheets had never been brought against them – certainly not on the charge of 'incitement to rebellion'.

The purpose was quite simply to neutralize our luster and grind us down financially and organizationally under the wheels of the legal establishment, thus compelling us to devote our time and energies to a courtroom entanglement instead of the political struggle.

Till then, the charge of sedition had never been brought against a movement struggling against government policy[1]. In view of the anti-democratic nature of this clause, the signature of the state attorney himself is mandatory, and Michael Ben-Yair was not anxious to affix his signature to the very first such charge ever brought in the State of Israel, a charge of 'incitement to rebellion' on the part of an opposition movement.

The article dealing with 'incitement to rebellion' has been on Israel's law books ever since the mandatory period. Originally it served as an instrument in the hands of Great Britain for control of the colonies such as India, Rhodesia, Singapore, and also – Palestine.

True, the State of Israel adopted the British laws, including the article dealing with 'incitement to rebellion', but in practice no political application of this law had ever been made. True, the fourth clause of this law, dealing with racial incitement, had been applied once before. Benjamin Kahane was sentenced for incitement when he published a proclamation calling for the bombing of the Arab town of Kfar Kassem. But exploiting this law against an extra-parliamentary group struggling and demonstrating against the government's policy – no Israeli government had dared to do so prior to this case.

It has always been agreed that sweeping use of the law against citizens opposing the government's stance (and not involving ethnic bias) stands in contradiction to the most

---

[1] The single case in which the charge of sedition was made concerned Benjamin Kahane, who had circulated a manifesto calling for the bombing of Kfar Kassem. It was a dissimilar case, since Kahane had not created a problem for the authorities. In his case, the judicial system relied on the fourth clause of the law defining 'sedition', while in our case, all the other applications were cited – causing hatred, scorn, or disloyalty to the State , etc.

basic democratic values. Indeed, not a few leftist spokesmen spoke out vociferously against the incitement charges brought against us.[1]

Theoretically it is quite possible to accuse nearly every citizen of 'incitement'.

All the administrations in Israel had always refrained from such an act, but in Israel under the Rabin government, the 'peace process' was placed at the very top of the ladder of national values. The 'process' had become a sort of 'religion' unto itself, overshadowing the principles of democracy.

At the very start of the legal proceedings, advocate Yosef (Sefi) Elon (brother of Rabbi Benny Elon) argued that the only way one can reconcile the law regarding 'incitement to rebellion' with living in a democratic country is by investing it with a most limited, clearly defined and unambiguous interpretation: 'incitement' is violence, speech with a violent purpose, and actions which are meant to provoke violence.

The court did not accept Sefi's position. The court did erase a number of clauses in the charge sheet, clauses by which the prosecution attempted to frame us with the accusation that we had acted violently against Arabs, a totally false, baseless accusation. But the basic decision in principle that the court should have taken – a decision that boldly states that such a charge-sheet has no place in a democratic society – was not taken.

We are talking about a period following closely upon Rabin's assassination. The gravely disturbed atmosphere in the country proved to be too compelling, and the court did not display the courage required at such a time.

The moment the court agreed to deal with the charge – the outcome was inevitable.

Let the reader re-read the four sub-sections of the law dealing with 'sedition' quoted at the head of this chapter.

Are you sure that you will never find yourself on the bench of the accused – for 'incitement to rebellion'?

Have you ever fomented discontent with or mockery of any administration?

The article of the law dealing with 'incitement to rebellion' provides the authorities with a legal instrument enabling it to bring its opponents to trial. Every individual in Israel is potentially an inciter – every journalist, every columnist, and every woman

---

[1] Such a tract has recently been published by Prof. Kremnitzer, who is rated in the judicial system as an authority of the highest rank, and who is, of course, not identifiable as 'right-wing'.

chatting with her neighbor while hanging up wash. One cannot find a single person who would not 'qualify' for one of the clauses under 'incitement'.

Of course this law is not applied offhandedly, but the principle that one is presumed innocent until proven guilty is overturned when this law is enforced.

We all incite.

Now go ahead and prove that 'you haven't got a sister'.

Go ahead and try to prove that you were only out to rectify a bad situation.

Go ahead and prove that you conducted yourself in 'legally acceptable ways' (civil disobedience, for example – kosher or not?).

Prove that the situation called for such conduct – that the country was truly in danger and that you were only determined to come to its aid, that a back flag was flying unfurled above the government's policies.

For, after all, what one person sees as a black flag, might be seen by others as a shining white one...

It was a week after the demonstration in Paris Square. Not only my house, but many others as well, were subjected to intensive searches. Shmuel Sackett and everyone else who was suspected of affiliation with our movement underwent at five o'clock in the morning the same troubling experience of being awakened by pounding on the doors and having the house searched. As for me, I had no idea of how vast a quantity of written material I had accumulated over the previous two months. The detectives left my home and kept returning, carting away countless cartons full of printed matter.

The feeling of impotence before the members of my family, whose questioning eyes were directed at me, made me feel physically throttled by this degrading invasion of my privacy. The detectives raked through the whole house, and our children reacted in their own way. Twelve-year-old Na'ama closeted herself away in her room. Nine-year-old Ayelet went out to where the investigators' car was parked, and used the camera she had received on her birthday to take snapshots of them from every angle. She was determined to turn with this evidence of intrusion to the proper authorities and make these people pay for the inconvenience caused. Aryeh and David were too young to understand what was taking place around them. They blinkingly viewed what was going on, trying to relate the image of 'the decent policeman', upon which they had been reared, with the reality they were witnessing.

Beyond the disagreeable personal reactions, there was indeed a comic element in the situation. The detectives, who were experienced in searching for criminal evidence such as drugs or stolen goods, were quite perplexed as to what exactly they were supposed to be looking for. "Just what am I expected to search for?" muttered the detective rummaging through my office in bewilderment, when the unit commander asked me in all seriousness whether I had arms stored away in my house.

Tzippy suppressed her rage, while I masked my feelings entirely and tried to diffuse the tension by affecting a jocular mood. "Good thing you fellows have come," I commented to the detectives removing cases of documentary material from my house. "So much rubbish has accumulated in my home, I'm grateful to you for cleaning up the mess." Tzippy was not amused. Fortunately, she maintained her composure and refrained from bursting out at the visitors.

This search of my home did not come as a surprise. I realized that such a development would take place sooner or later. Nevertheless, I made no attempt to conceal even one sheet of paper. I made sure to preserve my self-assurance as a free citizen, refusing to act like a wary, frightened mouse hiding from the establishment. I felt it was most important for me, for my own peace of mind, to continue to manage my affairs openly. Every paper I had written had already been widely publicized long before the detectives arrived. Indeed, as I was to learn during the later police investigations, the police were among the 'regular recipients' of my faxed messages, and every update flowing from my home computer made its way directly to the office of the national headquarters. Try as hard as they could, the detectives could find no material that had not already been publicized.

Their frustration and confusion was evident. They finally decided to confiscate my personal computer, in addition to the printed matter, hoping perhaps to find in its memory bank some plan related to a military overthrow... Not taking any chances, they even confiscated my old printer. I tried explaining to them that they would get nothing out of that, but to no avail. They insisted on doing a thorough job. To this day this equipment remains as evidence in the courthouse.

When they had completed the removal of the material onto the police van, they informed me, Shmuel, and the other neighbors whose homes had been searched, that we were under arrest, and we were officially escorted to the criminal investigations center of the Petach Tikvah police.

When the police van exited the settlement we were shocked to see a very large force of the Special Police Patrol Unit. It reminded me of the preparations made, during our military service in the reserves, for entry into the Arab village of Tamun in Samaria, on a search mission. I knew why a company was needed to enter a hostile Arab village, but the sight of such a company at the ready on the outskirts of Karnei Shomron was a devastating scene. The police vans, camped at the settlement's gates, were set to break in as if they were charged with overcoming a force of terrorists holding a group of hostages. They were equipped in an awesome manner. I don't know what had entered their minds, but apart from ladders and storming equipment, one could discern a number of them carrying rifles with telescopic sights.

"Have you all gone mad?" I asked the accompanying guards.

"We take no chances," was the laconic reply.

'Hamas collaborators' was the term the prime minister used to label us, at the time when that organization was sowing death and destruction throughout the country. With these simple words, the Prime Minister stigmatized the opposition that was active in those days – 'Zo Artzeinu' – as its own enemy, and these words percolated down through the police.

At seven o'clock, while still on the way, the driver of our police van, who was taking us for questioning, switched on the morning newscast, and, lo and behold – the broadcaster knew every detail about what had transpired in my home over the previous two hours. It was obvious that the police and the State Attorney's Office thought it important to announce to the people of Israel that a search had been made in the homes of the heads of the movement, and that the lawbreakers had been arrested. Once again it became clear to me that there were those who knew how to exploit the media for their political ends, even when they were ostensibly acting in the national interest.

We arrived at Petach Tikvah and were led into separate rooms.

★ ★

We were fully prepared for the police investigation, since we had readied ourselves for such an encounter from the very beginning, at all our gatherings and in all our manuals.

The investigating teams were very polite, and tried to create a friendly atmosphere in order to dissipate feelings of suspicion. We were left to wait until they had finished a preliminary thumbing through of the vast amount of collected material. Their object was to interrogate us as quickly as possible, before we even had a chance to recover from the morning's episodes. However, the whole affair was totally ill advised, as we couldn't add any information to what had already been publicized throughout the country. But procedures demanded an investigation – for otherwise, what would be done with all that material that had been gathered?

I knew exactly what the purpose of all that affected friendliness was, but I felt sufficiently self-confident to play their game and try to exploit it for my ends. Till the official investigation began, I chatted freely with the investigators, cracked jokes at my expense, and at theirs, and tried to bring them down to reality. It worked. Then, at a certain point, the official investigation commenced – and I, like my friends in the neighboring rooms, conducted myself according to our prepared 'guidelines'.

Investigative procedure requires that the interrogator inform the detainee that the cross-examination has commenced, and warn him that his answers may be used against him. At this stage, the questioner records his question in his report on the inquiry, reads it aloud to the person questioned, and then writes down the response. The entire procedure takes a long time, so that a few dozen questions can drag on for a full day.

The interrogator sitting opposite me jotted down his particulars, wrote his question, and then read it aloud to me: "Is it true that you and some other individuals established an organization known as 'Zo Artzeinu'?"

Feiglin and 5 'Zo Artzeinu' activists taken in custody on suspicion of sedition, and released on bail

Photo shows Moshe Feiglin (right) and Shmuel Sackett arriving for interrogation in the Petach Tikvah Office of Criminal Investigation
Ha'aretz, September 19, 1995

"See here," I replied. "You are fully aware of every word that has issued from our mouths. You know exactly how we conduct ourselves, and I have no intention of acting differently. I will not cooperate and will not answer any of your questions. You're wasting your time. I am certain that this police unit was established in order to deal with real problems and not for political purposes, and it pains me to see an entire staff engaged in a political inquiry of this sort.

"You will get the same answer to each and every question directed to me: 'This is a political investigation. I have nothing to say.'

"I therefore suggest that you drop this farce. If you wish – you can detain me in custody, or release me, as you see fit. Your time and mine are precious, and it's a pity to waste them."

The interrogator was not particularly impressed by my brief declaration. As far as he was concerned, it was a matter of following orders and routine.

"So what is your answer?" he repeated.

"What is the question?" I played along.

He repeated the question: "Is it true that you and some other individuals established an organization known as 'Zo Artzeinu'?

"This is a political investigation. I have nothing to say."

The interrogator patiently recorded my response, and proceeded to the next question: "Did you call upon the public to go out and block road traffic in protest against government policy?"

"This is a political investigation. I have nothing to say."

That was how the weird interrogation began, with a long series of pointless questions, which served merely as a softening-up prior to the more substantive questioning.

"Did you claim that the government of Israel was not legitimate?" he queried, after having jotted down his question.

The ability to persist in non-cooperation with an inquiry is really tested when you are accused of things you have *not* done. True, I had argued that the Rabin government had lost its moral legitimacy. It had been voted into power by deceit and falsehood, having committed serious violations of a wide range of laws. It would be very easy to twist my words and later present them to the court as a call for a real insurrection against the government of Israel.

So now I was being offered the opportunity of explaining my position calmly, every word would be recorded conscientiously by the diligent detective, and the court (if eventually there were a trial) would then have a correct and precise version of our position.

On the other hand, it was I who had instructed our activists to refrain from speaking out in an interrogation, and so I found it hard to act differently.

These were the thoughts that flashed through my mind when the questioner read off his question.

"This is a political investigation. I have nothing to say," I responded without undue hesitation.

"Did you plan on embarking on violent action in the pursuit of your goals?" he asked, aware of the dilemma I was facing and hoping to prod me into speaking up.

"This is a political investigation. I have nothing to say."

And so it went for hours. In the afternoon, the interrogator informed me that he was through for the day, and asked me to sign the transcript. I refused.

"But you have not said anything! So what difference does it make if you sign?" he practically pleaded.

"Forget it – don't waste your energy," I answered, and joined my group from Neveh Aliza, who were waiting in a separate chamber.

At the next stage, the interrogators decided to change their approach and shifted to threats: "If you don't cooperate, we will have to keep you under arrest."

To this day I haven't the faintest idea why it was so crucial for them to get answers which in any case they were fully familiar with, especially since all the evidence of our terrible crimes was already in their possession. Anyway, the threat made no special impression on us. When some of my arrested neighbors began to tire, we perked up their spirits, pointing out that the victors in this contest are those who display the most grit and patience.

The police then decided to play the game to the very end, and we were hauled to the jail cells of the Petach Tikvah police. The scene we saw was quite grim. Two prisoners in solitary confinement sat with arms and legs shackled. "They tried to commit suicide," explained the ledger-keeper upon seeing the expression on our faces. The explanation did not contribute to our peace of mind.

"After we topple the government, we will be qualified to publish a newspaper column devoted to criticism of eateries, and focus on the food served us in the various jails," I announced loudly. "We are already experts regarding the menu served in the jails of Tiberias, Rehovot, the Russian Compound in Jerusalem, Beit Shemesh, Petach Tikvah..."

"I have only one request," Shmuel said, in a similar vein, as he turned to the detective accompanying us.

"What's that?" responded the grim-faced detective.

"I would very much like to get a cell with a switch for turning off the light," Shmuel answered.
"What's on your mind?" responded the detective suspiciously.

"Look," Shmuel explained in his 'Anglo-Saxon' Hebrew accent, with a broad grin on his face. "Tonight our followers are going to engage in a 'Protest by Lights' campaign: all over the country, everyone will turn off the lights – and we too would like to participate..."

They let us wait in the entrance hall, and half an hour later released us all. It was obvious that they had no justification for our detention, and when they realized that our being kept in custody served no purpose, they let us go home, but not before setting the dates for the renewal of the investigations. It transpired that the 'guidelines' that 'Zo Artzeinu' had distributed in advance to all its activists had been very helpful, and saved the day for all those who had followed them. Those few who had acceded to the requests of the interrogators found themselves in much worse circumstances than those who rejected any cooperation with them.

The investigations went on for weeks. One or two days every week were devoted to endless questions, my answer being invariably the same: "This is a political investigation. I have nothing to say."

At one point I allowed myself a humorous retort, and when the interrogator finished reading me the question, he got the following response: "Tiapiihants."

"What? What's that?" the interrogator quickly asked, upon hearing for the first time a different sort of answer. He probably was hoping that I had changed my approach.

"Tiapiihants," I repeated.

"What on earth is 'tiapiihants'?" inquired the interrogator with growing interest.

"Those are the initial letters of my standard response, 'This is a political investigation. I have nothing to say,'" I explained most seriously. "You see, I really am sorry to cause you so much labor, all this writing. I am trying to make things easier for you."

"How should I write this answer down in the report?"

"Exactly the way it sounds."

From that point on, throughout the report, the enigmatic reply 'Tiapiihants' appeared again and again...

The questions related mainly to the nature of the material taken from my home.
"What did you have in mind when you wrote 'We represent the true will of the nation'? What exactly did you mean in your letter to..." and the like. At one point I

began making a practice of bringing books with me, and politely asked the interrogator for permission to make good use of my time. He responded most politely, and that was how I managed to complete reading several neglected books, books I had never found the time to peruse. Once every ten minutes or so, it was time to respond to a question; that was when I interrupted my reading to blurt out the standard 'Tiapiihants' – and both of us resumed where we had left off...

Under no circumstances did I allow the activities of 'Zo Artzeinu' to grind to a halt. I realized that the purpose of the investigations was to weaken our capacity to perform, and to cause peripheral circles of activists to drift away, for fear of clashes with the forces of 'law and order'. As for us, the inner core, I did not permit the pressure to affect us in any way, and throughout this lengthy period we carried on with every possible activity, totally ignoring the apparatus that was being activated against us.

With the passing of time, the investigators became accustomed to us, and it seems to me that they actually enjoyed meeting the strange birds that had fallen in their domain. On one occasion, one of them passed me by in the corridors of the national headquarters of criminal investigation, while I was waiting for the start of the inquiry, and chuckling showed me a copy of the faxed message I had sent to our activists the evening before.

"Would you happen to know who sent this particular fax?" he asked, a broad grin covering his face. I was well aware that, apart from the investigations, I was under constant surveillance, and, on one hand, it even pleased me, because it was important for me that they should all realize that as far as we were concerned – 'business as usual'.

Matters got to such a point that in the course of one telephone conversation at home, I was suddenly interrupted by the voice of Superintendent Ofer Gamliel, head of the investigating unit at the national headquarters of criminal investigation. It did not faze me in the least; I reacted as if it was the most natural thing in the world. The opened mail, the searches of my home, and the general aura of Bolshevism did not succeed in throwing me off balance and disturbing my tranquillity. I had won this war. They continually circled around themselves, but I did not develop any trace of paranoia symptomatic of underground activists. I remained the same free individual.

One day the show closed earlier than usual and the investigator on duty informed me ceremoniously that the entire inquiry had come to an end, and that I would no longer be called for interrogation. I did not know whether to rejoice or not. Of course I was relieved that the molestation had ended, but I also understood the reason for that. 'Zo Artzeinu' in those days had already disappeared from the headlines. The severe violence exercised against the activists, and the media defamation, had had their effect.

Of the vast multitudes that were ready to be arrested, there remained only a few dozen who were still willing to endure vicious police blows. Of these, even fewer were left who were prepared not only to suffer such blows but also to hear on the media that it was they who had acted violently. 'Zo Artzeinu' was no longer in the headlines (public pressure did not disappear, as already noted, and there were those who found alternative means of expressing their discontent after we vacated the stage). Apparently it was felt that there was no longer any need to squander the resources of an entire investigative unit of the national headquarters. It was now apparent that no charge sheet would be handed in after all. Such a sensational and precedent-setting trial for 'incitement for rebellion' would once again bring us into the headlines, expose the government's shame in the very area of citizen's rights and 'liberalism' which, theoretically, it had emblazoned on its flag, while we would gain a splendid platform on which to present our position, free of charge.

I parted from the investigator cordially and returned home.

A few quiet weeks elapsed, without any special annoyances, and it seemed that the period of investigations was indeed over for good. Yigal Amir's bullets put an end to the tranquillity, and quickly restored us to the inquiry chambers.

I was not taken by surprise by the order to reappear for investigation. I actually anticipated something much worse.

The entire country was in an uproar. Half of the population was now accused of murder. The heads of the opposition vied with each other in condemning their associates, and instead of attempting to correct the distorted portrayal streaming from the TV screens, adopted the approach of "it wasn't me, it was him". Bodyguards were attached to all the leading leftist figures, sirens wailed, and scores of sharpshooters, armed with automatic weapons in plain sight, took up positions covering every VIP.

An air of fear seeped into every nook and cranny. A barber in the Rechavia neighborhood in Jerusalem finished trimming the hair of one client and called out, "Who's next?" whereupon one of the waiting clients uttered a most inappropriate joke: "Shimon Peres."

Someone rushed to inform the police, and the man was immediately arrested.

Yitzchak Newman, a student at the defamed Bar Ilan University, opened an internet address, in which he detailed all of Rabin's misdeeds. Newman, a young fellow who was living in the country all alone, was ejected from the university, despite all his pleas and apologies. He then found it impossible to be accepted at any other university. He became depressed, and a few months later committed suicide. His mother arrived from the USA for her only son's funeral. Shmuel had known Yitzchak, and was called to identify the body. Very few people dared to participate in the funeral; Shmuel and I were there.

There were indeed victims of incitement.

Dozens of rabbis and Religious Zionism Yeshiva heads were summoned for investigation. The filming of the rabbinical procession to the offices of the investigation was acutely degrading. An entire generation of crocheted-kippa wearers saw their leaders led to the investigation chambers as virtual criminals – but could only watch.

Religious youth walking the streets of Tel Aviv preferred to remove their *kippot*. Rightist activists were accorded special treatment. My home telephone took all sorts of threats. At one stage, we prohibited our children from lifting the receiver, in an attempt to shield them from this intimidation. I attached an answering machine to my phone, which recorded – as a memento – the threats of murder and the gems of language issuing from the leftist sewers.

Rightists were arrested all over the place, but the heads of 'Zo Artzeinu' were left untouched. Someone apparently realized, after all the surveillance and investigation, that 'Zo Artzeinu' was truly opposed to any form of violence, and that its approach was not to be equated with the feeling of primitive paranoia that justified a descent into violence on the part of fringe elements.

My anticipated arrest was not forthcoming, but I was again summoned for interrogation in the offices of the national headquarters of criminal investigation. Upon arriving, I caught a glimpse of masses of newsmen waiting for the next Yeshiva head to pass by, humiliated and forlorn. It was a revolting sight. A jumble of microphones on extended poles, recording and filming devices, wild-haired heads, photographers' jackets packed with equipment, antennas, ear-rings, charming women broadcasters, mobile phones, local and foreign crews – my eyes took all this in. It reminded me of a pack of wolves lying in wait for their next victim.

They identified me as I drove around looking for parking place. Finally, here was a refreshingly new subject. Here comes one of the active murderers. Rabbis were no longer a fascinating 'item'. An electrical charge of excitement ran through the crowd as I parked my car. I had no intention of keeping mum and appearing in public as one who does not dare open his mouth. I knew what they would ask, and I concentrated on giving an appropriate answer. By the time I approached the entrance, the newsmen were ready for me. They blocked the entrance, and all sorts of questions were thrown at me. I could not make out individual faces, just a sea of microphones shoved in my face.

"Why have you been summoned?"

"I have no idea," I answered, feigning bewilderment.

"How do you feel being led to investigation?"

"Great."

(Silence…)

"What do you mean by 'great' – you're now going to be subjected to interrogation!?"

"I fail to grasp why I have been singled out for this great honor. All of Israel's great rabbis and distinguished leaders have been walking this lane over the last few days, and little me – I am simply going in their footsteps. *'This is the gate … into which the righteous shall enter',* I proclaimed (quoted) loudly, and theatrically turned towards the entrance. "I am not really worthy," I murmured.

The tight pack were taken aback. The ridiculous situation rocked the self-assurance of the journalists, and I slowly stepped inside.

In private talks with some of the rabbis, a few who had been degraded in this manner expressed their thanks for restoring their self-respect. I reproached them for having come at all, but I understood that in view of the general atmosphere they feared causing a disturbance and therefore preferred to be subjected to the indignity and show up. They were not accustomed to interrogation by the police, and did not have the 'chutzpah' that I had learned to call up in such situations.

The inquiry began.

"Is it correct that you participated in the most recent program of 'Popolitika'?"

"This is a political investigation. I have nothing to say," I replied as usual.

"Did you, in the course of the program, rip up your population census form?"

I wanted to respond with the 'acrostic' that I had concocted in the past, but the atmosphere now was quite different. It was evident that the interrogator was deeply affected by the general propaganda, and was convinced that the person sitting before him was an accessory to the crime.

I decided to do without the humor. "This is a political investigation. I have nothing to say. "

"Did you claim that Rabin was leading us headlong into a disaster?"

For the first time I began to lose control of my nerves. "Tell me," I said to the

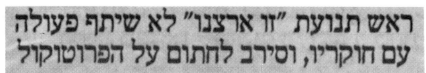

investigator, "don't you feel a bit awkward asking me such questions? You are supposed to be a policeman in a free country, and you ask me about criticism voiced on a television program?"

"Did you claim that Rabin was leading us headlong into a disaster?" he repeated in a tough voice.

Zo Artzeinu head fails to cooperate with investigators, and refuses to sign transcript

Moshe Feiglin, suspected of incitement and sedition, released after interrogation at Criminal Investigation Offices

...Feiglin noted that he had refused to sign the transcript of the interrogation, nor did he sign a personal bond upon its completion. "I do not feel obligated to cooperate in a political investigation," he declared. He also announced that he by no means regretted his actions...According to him, the interrogators produced quotations from media interviews in which he had claimed that the government was acting illegally..."I said: 'Why wasn't Prof. Yeshayahu Leibowitz interrogated when he labeled IDF soldiers "Judeo-Nazis"? Why is there no interrogation of tenured professors who call the Jewish children of Hebron "Hitler youth"?' Had I also witnessed the hauling to interrogation of those who express themselves in such extreme leftist rhetoric, I would have cooperated, for then I would have been convinced that justice was indeed being sought. But only one camp has been interrogated, while the other camp remains apparently guiltless...I compared, psychologically, the conduct of our leftist government to the behavior of the Jewish authorities in the Ghettos..."

"Tell me, aren't you ashamed?" I responded.

"I – ashamed? *You* should be ashamed!" he suddenly exploded. "See where your actions have led."

I realized that this man's channels of independent thinking were totally clogged up, just like those of most of the public at that time. I took a deep breath and returned to my shell: "This is a political investigation. I have nothing to say. "

The investigator expressed his regret over his lack of professional detachment, and continued to record my answers according to procedures.

It was now absolutely clear to me that the inquiry had not been resumed without design. It was evident that the government was out to exploit Rabin's assassination to eliminate its political opponents by any possible means. In the wake of the gloomy atmosphere that had been created, there were no longer any qualms about holding an anti-democratic trial and pressing precedent-setting charges of 'sedition'.

It was Tzippy, watching the evening news broadcast on 'Mabat' while folding the laundry, who called me quickly to come and see what they were saying about me.

"How come you have to learn from TV that charges have been brought against you?" Tzippy asked angrily. My wife's naiveté brought a smile to my face. I was already well acquainted with the *modus operandi* of the State Attorney's Office, so that I was not surprised. I had to explain to the reporters who began phoning that I had no idea what I was being charged with, since I had not received the charge sheet. "How can that be? We all have copies of your indictment." "It's high time you realized where you live and begin fulfilling your function as watchdogs of democracy rather than serving as 'poodles of the regime' " – I vented my frustration on them. The political circumstances leading to the presentation of the charge-sheet prompted the attorney-general, Michael Ben-Yair, to deliver the charge-sheet to the media two days (!) before it was handed to me.

The following day I was contacted by Tali Nir, Channel Two's reporter on legal matters. She began posing questions, but, having regained my composure, I patiently explained that I had received no charge sheet. "It seems that this charge-sheet was meant for the media more than for me – and that's why it was distributed among you so urgently even before they found it appropriate to present it to the accused himself," I said.

"You know what," she responded, "I will photostat a copy for you, give you enough time to study it, and then I'll ring back to ask a few questions."

I agreed. That was how I received Israel's very first charge sheet for 'incitement for rebellion' against a political protest movement.

For the first time in my life (with the exception of the quickie trial in Rehovot following the huge road blockages, in which I never even got to see the charge-sheet before the trial), a charge-sheet had been drawn up against me. Its content made me feel helpless in the face of the system closing in on me. The charge sheet was a cunning patchwork of accurate facts mixed with baseless slander. I was not overly concerned with what the final outcome would be. I had always been aware that I would have to pay a price for the struggle I had mounted, and I was ready to pay it. But judging from the way in which the facts had been falsified and handed to the media, it was clear that they were bent on character assassination, and that in this maneuver there lay a completely different purpose, a much more important one than merely placing us behind bars.

Thus, for example, in one of the clauses I was accused of causing the death of an Arab on Hartis Mountain near Beit-El. I had never been at that spot, and had no connection whatsoever with the incident in which the residents of Beit-El had to act in self-defense when attacked by an inflamed Arab mob. But the charge sheet that had been drawn up for political gain made no pretense of stating the truth. The three judges did compel the prosecution to drop that clause before dealing with the charges, but they were unable to erase the effect of the media's prominent quoting of this false charge as it had originally appeared in the charge sheet.

The situation I found myself in, facing a political campaign utilizing all the apparatus of government in its onslaught, created a great deal of frustration. As had happened on the 'New Evening' TV program, I could not stomach the attempt to brainwash the public by making use of a supposedly objective medium. But this time there was not to be a live interview in which I could leave my imprint on the impression created. Here we were dealing with a pernicious system that leaves one with no recourse, no avenue of defense. The media simply quoted from the charge sheet – which is definitely their prerogative. Any attempted explanation on my part would have sounded like the pleas of a common criminal, so there was no point in playing the game.

The State Attorney's Office succeeded in inflating the sensational effect of presenting the charges by requesting that the trial at the Jerusalem Magistrates' Court be conducted by a special three-judge panel (an unusual step at this instance), and by issuing a refraining order for departure from the country. I had absolutely no intention of fleeing the country, and had no intention of cooperating in this attempt to paint us as escaping criminals. I appeared at the preliminary proceedings with my 'arrest kit'. I explained to the assembled reporters that I did not plan to flee, and if I were asked to deposit my passport, I would prefer to be jailed immediately. Finally, the court decided only to accede to the prosecution's request that a panel of three judges deal with the case, which would be held continuously, day after day.

★ ★

"*Nu*, so what have you 'Others' got to say?" I twitted Shmuel, as we sat down to discuss the ramifications of the charge-sheet that had been drawn up against the two of us and against Rabbi Benny Elon under the heading: "The State of Israel vs. Feiglin and Others".

"Wait for the verdict," Shmuel retorted, "there too there will be a distinction between Feiglin and 'others'."

In view of the fact that the indictment was obviously politically inspired, I hoped to conduct my defense accordingly and take advantage of this platform for a continuation of the struggle. We were charged not only with 'incitement for rebellion', but also on eight counts of 'instigation': instigation to violate a legal demand, instigation to disturb a police officer in the performance of his duties, an attempt to instigate extortion under threats (??), and the like.

It was apparent that even if we were exonerated from the main charge, the prosecution would find a way, at all costs, to have us convicted. The prosecution also made it clear that it intended to appeal a sentence of acquittal, 'up to two instances of appeals to the Supreme Court', as the advocate put it. It was obvious that we were a clearly marked target and that Michael Ben-Yair, who had signed the charge sheet, had no intention of seeing his prey escape.

"Look," I said to Shmuel, "in any case we have no funds to cover the costs of lawyers and drawn-out and exhausting trials. Since we do not propose to deny the facts, let's own up to them at the outset and save ourselves time and expense. By doing so, we can focus the court deliberations on the issues *per se*, while the trial still occupies center stage in the media's attention."

Shmuel heartily agreed with me, but Rabbi Benny Elon thought otherwise. "This is a major confrontation – so why should we acknowledge anything? Let them wear themselves out in an attempt to prove everything. I for one want to interrogate each and every one of their hundred witnesses; I want to tire them out in court."

Benny chose to be represented separately in court by his brother, advocate Sefi (Yosef) Elon, which left Shmuel and me in a quandary. If we chose the line of defense we had decided upon previously, and admit to the facts, we would be cutting the ground from under Benny's stand. This we did not want to do, nor did we want to appear to others as disunited. Sefi was not interested in representing us as well. Reluctantly, we engaged a Jerusalem lawyer whose services we could afford, and thus, on January 17, 1996, at nine in the morning, we appeared at the first court session, three defendants and their two advocates.

The Jerusalem Magistrates' Court, situated in the Russian Compound, is housed in the Russian pilgrim hostel built at the close of the previous century. The courtroom assigned to our case was that of the president of the court, Judge Amnon Cohen, who was joined by Judges Zilbertal and Dotan. As soon as we arrived for the security check at the entrance, we realized that 'things were going to get heated up'. At the entrance, in pouring rain, a group of protesters flanked by policemen stood in demonstration. I begged the protesters to desist, so as not to get drenched in the rain, but they obstinately stayed put. Inside there snaked a long, dense queue filling all the corridors of the building up to the president's courtroom. My immediate circle included me and Tzippy, Shmuel and his family, Julie Torenberg, a former Lehi underground fighter, who was already in her eighties but persisted in making her way up to Jerusalem by bus for every court session, media folk, 'Zo Artzeinu' activists, law school students interested in such a precedent-setting trial, and ordinary, curious citizens.

The queue did not advance, and I was afraid we would arrive late for the opening. The building's security men had set up several improvised checkpoints, but it was impossible to admit such a large crowd into the chamber, so that only immediate relatives of the accused were permitted entrance. Shmuel saw that the elderly Julie was being shoved back, and suddenly began shouting: "Mom, Mom – I won't go in without my mom." That was how Julie effected entrance under the guise of Shmuel's mother. Inside the courtroom, everyone settled down on long benches, and then it transpired that I, of all people, the groom of the celebration, so to speak, had no vacant seat.

The announcement "All rise!" hushed the packed crowd, and everyone stood up expectantly as the three judges made their entrance.

When everyone had taken his/her seat, Judge Cohen looked at me and asked, "Why aren't you sitting?" I shrugged, "There's no place for me." Someone had to vacate his seat, and I took his place in one of the rear benches.

The trial dragged on for several months. With the passing of time, I became ever more convinced that I had been right when I proposed admitting the true facts. Dozens of prosecution witnesses took the stand. Countless technical objections were raised by the lawyers. Long, convoluted and silly argumentation over each and every clause and item wearied the judges and created a hostile atmosphere. Our advocates did succeed in shaming the many policemen whose testimony was exposed as pure fiction, but it remained impossible to deny the veracity of the overall picture, since no one tried to claim that the demonstrations had never taken place at all.

The list of witnesses included mainly police officers who were not averse to outright lying[1], but it was not always possible to provide contradictory evidence to prove their falsifying. In addition, a number of newspaper correspondents who had interviewed me were called to testify (the ethics of journalism did not concern them, and they did not hesitate to bear witness against me), as well as detectives who had gathered material regarding the movement by undercover means.

One of the newspaper correspondents who testified against me was Yael Guertz of *Yediot Acharonot*. Yael had listened in, without my knowledge, to an off-the-record argument I had conducted with a newsman named Tamir, during the Intermediate Days of the Succot festival.

"Do you believe that it is appropriate to call Rabin a murderer?" Tamir asked.

"No, it is wrong to do so," I answered. "However, just between us, there are grounds for doing so... After all, he was involved in the murder of sixteen people."

"Are you referring to the 'Altelena Affair'?" he asked.

"Yes," I answered, without paying attention to the fact that Guertz was taking notes.

---

[1] The most prominent of them was the Commander of Operations of the Jerusalem Police District, Col. David Krauza, who testified that the 'Zo Artzeinu' demonstrations were "the most violent demonstrations he had ever seen...".

In the court, Guertz testified that I had alluded to Rabin as a murderer.

So it went. From this technical testimony of someone who had recorded our conversation, to the testimony of the helicopter pilot who had flown me over the intersections, to the testimony of a senior police official, to the testimony of a policeman at a remote crossroads, with endless interrogations and counter-inquiries, the trial went its ponderous way over the long and tedious months.

Before the defense began its case, Benny Elon was elected a Member of the Knesset, and legal procedures against him were frozen. Shmuel and I were left to cope with a trial that took a turn that we had not desired. Public interest practically vanished, with only a few individuals taking the time and trouble to come up to be present at the exhausting sessions. The media stopped issuing reports, and we were worn down by the endless trips to Jerusalem.

The line of defense taken by our advocate did not suit my purposes, and I looked about for a way to save something of my original plan regarding the conduct of the trial. When the turn of the prosecution ended, I decided to represent myself in my own defense.

I was advised from all sides not to do so. Even in an ordinary case, it is far from wise to forgo legal counsel, all the more so in a case that was so complex and lacking precedent as ours.

If I had had at my disposal the hundreds of thousands of dollars required to engage the services of a battery of top-notch attorneys (which is what was really needed in such a case), I might have dropped the idea – but such sums were never available to us, and I despaired of this dull, exhausting duel. I wanted to focus the case on the truly important issues, and was not interested in courtroom tricks of the trade and maneuvering.

It was agreed with Shmuel that I would defend myself, and that Shoan (Shmuel) Kasper, our young friend from the days of our arrest in Tiberias, would represent Shmuel for a minimum fee. This would enable me to speak out as I saw fit, while Shmuel would still have defense counsel. Kasper shared the work with the lawyer Naphtali Werzberger, and despite initial trepidation, the interaction between the lawyers and myself went very well.

I spent the week before this stage of the trial working feverishly on my opening brief. I delved into various sources, and appeared with a portfolio bulging with relevant exhibits. On the day when I was to begin my testimony, the general public was already indifferent to the proceedings in the case of 'Zo Artzeinu', since we had been overshadowed by the Savion lady who had planted explosives in her millionaire husband's limousine. Nonetheless, the courtroom was crowded with many activists, who took their seats on the benches.

Although I had already become accustomed to making public speeches and to appearing at public gatherings, I felt myself going all weak at the knees. This was a playing field I had never before played on, and a fear gnawed at my heart: Would they let me speak, and would I succeed in keeping to the line I had designed in advance?

The name of the game in the trial could be encapsulated in one word: Relevance. For seven full hours I was on my feet, delivering my defense arguments, which carried over to the following morning. When I was through, I was given to understand that my performance was equal to that of a professional advocate, which also accounts for the fact that, despite the prosecution's objections, the judges barely interrupted my talk.

I started with a description of the background behind the reality that led me to begin the struggle: How the leftist government had destroyed the Jewish and Zionist dream in our land. How the Rabin government had wiped out the heritage of our common past, and even delivered into the PLO's hands the relics of the Hasmonean coins from the period of the Great Revolt, together with all the archeological antiquities of our past, which have now become part of the history of 'the ancient Palestinian people'.

"They not only sold our future for the Oslo broth of lentils," I concluded the preliminary part of my speech, "they sold our past as well, turning us into merely colonial conquerors, without roots and destiny."

"I object to this whole speech," declared the prosecutor, getting to his feet. "The indictment does not deal with ideas but with deeds. The defendant has just delivered a political speech."

The judges turned to me, as if asking, "Sounds logical, what have you got to say to that?"

"My line of defense," I rose to declare, " is that all the activities of 'Zo Artzeinu' fall into the rubric of 'passive civil resistance', known popularly as 'civil disobedience'. Civil disobedience is the last resort available in developed democracies to a citizen when he discovers government wrongdoings that his conscience cannot abide. After he has tried every other avenue of legal protest, a responsible citizen who does not wish to revolt and definitely does not wish to engage in violence has only this recourse.

"Civil disobedience cannot be classified as 'incitement to rebellion', since its whole purpose is to undo wrongdoings, precisely as described in the relevant clause of the law (number 138). I shall prove to the court that ours was indeed a case of civil disobedience, which means that it cannot be categorized as 'incitement to rebellion'.

But in order to do so, I must first explain to the court precisely what those iniquities, against which I and my comrades campaigned, actually were."

The judges accepted my arguments and I went on. After describing at length the danger ensuing to Judaism and Zionism, brought upon us by the Rabin government, I proceeded to detail the security and economic dangers.

I presented the statistics showing the terrible ravages that the 'peace process' had brought upon us; the inevitable war after Arafat has received everything promised him and established his state just 16 kilometers away from Netanya; his declarations regarding a *Jihad* against us; the murderous use of the Israeli arms, which we had provided him, against our own soldiers; the horrifying endangerment, which the Rabin government had created, to the lives of the Israeli citizens who dwell in Yesha settlements, which would, according to the agreements, become isolated islands surrounded by a hostile, armed Palestinian state; the undeniable danger to all the towns and villages of the coastal plain which would come within range of even the most primitive weapons in the hands of terrorists.

For a long time I dwelled on all the perils created by the government's policy.

I then went on to describe all the legal demonstrations and protests which the country had experienced over the past three years, and the government's total indifference to every legal, popular expression of disaffection. I quoted extensively from Rabin's expressions about his own people. 'Propellers', 'half-wits', 'Hamas collaborators', and all the other linguistic gems employed by the insensitive prime minister – all these were laid before the court one after the other.

Whenever my words related to Yitzchak Rabin, the prosecution immediately raised the objection of their being irrelevant.

Undermining the sacred myth of the revered Rabin, around whom flourished a veritable devotional ritual following his murder, compelled the prosecutor to jump to his feet the moment I mentioned his name.

But I insisted that Rabin's expressions contained the seeds of civil disobedience, which can only break forth against a background of extreme indifference to the legitimate protests of a significant segment of the public.

At a certain point, I had to explain the comments I had made to media correspondents, who avidly testified against me.

Here I was in a predicament. I had not been at war with the Prime Minister, who was lying in his grave, but on the other hand I could not retract a word I had said about him, and I had to justify them in court. My quandary was greatest when I had to relate to the testimony of Yael Guertz, who claimed that she had heard me say that Rabin was a murderer.[1]

I had never used that term, and I made this clear to the court. "However," I added, to the judges' shock, "this man was indeed involved in the heinous murder of sixteen new immigrants, survivors of the Nazi concentration camps, and should the prosecution raise its objection to this statement, I can bring a witness to testify to the truth of what I have just said...!"

I had indeed such a witness. The witness, a prominent and respected person, had, during Rabin's tenure as ambassador to Washington, participated in the reception held in the Israeli Embassy on Independence Day. At the height of the festivities, every one of the participants was asked to relate exactly what he had been doing on the day that the Declaration of Independence was proclaimed.

When it was Rabin's turn, he did not do so; instead he chose to speak of an incident that occurred on a different date. He spoke about what took place when the Etzel ship *Altelena* arrived at the Tel Aviv shore.

"After the ship had been fired upon, it began to sink," Rabin told...

"We 'bumped off' the men who remained on deck, and we 'bumped off' the men who jumped into the sea and began swimming to the beach..."

That was how Rabin boasted in front of the Embassy staff of his role in the murder of the survivors of the Holocaust who had finally reached the shores of the Land aboard the *Altelena*.

He had simply carried out orders. He obviously did not view his role as one of murderer, and was sufficiently proud of his deed to have selected this particular incident as one worth recounting to his comrades.

I know of no other military action in the line of fire in which Rabin took command.

---

[1] Anyone who is taken aback to learn that an individual in a democratic country is brought to trial for having labeled the head of the government a murderer does not realize the nature of the general climate in which this trial was conducted. At that time, the heads of the right-wing parties were all falling over each other in an attempt to display their liking for Rabin. The incitement directly connecting anyone who had opposed Rabin's policy with the despicable crime of murder committed by Yigal Amir filtered down into the court.
The fact that the heads of the Left had routinely called Erik Sharon, Menachem Begin, and other outstanding Rightist personalities, 'murderers' – did not matter, of course.

There was profound silence in the courtroom. The utter confusion of the judges was apparent. They all directed a questioning look at the prosecutor – was it conceivable that the State Attorney's Office would not object to the assertion, made before three judges in Jerusalem, accusing the revered prime minister of – murder?

The prosecutor made a split-second decision, and to my delight and to the relief of all present refrained from looking up and from expressing objection to my provocative words. There was thus no need to call upon my witness, and I was able to proceed to the next subject.

I was pleased that no reporters were present at that time. The statement was duly recorded in the court records and I had no intention of publicizing the issue. I knew that should an alert newspaperman seize upon my words, it could easily become a media bombshell, which I did not desire. The overall atmosphere in the country was beginning to show signs of recovery from the catastrophe of the assassination and the highly charged accusations ensuing from it.

I finished testifying, and Shmuel, who took the stand after me, then gave the judges a performance the likes of which are rarely seen in courtrooms. The heavy atmosphere engendered by my testimony was transformed, and gales of laughter swept the judges and spectators. The image of a tough and violent underground movement quickly dissipated.

"Don't worry," Shmuel assured the judges, "my speech won't last even a quarter of the time taken by Moshe."

The prosecutor queried: "Did you understand everything that Moshe wrote?"

"Are you nuts?" he answered. "He never stops writing. Who has the time to read all that blah-blah?"

One of the most important parts of Shmuel's testimony focused on a description of his participation in the demonstrations on behalf of the Jews of the USSR, when he was still a US resident. It was important because it taught the court how, in a truly democratic regime, non-violent protests were legally dispersed. We had believed that the accepted model in democratic countries would be emulated in Israel, but we were rudely disabused of such expectations by the thugs under the command of Chavivian, Revivo, and Krausa (commanders in the Jerusalem police force).

"...We squatted, maybe a thousand people, on the main thoroughfare of Washington D.C....

"There's a lot of traffic on that road... even our sacred city of Jerusalem can't boast so much traffic... (Shmuel succeeded in eliciting smiles from all those present.)

"It was below zero weather; we prayed that the police would hurry up and remove us. But they have their rules. A police officer came up to me, stood in front of me, and began reading me my rights from a sheet of paper.

"'Sir, I wish to inform you that you are now violating such and such a law. Now, Sir, I will repeat this message three times.' I desperately wanted to tell him that this repetition was unnecessary, that I was cold, and that I wanted to be hauled away. But he went ahead, and read the warning three times. Finally they came, lifted me and took me to the police van. That is what they did with each and every one of the thousand folk plunked down on the road.

"All traffic had come to a halt, while the police continued to work according to the rules."

The ineluctable comparison between the conduct of the American police and the way civil rights were 'respected' in Israel gave the judges much food for thought. Thus, within less than two hours, Shmuel restored the popular, positive image of our movement, which the prosecution had tried to destroy, The judges' reactions reflected the contents of an avalanche of supportive letters which arrived from Jews of the diaspora, letters expressing abhorrence of and repulsion for the anti-democratic character revealed in the State of Israel. Prominent in organizing this support were Ms Pearl Witkin and her friends in New York. It was heartwarming to realize that we were "not waging a battle alone".

The list of defense witnesses we had brought was much shorter than that of the prosecution, and their testimony, over a period of six days, dealt mainly with seven subjects:

The organized violence of the police and other branches of government.

Our demonstrably extreme punctiliousness in observing strict passivity and non-violence.

The popular nature of our struggle (in contrast to underground activity).

The general feeling of powerlessness in face of the government's indifference to protracted protests.

The inability to convey the feelings of the majority through the 'mobilized' media.

Scrupulous adherence to the principles of civil disobedience.

The bilateral agreement between the Left, before it won the elections, and the terror organizations, in outright violation of the law.

We made no particular effort to locate and prepare witnesses. Those who heard of the trial and wanted to testify took the initiative and spoke to me several minutes on the phone, and I quickly decided whom to select. I met many of these witnesses face to face for the first time on the witness stand. It often seemed to me that Providence had come to our assistance, for the group of witnesses as a whole gave a very true picture of what had really taken place. Even I – who had cooked up the entire meal – had not realized what exactly had transpired until I heard their testimonies in court.

The witnesses came from every walk of life, religious and secular, intellectuals and ordinary folk, recent settlers and veteran settlement members, an engineer from Netanya and a professor from the Weizmann Institute of Rehovot. The judges suddenly became cognizant of the fact that our supporters were not riffraff, a gang of hoodlums, as the prosecution was trying to depict them, but rather a true cross-section of all of the Israeli people. Among those who took the stand were professors who had taken part in blocking the roads, who explained at length how respectable citizens had reached such a point.

During the first two days of testimony, the witnesses testified mainly to the awful brutality of the police, and their systematic violations of the law. Women who strolled along the pavement with their baby-carriages and found themselves attacked by mounted police who overturned their carriages and nonchalantly continued on their way; elderly people who were beaten by the fighters of the Special Police Patrol Unit under the command of Chavivian and Revivo; teenage girls whipped by the police, etc. etc. The spine-chilling descriptions shocked the court. I personally had never been subjected to such brutal police treatment, because they treated me with a certain degree of respect. Perhaps my frequent appearances in the media served as a protective flak jacket, or perhaps they knew that violence against me would achieve an unwanted effect. But against anonymous people, a terrible violence had been perpetrated, the shocking details of which I was now able to comprehend.

The prosecution claimed in its summation that these manifestations of cruelty were 'exceptional', and would be dealt with. When my turn came to summarize, I said that "yes, indeed, there were 'exceptions'; there were policemen who conducted themselves according to the law, as human beings and not as animals."

At a certain stage I saw that the prosecution was feeling most uncomfortable. They found it necessary to promise the court that the findings revealed in these proceedings would be properly handled – but nothing of the nature actually occurred, of course.

To illustrate to the court the malicious functioning of the Israeli media, we called on Professor Eliyahu Pollack, founder of the association 'The Public's Right to Know'.

..."I am a native-born Israeli, scientist, have been engaged in physics and chemistry for over twenty years, professor in the faculty of physics and chemistry in the Weizmann Institute, a citizen who had never been involved in any sort of public activity apart from participation in teacher-parent meetings in school..."

After he went on to explain how it came about that he and fellow professors joined the activities of 'Zo Artzeinu', Professor Pollack detailed how the media had betrayed its mission:

"...We arrived at the conclusion that something was radically wrong with the media. About 80 of us professors stood in the street opposite the building of the television studios in Romema and demonstrated... (No one came out to interview us) there was no microphone, no tape recording, and no TV crew – nothing. We requested a meeting with the head of the broadcasting authority, Mr. Kirshenbaum.

"(We asked him) 'Eighty professors are standing outside and demonstrating against Israeli television – and you don't find it necessary to cover this event? The public doesn't have the right to know what is taking place?' His reply was that they had a policy of not covering demonstrations held in front of their building. Why? 'Because it interferes with our work.'"

Among the witnesses were individuals who had participated in civil disobedience in the United States and found parallels between the American experience and our own activities. Their testimonies, such as that given by Israel Medad (Winky), who had taken part in, and even researched, the phenomenon, aroused the judges' great interest.

"... I met my future wife for the first time at a protest vigil held opposite the Russian UN mission. I clocked up many hours of squatting on pavements, marching, and organization, in all areas. I even traveled to Russia to promote the campaign (of Jewish emigration from the USSR).

" (In everything related to civil disobedience) I also have a lot of expertise in the theoretical aspects, that is, the teachings of Ghandi, Martin Luther King, Bertrand Russell, and others.

"While studying at Columbia University, I took part in sit-down demonstrations and blockage of roads in protest against the Vietnam War and the violation of civil rights in the USA.

"I participated in most of the mass demonstrations in the USA, and in many of the activities of 'Zo Artzeinu', and in my opinion what I noted here regarding observance of the principles of civil disobedience did not deviate from what I had observed in the United States."

Q. "What is the purpose of all these activities?"

A. "The immediate aim is to point out injustice. In a democracy, the government rests on two systems: A legal system and a civilian system based on political support. Democracy does not come to an end the day after elections. The citizen has the right to change and influence the government between election campaigns...

"The government is a political body that rests, among others, on the public's approval. That is why the citizen may try to exercise influence...

"I advised the leaders of 'Zo Artzeinu' to adopt the methods of passive civil resistance in order to mobilize maximum public pressure against the government's policies."

The case for the defense was brought to a close with the testimony of the newspaper correspondent Yehoshua HaMe'iri, who presented proof of the ties between the PLO and the heads of the Labor Party, at a time when it was still in the opposition. Part of the indictment against me referred to my accusation that the Rabin government rested on a criminal foundation. HaMe'iri's testimony was therefore extremely crucial to the justification of my allegations that the Rabin government had been elected thanks to illegal manipulations with a terrorist organization. HaMe'iri detailed with great precision the places and dates of the meetings between personages such as Avrum Burg, Yossi Beilin and Shimon Peres's closest advisers, and the heads of the bloodthirsty organization. These meetings, most of which took place in Cairo, were blatantly illegal acts, but the Shamir government at that time was too weak to capitalize on what was going on. HaMe'iri also presented proof that these meetings paved the way for the Labor Party's subsequent victory in the election, since all the stipulations of the Oslo Accords were promised Arafat in advance, in return for the support of the Israeli Arabs for the Labor Party.

Justice Dotan: "Was the nature of these meetings revealed to the public?"

HaMe'iri: "Yes, this too was published. What was discussed was an attempt to ensure a Labor Party victory in the elections."

★ ★

The testimony of the witnesses was now over.

Actually, I could have exhausted the court by producing countless witnesses who had been present at the various activities, but despite my formal right to do so I had no intention of dragging out the trial needlessly. The judges knew that I was capable of stretching the trial out without end, and they even hinted at their concern. In the prosecution's summation, he tried to present our actions as falling within the definition of the law on sedition. He did not cope with the reality that most of the population could be equally liable. He similarly evaded the central defense thesis that civil disobedience cannot be considered an act of rebellion in a democratic society. Instead of dealing with our arguments, he simply announced that civil disobedience, no matter what its merits, is not relevant in democratic countries (!?).[1]

I prepared myself for the summations. I could have relied upon the professional summations of Shoan and Naphtali, but I thought it important to add a personal touch of my own. My summation was relatively short.

I reminded the judges of the government's indifference to what half of the nation was saying, the many lies exposed in the testimony of the police officers, and, once again, the principles of non-violent civil disobedience which were our guidelines. In conclusion, I argued that, in light of the government's violence, it was fitting for the court to rebuff the prosecution's claims, thus sending an unambiguous message to any future government that might be tempted to exercise similar brutality against its own citizens.

Ending my words, I asked the judges for permission to read aloud a short passage from *The Little Prince*, one of the world's humanist classics. I presume that *The Little Prince* had never before been quoted in an Israeli courtroom. The trial that had begun as an indictment of an extremist, violent group would now come to a close on a completely different note. When I picked up the thin book to read, those present, amused by the scene, could not refrain from smiling.

"Sire – over what do you rule?"

"Over everything," said the king, with magnificent simplicity.

"Over everything?"

The king made a gesture, which took in his planet, the other planets, and all the stars.

"Over all that?" asked the little prince.

"Over all that," the king answered. For his rule was not only absolute: it was also universal.

"And the stars obey you?"

"Certainly they do," the king said. "They obey instantly. I do not permit insubordination."

---

[1] See page 64 for a detailed account.

"I should like to see a sunset...Do me that kindness...Order the sun to set..."

"If I ordered a general to fly from one flower to another like a butterfly, or to write a tragic drama, or to change himself into a sea bird, and if the general did not carry out the order that he had received, which one of us would be in the wrong?" the king demanded. "The general, or myself?"

"You," said the prince firmly.

"Exactly. One must require from each one the duty which each one can perform," the king went on.

"Accepted authority rests first of all on reason.

"If you ordered your people to go and throw themselves into the sea, they would rise up in revolution.

"I have the right to require obedience because my orders are reasonable."

For over six months the judges meditated over the issues. At last, the expected notification arrived, and we finally seated ourselves (again very crowded in) in the small courtroom to hear the verdict.

Preliminary assessments by all the advocates and spectators were that, because of the severe ramifications for Israeli society as a democratic society, the court would not dare convict us of 'incitement for rebellion', but would, in order to placate the prosecution, convict us of the other clauses in the charge-sheet, those dealing with various counts of instigation.
To everyone's amazement, the court's decision was diametrically opposite. The court exonerated us of all the charges of instigation, and instead convicted us of the main charge. We stood guilty of incitement to rebellion.

The court did not accept our main argument, and did not view civil disobedience as a legitimate course of action that cannot be classified as a violation of the law against sedition in a democratic regime.

The stage of argumentation as to punishment was set for the period following the holidays of the start of the year 5758 (1997-98). It was now clear to me that I was headed for a sentence of imprisonment, perhaps even a long term.

The State Attorney's Office celebrated its victory for two weeks. The excitement there was palpably great. They had been greatly worried lest a loss in this case would bring them a great loss of face. They had no intention of letting their prey escape with only a symbolic punishment, and needed a harsh punishment in order to emphasize that the conviction was not on a technicality. They informed us that they intended to demand a long prison term.

Tzippy and I returned home, very depressed.

It was now necessary to organize our personal matters in light of what lay in store. We had to prepare the children, to try and organize ourselves economically, all this in preparation for imprisonment the length of which we did not yet know. We decided to spend the holidays at home, and to try to spend as much time as possible in the company of our children before the session dealing with our sentencing, set for November 27, 1997.

But my fate determined otherwise – and I spent all the Intermediate Days of Succot in a prison cell.

The court that had rendered its verdict in my case had not weighed its profound consequences, the democratic character of the State of Israel, and the serious blow that this precedent would inflict upon freedom of expression.

The State Attorney's Office did not procrastinate. Shortly after the verdict was announced, I was told, to my surprise, that I was expected to appear at a police interrogation. All they told me was that the investigation had to do with something I had said on a radio broadcast on radio Channel 7 a year earlier.

On Sunday, I returned home from morning holiday prayers. Over the Shabbat, our *succah* (booth) had been totally drenched by a storm.

I put aside my prayer shawl and *lulav*, and entered the succah for breakfast.

The sun was finally shining, the succah was still standing in its place, smiling at me through the raindrops, and I made the blessing and absorbed the atmosphere and fragrance so special to the holiday.

I then studied the '*daily page*' (prescribed daily study of the Talmud); meanwhile my youngest son awoke, and joined me in the succah.

I felt unusually elated, but I had to cut the idyll short, because at 10 that morning I was due to meet the police investigator at the station in Kadum.

I arrived for the investigation.

It had nothing to do with one of the operations of 'Zo Artzeinu', but with an inquiry opened against me because of something I had said, the nature of which I was not yet informed. I was afraid that perhaps I had once uttered a slip of the tongue without realizing it, and that now someone out to get me was seizing upon it. I decided to cooperate fully with the police, in order to get the whole matter over and done with quickly.

It transpired that an extreme leftist activist, a pitiable fellow named Adam Keller, had heard me call a year earlier, on a Channel 7 broadcast, for the release from prison of Nachum Korman and Yoram Skolnik, especially in light of the sweeping release of Arab murderers by the government.[1] I did indeed believe that, and did issue such a call a year earlier. This view was very popular and was expressed constantly by ministers and members of the Knesset. Keller accused me of supporting murder, and presented a complaint to the police. The unbiased State Attorney's Office of the State of Israel waited a full year before acting on this individual's complaint, and now that it had achieved my conviction for incitement to rebellion, it recommended looking into this expression of opinion. The police were now about to interrogate me under the awesome clause relating to membership in a terror organization or something similar...

It is doubtful that the Jerusalem judges had foreseen how quickly their decision in our trial for sedition would loosen the fetters that had heretofore restrained the Israeli 'thought police'.

With great patience I explained to the police interrogator that I am not a member of any terror organization (that was precisely the wording of the question: "Are you a member of a terror organization?").

I further explained that I do not support murder, Heaven forbid, and that – "Yes, I definitely do support the release of Korman and Skolnik from prison, and that ascribing support of murder to anyone as a result of his taking such a position is nothing but the antics of an extreme leftist activist employing the police in order to waste my time."

I finished my explanation, signed my statement, and, confident that this ridiculous file would be closed as soon as someone with a bit of intelligence in his cranium would examine it, got up to leave.

However, a surprise awaited me.

---

[1] Especially in view of the fact that the two had found themselves in their position by chance, without any intention of killing anyone, and especially since one of them was a security officer who was simply carrying out his duty faithfully – acting against stone-throwers, one of whom was hit and killed.

"Just a moment," said the interrogator, "kindly sign here..."

"What this?" – I asked.

"It's a personal bond committing you to report to the police whenever requested..."

Up to that point, I had cooperated fully, of my own free will, with all the police requests. After all, it's their duty to deal with every complaint, even with such a ridiculous complaint against me.[1]

The police were functioning, as it were, properly, and I played along, and cooperated, as a decent citizen should.

But now, I was being asked to sign a document the significance of which was that I, of my own accord, was prepared to forego an iota of my personal freedom as a citizen with equal rights in the State of Israel – and all this simply because I had called, on Channel 7, for the release of Skolnik and Korman, which had so infuriated Adam Keller that he had submitted a complaint against me.

I refused to sign.

I explained to the commander of the Kadum station, someone named Gurevitz, that I had no intention of fleeing the country, that I wanted to cooperate exactly as required by law, neither more nor less, and that all the officers on the spot acknowledged that my having lost out a full day with my kids was sufficient. I pointed out to him that had the police felt that I was so dangerous as to warrant restriction of movement, surely they would not have waited a full year before addressing this bothersome complaint, and I asked that he desist from detaining me any further and allow me to return home.

Gurevitz was stubborn. "Either you sign or I will arrest you..."

I am very familiar with the psychological pressure experienced by the Faithful to the Land in such situations.

---

[1] In reality, only complaints regarding expressions of opinion by right-wingers merit attention. I myself have submitted reasoned complaints regarding malicious, forbidden expressions of opinion on the part of left-wingers, all of which have been rejected without any inquiry whatsoever. Can anyone imagine that an extreme rightist would submit a complaint against one of the harsh statements made by Sheli Yachimovitch on the radio, and that she would be summoned to the police, interrogated, and even requested to sign a guarantee to show up when required?

Outside there's a holiday – the family is waiting. Who is going to be such a 'simpleton' as not to knuckle under to such extortion, sign, get back to his home, and forget the whole episode?

That is precisely how the Faithful to the Land turn themselves into second-rate citizens. After all, they do not belong to any of the élite strata – no one will bother about their civil rights on such media programs as '*It's All Talk*' or the nightly news program '*Mabat*'. So they sign, even though they do not feel the request was warranted, and return home, but a bit more stooped.

True, they are free to move about and are not behind bars, but actually they are tyrannized, not really free citizens, not citizens whose opinions carry the same weight as those of others and whose civil rights are faithfully preserved.

In short, I was such a 'simpleton', and did not sign.

Gurevitz ordered me taken before the judge on duty in Petach Tikvah, and thus I arrived after the day's tiring proceedings before Judge Shapira in Petach Tikvah.

Judge Shapira did not allow me to speak. The combination of a bearded settler in a white holiday shirt, together with the accusation of membership in a terror organization, sealed my fate before I could open my mouth.

"It is not clear why the suspect obstinately refuses to sign," wrote the judge impatiently, giving the police the authority, should they deem it necessary, to keep me in custody until Wednesday.

When the judge had signed her learned decision – and the nature of the decision was already clear to me – I presumed to asked her:

"If your honor has written that it is not clear to her why the suspect refuses to sign, how is it that she has come to a decision before clarifying what is not clear to her?"

The judge was a bit taken aback, but made do with the words, "Yes, yes, if you are so adamant..."

"Should he not sign by Wednesday – please come prepared for the proceedings," she managed to add to the police representative as I left on my way to detention.

Apparently, the honorable judge suddenly realized that this troublesome character might indeed not sign and have to remain in custody all the time, and then, should the police be unable to rationalize its demand for this miserable guarantee, it would become embarrassingly clear that both the police and Judge Shapira had caused a man to be held in custody without justification. They had thus created a situation in which both the police and the court had climbed up a very tall tree as a result of this customary behavior – not to preserve too rigidly the civil rights of the Faithful to the Land, who, as is accepted in our established circles, do not really deserve true civil rights and who have already resigned themselves to this reality.

I did not sign, the police could not release me – for by doing so they would be admitting that there had not been grounds for making such a demand in the first place – and I was led to detention. I spent all the remaining days of the holiday, from Sunday through Wednesday, in a small, dismal cell. I was prepared to spend many more days there, but thank G-d, it was deemed sufficient.

It dawned on the police that the longer that time passed, the greater would be their discomfiture, for this obstinate fellow would not sign. They therefore requested that I write a letter stating my reason for not signing, and informed the court that this letter satisfied them.

I was released from custody a few hours before the start of the Simchat Torah Festival, without, of course, having signed any commitment.

I had come for interrogation on Sunday, and was released on Wednesday, a citizen with equal rights in the State of Israel, just like Adam Keller or Chaim Yavin (of Israeli TV), but it had cost me the little remaining time to be with my family before my sentencing in the Jerusalem Court.

Needless to say, no indictment will ever be presented against me in the afore-mentioned matter; even Judge Shapira would have to pronounce me as guiltless and as clean as snow in such a trial, and the State Attorney's Office, the police, and the Petach Tikvah court, had shamed themselves sufficiently in this case.[1]

In a small cell, to the incessant cries and catcalls of Arab car snatchers emanating from the neighboring cells, I had all the time in the world to contemplate how it had

---

[1] About one month later, Rabbi Israel Eichler, of the 'Kol Chai' radio channel, initiated a general request for information from the Ministry of Justice as to why this very odd investigation had taken place. The State Attorney's Office evaded providing a pertinent response, but from their answer it became clear that the initiative had come from 'the department for the enforcement of the law against revolters and law-breakers engaged in incitement and instigation' (Yes, such a department exists in free Israel), headed by Ms. Talia Sasson. It then became clear to me that the entire episode of suffering and arrest stemmed from a personal desire for revenge. On the very same radio program in which I had called for the release of Korman and Skulnick, I had poured scorn on the very existence of such a department in the State of Israel, and I mentioned Ms Sasson by name, as head of that Orwellian department. It is obvious that Ms Sasson exploited the governmental tools available to her to get even with me.

transpired that, having once called for the release of fellow Jews from prison, I now found myself in a prison cell.

Perhaps I had it coming, for I had not really mentioned Yoram Skolnik and Nachum Korman enough during the previous year in my regular programs on Channel 7.

★ ★

"The activities of 'Zo Artzeinu' came to an abrupt halt as a result of Rabin's assassination. If Rabin had not been assassinated, 'Zo Artzeinu' would have persisted in its mass campaigns, with high chances of achieving its nefarious designs."

Thus did the prosecution begin its arguments for punishment.

Obviously, interpolating Rabin's murder into the arguments for punishment was cleverly contrived to score political points.

Taking up quite a bit of time, the prosecutor embellished the severity of our deeds, demanding that we pay the maximum penalty of ten years' incarceration.

I listened patiently to his words, and when it was my turn, I tried to rebut his arguments to the best of my ability.

"Permit me to correct you," I said to the prosecutor. "If you check the dates, you will realize that the mass activities of 'Zo Artzeinu' winded up a few months before Rabin's murder.

"Let me tell you now why they ended. They terminated because the tens of thousands of citizens who were prepared to pay the heavy price of going forth in demonstrations and sitting in jail were not prepared to risk bodily injury as well, as a result of deliberate police violence.

"Women with baby carriages were no longer ready to endanger their offspring. Elderly men of seventy who had suffered blows for the first time in their lives felt that they had done enough. The general public grasped that Israel was not the developed westernized democracy that they had previously imagined. The public understood that the rules of the game here were very violent. They realized that no matter how passive their conduct, the media would persist in depicting them as violent. And so the huge masses kept away from further demonstrations, simply out of a very basic physical fear."

The court had already heard dozens of testimonies from witnesses to this governmentally authorized hooliganism, so I had no need to recapitulate the descriptions – they all knew exactly what I was talking about.

"It was not Rabin's murder that put an end to the demonstrations," I said to the court. "Quite the contrary, the cessation of demonstrations led to the murder.

"When the last recourse of legitimate and democratic protest was blocked, while the tremendous public pressure in the face of the awful arbitrariness of a government that was disdainfully crushing all that was dear and sacred to most of the nation remained bottled up and found no avenue for expression, at a time when we had all become irrelevant 'propellers' unable to give vent to our opposition, it was only a matter of time till a madman from the extreme fringes of the extremist camp would rise up and commit that despicable deed."

(By the way, Yigal Amir himself had testified that this was precisely the road he had traveled – but why let the facts negate the theory...)

I was now expected to argue the question of the severity of the punishment I deserved. I decided to forgo doing so. I explained to the court why I forbore from raising my arguments.

"If I had sought to evade punishment," I declared, "I could have found excellent ways of doing so.

"I could, for example, have gotten myself elected to the Knesset and avoided this trial altogether; I could have had myself represented here by a battery of lawyers who would have exhausted you *à la* Der'i (a trial that has been dragging on for years)... I could have brought countless character witnesses – from the days of my army service, many professors, rabbis, and the like. But I was prepared to forgo all this because, with all due respect to the court, there is a court that concerns me ten times more than this court." The three judges listened intently to these words, which seemed to imply audacious disparagement of their role. "The court that worries me so much are the eyes of my children, who in ten or twenty years hence will look at me with the question – 'What did you do then, before the great catastrophe, when it had already become clear to you precisely where the nation was headed..'

"What will I answer them then?" I asked the court. "That I took a seat in the Knesset and voted against... that I engaged the services of an efficient advocate, and allowed him to water down everything that I had cried out till the trial, that I returned home with a vindication by the court, that I apologized for all I had done, and that I had brought character witnesses to prove that generally speaking I am – O.K....

"If you imprison me," I closed my presentation, "you will be punishing mainly my wife and children, but when facing the court of their questioning looks, I shall always be able to look them squarely in the eyes."

★ ★ ★

Conclusion and Beginning

Chapter 12

> "...Who lost (the elections)?
> – Peres: We Israelis.
> And who won?
> – Peres: You may say – the Jews.
> The Jews beat the Israelis..."
>
> Daniel Simon, in an interview with Shimon
> Peres, for his book *A Different Land*

While our time was taken up in endless sessions in the Jerusalem courthouse, with no end in sight to this 'farce', the State of Israel entered the stormiest election campaign that it had ever undergone.

Those elements of the population that were loyal to traditional beliefs, swamped by a tidal wave of post-Zionism which threatened to drown them, reached out for any straw that could save them. Stigmatized as responsible for the assassination of Rabin, with everything they held sacred and precious trampled upon before their very eyes without their being able to affect or protest the course of events, they jumped at the small window of opportunity presented by the candidacy of 'Bibi' Netanyahu.

The citizens whom we had become accustomed to seeing at the 'Zo Artzeinu' meetings, conventions and demonstrations, now all mobilized themselves for the political campaign against the leftist government. I found myself unable to join the bandwagon. Around us, the country was in a state of ferment and agitation, but we deliberately kept our distance. I could not bring myself to paste a sticker on my car proclaiming 'Bibi Is Good for the Jews'. I did not believe that. Nor did the sticker 'I Feel Sure with the National Camp' express my conviction. I did not at all feel sure of this fickle and spineless camp, and I did not believe a word uttered by its spokesmen. In the various parties of the national camp, I did not discern any serious ideology that could serve as an alternative to the 'post-Zionism' of Meretz. To me it was quite clear that lacking a solid ideological foundation, 'Bibi' would quickly slide down the same slippery slope from which Begin had tumbled before him, and would find himself actually following the course paved for him by the forces of the Left.

We did not wish to publicize our position. The public was so frustrated, so eager to clutch at any spark of hope, that puncturing this illusory balloon would have been nasty. Besides, did anyone have a better alternative? Surely you don't expect us to vote for Peres!?

I therefore confided my thoughts to a very limited circle of intimate friends and adopted the relaxed position of uninvolved spectator looking on from the sidelines.

We were quite alone. For me, the political 'Right' had no appeal. I found myself wriggling out of various offers to join one of its parties. At the same time, I realized that here was an opportunity to get rid of the yoke of the leftist regime – so how could we remain passive?

The most pressing issue at that time was Hebron. Peres wanted – wanted very much – to hand Hebron over to Arafat, as he had promised, but he was afraid of taking that step. Unlike Rabin, Peres was endowed with much wisdom and sensitivity to public opinion. He knew how far he could proceed, and was not tempted, as his predecessor had been, to plunge forward like a bull in a china shop trampling all in the way.

True, he had exploited the national trauma of Rabin's assassination and the reflexive defensive stance taken by the faith-keeping public sector (in reaction to accusations of having been 'involved') to deliver all the major cities in Judea and Samaria into the hands of the PLO without opposition. But Hebron was an altogether different matter. The hundreds of thousands of visitors who streamed to the Machpela Cave, the plucky little Jewish community that tenaciously clung to its land in the heart of Hebron, and the general support provided to the settlers by the broad faith-keeping public – all these deterred Peres, and he stopped in his tracks. The problem became acute because the army had already been sitting on their kitbags for a long time, and the high command, pressing to leave quickly, fed the media 'professional' assessments favoring withdrawal.

Tension was high. We decided to initiate a 'campaign' for Hebron that had no direct connection with the approaching elections and the candidates. The seat of King David before he moved on to Jerusalem, with its remarkable monument to the founding fathers and mothers of the nation, the Machpela Cave, a site without parallel in any other country, had become a desolate Arab town unworthy of our presence, in the eyes of the leftist elements. We, on the other hand, wanted to instill in the general public a deep sense of personal belonging and relationship to Israel's first capital city. We decided on an operation with the theme, 'You Gave Away Hebron – You Took Away My Home'. Our plan was to pitch tents on traffic islands at major intersections throughout the country, tents with all the marks of belonging to the 'homeless': a small pup tent, a field bed, and a clothes-line with a few clothes drying in the wind. We wanted passing motorists to realize that even residents *within* Israel's 'green line' felt the loss of a home, with our handing over the city of our forefathers to the hands of aliens.

Persuading the public to carry out this undertaking was no easy matter. They were all busy with the election campaign. Though the operation was executed successfully at a number of spots, it did not really spread throughout the country. As was our practice,

Shmuel and I were the first to do what we asked of others. We set up a small tent in the center of the traffic island at the Ra'anana junction, posted up placards 'You Gave Away Hebron – You Took Away My Home', and plunked ourselves down to the humdrum daily routine of the homeless. A concerned policeman who arrived on the scene convinced himself that we were not a public nuisance in any way, and left us alone. When we felt hungry, we ordered pizza to be brought to our 'new home', and sat down to our evening repast. Astonished drivers stared at the couple of 'homeless' crunching their pizza in full view, and tried to figure out what connection that sight might have with the various election campaign posters adorning the area. "Hey, just a second – which party do you fellows represent...?" queried one puzzled driver.

Only in retrospect did I realize how effective this operation was. To this very day I encounter people who identified me at that intersection, and who tell me how much our gimmick had led them to think about the issue.

But at that time, our little demonstration was proving to be quite frustrating. The stony, unsmiling faces of the drivers behind the windshields in their air-conditioned cars seemed to us to be devoid of sympathy. When night fell, Shmuel had no trouble falling asleep on the field cot. I could not sleep. I continued to observe the fleeting cars and the layer of soot from their exhausts that accumulated on my body.

In the early morning I spotted the cars which had returned the previous night from work in Tel Aviv to their homes in Ra'anana and Kfar Sava as they once again set forth to work. The faces of the drivers did not betray their thoughts – they were probably surprised to see us still installed at the intersection. Shmuel finally awoke from a restful night's sleep, and we sat on the field cot facing the rising sun, trying to warm up from the cool of the night and the morning dew.

"Actually, why are you going to vote for 'Bibi'?" asked Shmuel suddenly. "You have done such an excellent job of analyzing the situation and explaining why he is not going to change things, so why vote for him?"

"First of all, I have no alternative," I answered. "In a situation in which one person consistently and deliberately works against everything that I hold dear, and his rival will do the same things but only under duress – I prefer first of all to get rid of the former, and the only way to do so today is to vote for 'Bibi'. Apart from that," I added reflectively, "if Peres should win, he will hand over Hebron to Arafat immediately after the elections, while with 'Bibi', it would take three months... and three months is a long time in Israeli politics."

"After the elections, how do you visualize our role?" continued Shmuel. "Do you believe we will have any role at all to play?"

"It does not matter at all who wins," I responded. "What is important is that somebody should begin to construct a viable alternative which could challenge both the Left and the Right, an alternative based upon our Jewish identity.

"After the elections we will carry on from the very same point we were at when we met in my home, and which the Rabin assassination cut short."

Miraculously, Netanyahu was elected Prime Minister.

A tremendous eruption of jubilation swept the Right, while a wave of despondency swept over the Left. The government-controlled radio played mournful strains, as though it were a sad memorial day. My assessment was incorrect.

'Bibi' handed over Hebron only after six months, not three, as I had anticipated.

"It seems to me that everything must be investigated. Commissions of Inquiry have been established in the past over much less consequential matters. I want the Commission to be required to look into the severe security lapse resulting from the Oslo Accords....

"Why have thousands of terrorists been released from imprisonment? Why were thousands of weapons given to the Palestinians? Why did we continue to carry out withdrawals despite the violations of the agreement with the PLO?... This will be a Commission of Inquiry ranking with the most crucial the State has ever known. If it is not done now, I am sure it will be done eventually..."

Benjamin Netanyahu – Promises to set up a Commission of Inquiry to investigate the Oslo Process

In an interview on Channel 7, on the 16th of *Tevet*, 5754 (December 30, 1993)

Hebron was handed over to the terrorists without any vocal opposition or noteworthy protest. In addition, the 'right-wing' Prime Minister obligated his government to withdraw from the entire area of Judea and Samaria that did not include settlements or army bases – to be accomplished in three stages, reinforcing Israeli commitments to all the stipulations of the Oslo Accords – which he had previously called into question...

Had he wished, Netanyahu could have freed himself from the Oslo fetters elegantly and easily.

On the Intermediate Days of Succot, 5757, arch-terrorist Arafat provided him with a simple ladder that would have enabled him to climb down the tree.

Arafat dispatched his soldiers, armed with Israeli weapons provided them in accordance with the Oslo Accords, and ordered them to open fire on Israeli troops. The ostensible justification for this step was that the Hasmonean Tunnel in the Temple Mount, which was being opened, weakened the foundations of the El-Aksa Mosque. Within several days, sixteen Israeli soldiers were murdered with the weapons delivered to Arafat by the Rabin government.[1]

For years, concerned citizens stood at street corners and intersections carrying placards proclaiming, 'Do Not Provide Them with Arms'. There is no longer any question as to who was right in this argument. Arafat had breached all the agreements in the most murderous and vicious manner, and the Prime Minister should have declared an end to all understandings reached with the PLO gang and the arch-terrorist who headed it. Instead, Netanyahu hastened to meet with Arafat and warmly shake hands, declaring that Arafat was a true friend. He then obligated himself to hand over Hebron, release women murderers who had been sentenced to life imprisonment by Israeli courts, as a gesture of good will, and to withdraw from the remainder of the areas in three quick stages – all this even before negotiations have begun on the final settlement.

What on earth was taking place?! Unbelievably, Netanyahu was taking steps that were diametrically opposed to the will of those who had voted him into office! All this in total contradiction of the security conceptions that he had formulated so learnedly in his books! While he was still in the opposition, Netanyahu had called for the establishment of a state Commission of Inquiry to investigate the blatant violations of the law and security considerations involved in the Oslo Accords, and particularly the supply of arms to the enemy. Why now, having been brought to power with the enthusiastic support of the camp of the Faithful to the Land, did he choose to carry on along the path of his predecessors, and in effect become guilty of the same violations against which he had railed and regarding which he had shortly before called for an investigation?

Why does a government of the Left, when it reaches power, do everything possible to further the ideology of the 'Peace Now' movement, while a government of the Right does everything possible to further the ideology of ... the 'Peace Now' movement?

---

[1] These were not the first Israelis to be killed with these arms, but in the past, publication of these 'incidents' had been suppressed with the helpful cooperation of the media. This time the confrontation was filmed and seen live on the screen, and the photos of Arafat's officers in battle uniform deliberately aiming at Israeli soldiers were viewed worldwide.

Many on the political Right have evaded any serious discussion of this question, arguing that Netanyahu is simply not the right man for the position. They claim that he is a spineless individual who is incapable of resisting pressure, and that he should be quickly replaced by a better candidate, such as Uzzi Landau or Benny Begin.

This would be a simplistic conclusion. Netanyahu has indeed furnished all the proof: His fickle nature, doubtful loyalty to his friends and closest intimates, with a government run like a kindergarten by opportunists without vision. In addition, the occupancy of top positions requiring integrity and honesty by unreliable characters has created a dislike and rejection of the man and his government. Public opinion polls reflected this in the growing popularity of the head of the opposition, Ehud Barak.

But a deeper look refutes this facile assessment. Netanyahu is no fool. His scholastic background is much broader than that of his two predecessors. His books are well researched and well reasoned, and there can be no comparison between them and the edited diaries of Yitzchak Rabin or the wild fantasies presented by Peres in his recent books.

Netanyahu worked his way up from the bottom, to become Israel's youngest ever Prime Minister, without establishment aid and against all odds. He resurrected his defeated party after its defeat in the elections of '92, instituted primaries, and won them, successfully confronted a hostile media front and unsympathetic élites – and despite the reverberations of the Rabin assassination overwhelmed them all.

Netanyahu got no breaks, and enjoyed no shortcuts to power; he did it all on his own. There were no swift kicks to the top, no fast advancement as a representative of an élite. He was endowed with patience, persistence, wisdom, cunning, powers of persuasion and long-range vision. He suffered all sorts of insults, but persevered toward the goal he had set for himself. No previous Prime Minister had ever had to work so hard to attain that position. No. One cannot glibly dismiss Netanyahu as a person who is 'simply not fit'.

And what about substance? Could it be that a lack of ideology lies at the root of the evil?

Netanyahu's family roots lie deep in the Israeli Right – but even those who are not impressed by this fact and attribute the problem to a lack of ideology cannot make the same complaint against the previous prime ministers of the Right.

Menachem Begin, the first Prime Minister of the Right, certainly had an ideology that directed his actions. The former commander of the Irgun, the humble man who struggled all his life to fulfill Revisionist ideology, was the first to liquidate the entire settlement project in the Yamit area, evacuating and uprooting an entire town and eleven surrounding communities – all as a sacrifice on the altar of the false peace that bewitched him. Begin, who in one fateful step had thus forfeited his claim to ideological persistence, awoke too late from his illusions, and from that point on began to deteriorate physically and psychologically, until he resigned, broken-hearted, from his position.

Yitzchak Shamir, former commander of Lehi, who replaced Begin, was made of sterner stuff. He was not befuddled by the Zabotinsky notion of *Hadar* (nobility) nor was he impressed by the thought of grand ceremonies on the White House lawn. He knew exactly what the Middle East 'peace' processes were leading to, and he had the advantage of being able to benefit from his predecessor's blunders. He was already able to gauge the extent of the catastrophic reality resulting from withdrawal from Zionist fundamentals, following the signing by his predecessor of the agreement with the Egyptian dictator.

For a long time, Shamir stood firm and unrelenting against the heavy pressures on the part of 'our great friend' over the ocean. One clearly recalls how he held fast during the 'reassessment' by Secretary of State James Baker. But Shamir did nothing to further Zionist expansion; he merely tried his best to hold the line against post-Zionism. In the end, he too could not withstand the pressures, and the latter part of his rule was characterized by the freezing of settlement activity. The Madrid Conference, which opened during his term of office, recognized the validity of the principle that 'everything was negotiable'.

Thus, left, right, the decline of Zionist ideology determinedly moves on – from Camp David (right) to Madrid (right) and from there to Oslo (left).

Both the Left and the Right undermine the foundations of Zionism, casually renounce our right and obligation to the Land of Israel, and willingly relinquish strategic and economic assets – no matter what the personal qualities of the political leader are.

Does this mean that the ideology of the Left has triumphed? Does this mean that whoever takes over the political reins sooner or later comes to the realization, palatable or otherwise, that there is no other course save the road to post-Zionism?

Does this mean that the leadership of the Israeli Right consciously lies to its constituency, knowing that upon reaching the levers of power they will have to adopt post-Zionism realpolitik?

If so, then, for all practical purposes, there aren't two political camps in Israel after all. Both the socialism of the Labor party and the Revisionist versions of Zionism have been supplanted by the new western liberalism that has spread throughout the world. What has remained of the former Israeli camps is merely the degenerated institutional apparatuses and élites that try to preserve the enshrined privileges of their members. Both have succumbed to post-Zionism.

Those who have remained steadfastly faithful to the roots and values of the Jewish people – the 'heart' of the nation – have been left out of the game.

The Faithful to the Land are like the pawns who have managed to capture the objective, only to discover that they unintentionally had been fighting against their own outposts, and that they had been duped into engaging in a war that was not theirs. They had assumed that the source of the evil, the cause of all the misfortune, lay with the Left. The struggle against the Left serves the interests of worthy causes, and one may ignore irregularities and contradictions when considering the overall goal – defeat of the Left. Somewhere along the way, a small, simple point was forgotten: defeat of the Left is not a value in itself.

Zionism is a value, Judaism is a value, a just and moral regime is a value, the sanctity of life is a value, and the Land of Israel is a value. Simplicity, industriousness, modesty, labor, trustworthiness, sacrifice, honesty, wisdom, happiness...

These are values that one should struggle for.

Are they to be found in our 'Right' or 'Left'?

Can they be found in the 'religious' parties, or anywhere else in the Israeli political spectrum?

Is it not apparent that the entire range of Zionist political establishments has been submerged by post-Zionism?

Post-Zionism has co-existed with Zionism from the very beginning. The ideology which strove to restore the Jew to his true being, to the Land of Israel, to an independent existence as individuals and as a national community in his old-new country, was from the very first challenged by a counter stream of thought. Those who think that this negativism sprouted in the back yard of Zionism upon liberation of the historic areas of the homeland following the Six Day War are mistaken.

Emancipation and redemption have always been followed by a backlash.

This is an historic phenomenon that goes back to the days of Moses and Aaron – "Let us appoint a chief, and let us return to Egypt."[1]

In that Biblical description we find an echo of today's egocentrism: "Let's do as we see fit."

---

[1] Numbers, 14, 5.

Even before the rebirth of the State, a small but dominant circle of intellectuals, clustered mainly round the Hebrew University of Jerusalem, argued that the Yishuv should not aim at renouncing and displacing British mandatory rule over Palestine.[1] Why, asked these scholars, should we provoke unending conflict with the Arab population? The British will see to safeguarding the rights of the members of all the religious persuasions, and all the national communities will develop without arousing nationalistic tensions with their neighbors. True, the rag at the top of the flagpole will be the Union Jack, but is that not a small price to pay for the tremendous advantages of true peace and harmony?

Following the establishment of the State, this approach was developed (based on 'pacifist' conceptions – not in the spirit of Ahad Ha'Am) by radical leftist cliques, the most notorious of which was *Matzpen*. This organization, which was active in the mid-fifties, accused Zionism of responsibility for all the ills that troubled the Middle East and called for a total rejection of Zionism and the dismemberment of the State.

The nucleus of *Matzpen* consisted of Hebrew University intellectuals (naturally) who favored the establishment of a bi-national state. All this occurred long *before* liberation of Jerusalem and the heart of the homeland in the Six Day War.

Upon reading Shimon Peres' book *The New Middle East,* one cannot but be amazed by the startling congruity between the post-Zionist theories propounded by those radicals of the fifties and the philosophy adopted by this "bigger-than-life leader". [2]

Content-wise they are indistinguishable, and the same holds true for the terminology.

The concept of 'integration into the region', the idea of a multi-national entity (*The New Middle East*, p. 78) – in effect, a kiss of death for the Jewish nation – all this, and much more, was adopted by the political leadership of the Zionist State, who, paradoxically, had now become the guillotiners of Zionism. This process did not take place overnight. Yitzchak Rabin and Shimon Peres of the nineties were not at all (ideologically) the same persons that they had been during the early decades of the state. Classic Labor Zionism, that of Beryl Katznelson, Ben-Gurion, and Yigal Alon, gradually made way for the post-Zionism of Uri Avneiri, Yossi Sarid and Shulamit Aloni.

Rabin and Peres never owned up to this fact, but their declarations and actions in their later years stood in direct contrast with the teachings of their mentors. They had consistently and totally adopted the ideology of Avneiri and Co. The latter had experienced humiliation, at times egg throwing, but persevered, to the point where approval of their stand gradually expanded and became acceptable.

---

[1] The reference is to the formation of '*Brit Shalom*', headed by no less a personage than the Rector (!) of the Hebrew University at that time, Prof. Magnes.
[2] MK Dalia Itzik

One of the main turning points in this post-Zionism road was the Yom Kippur War and the ensuing state of shock.

Classic socialistic, materialistic, somewhat militaristic Zionism, the ideology that called for yet another house and another goat, a 'cloak of concrete and cement', agricultural machines and machines of war, 'kolhoz'-like factory assembly lines modeled after the Ata firm, and kibbutz communes – this brand of Zionism became exposed as a weak reed. The margin between defeat and victory had been extremely narrow, thousands paid with their lives for the exaggerated sense of self-assurance, and soldiers returning from the battlegrounds were now convinced that classic Zionism had only been an illusion. Post-Zionism appeared then as more correct than ever, and many turned towards it.

As is true of all authentic revolutions, the cultural élites and intellectual circles were in the vanguard of this reversal. The way to the head went through the heart. The tired and disillusioned public was captivated by the charms of a simple and promising universalistic panacea. Nationalist songs like 'Ho, My Homeland', were replaced by 'Song of Peace'. The lovely song 'Look, Rachel, See, They Have Come Back Home' has made way for 'We Have a Land, Who Needs Another', and 'Jerusalem of Gold' has lost out to 'Bye-bye! I'm Off to London!'

While the early decades of the century were characterized by authors and poets of the caliber of Chaim Hazaz, Nathan Alterman, Uri Tzvi Greenberg, and Yehuda Karni, in the sixties and seventies they had already been shoved aside by A.B. Yehoshua, Amos Oz and the like. In the local world of literature, theater and entertainment, hardly a niche remained for authentic Jewish-Israeli creativity – any expression of a people newly restored to its homeland. Israeli culture became a culture of disenchantment, alienation and apathy.

At the same time, an opposite trend of renewal and invigoration began flourishing in a different sector of the Zionist movement.

Graduates of the Merkaz HaRav Yeshiva, members of *Bnei Akiva*, launched the *Gush Emunim* movement and initiated a campaign of settlement of the lands liberated in 1967. To classic socialist Zionism, they added the element of religiosity which, by settling in the heart of the Land of the Bible, produced a component that had been sorely lacking till then. Unfortunately, Gush Emunim took as its exclusive model the classic mold established by Labor Zionism. The dream of these settlers in Judea and Samaria was to be 'more royal than the king', true Zionists of the socialist mold. That is, they aspired to be neo-kibbutzniks, neo-Palmachniks, with sandals, shorts, blue shirts, mustaches, '*kova tembel*' – and *tzitzit* (prayer-shawl fringes)...

They began to cultivate their own distinct culture, but failed to inject anything new into the spiritual life of the nation, and did not affect the broader public. Isolating walls, similar to those of the ultra-Orthodox, sprang up around them. The post-Zionists, who had already rejected the shallow Zionist mediocrity and materialism, found the new version, with its dimension of Messianism, even more objectionable. But the Gush persevered in the classic manner, another house and another goat, plowing and standing watch in the heat and in the cold, dancing around a campfire with the cry *'Utzoo Eitzah VeTufar'[1]*, and believing that establishing 'irreversible advances' was what counted.

Indeed, one cannot belittle their admirable job of settling the hills of the heartland. Clearly, were it not for the settlement endeavors of Gush Emunim, Israel would have forfeited all these central areas, which had been liberated in the Six Day War, to the terrorist PLO. But the assumption that this process of resettlement was irreversible proved to be false.

By ignoring the need for concurrent intellectual development, by limiting their concerns to the narrow confines of physical construction, and contenting themselves with the learning within the walls of their study halls – Gush Emunim had, in effect, abandoned the spiritual and cultural needs of the general public to the hands of post-Zionists outside. Classic Zionism was on its deathbed, unable to cope with the ever-growing wave of post-Zionism. There were indeed solitary figures who tried to chart a different course, writers and thinkers such as Moshe Shamir and Israel Eldad, but the bookshelves were largely taken over by Amos Oz, A.B. Yehoshua, and their followers – Grossman, Shalev, and the like.

From the camp of the faithful, there arose in the last generation no outstanding author, no poet with a broad appeal, no artist, no generally admired singer or entertainer, no artistic photographer, no playwright, no film director, no new creative avenue, in short – desolation.[2]

For every house erected in Samaria, Amos Oz and A.B. Yehoshua produced another novel.

For every new neighborhood established in Judea, Sobol produced a new play.

For every settlement set up in the Gaza strip, another post-Zionist television show appeared.[3]

---

[1] "Take counsel together, and it shall come to nought" [a retort to Israel's enemies] -- Isaiah 8,10

[2] It is my duty to apologize in advance to all those engaged in these professions who may feel themselves insulted. Certainly we have outstanding figures among the members of the modern-religious camp, many of whom are professionally excellent, but their influence generally on the cultural scene in the State of Israel has always been minor in contrast to that of the post-Zionists.

[3] See: Dr. Yoram Chazoni, *Techeilet*, no. 2, published by the *'Shaleim'* Institute.

It is therefore no wonder that Jewish settlement in Yesha found itself alienated to a great degree from the people of Zion, who were not prepared to fight for it. The only consensus regarding the settlements concerned their security, since 'Jews are compassionate, sons of the compassionate', but the values which the settlement movement was to have expressed meant nothing to the residents of Tel Aviv. As long as the government played the role of defender of the lives of the settlers (at the cost of "our sons who have to be there because of them"...), it could proceed in its post-Zionist dismantling, a process which the hearts of the public had been conditioned to accept for over a generation.

The inner core of the hearts of the Jewish population of the State remained true to their Jewish identity and the principles of Zionism, but had no means to give it expression. There was no one to do so for them. The communications media remained under the tight control of people in whom this inner core of faith no longer existed. The average Israeli apologetically resigned himself to the peace process.

"We have no alternative. We must proceed."

★ ★

What exactly is the flaw in classic Zionism that made possible the rapid development of post-Zionism? Where is the fault, the crack, through which the anti-Zionist ideology infiltrated and subsequently conquered its heart and soul?

The answer lies in Herzl's classic reportage of the Dreyfus trial and its aftermath: the public humiliation of the French Jewish captain, the breaking of his sword and the tearing off of his epaulettes and insignia. The formerly assimilationist Herzl drew the conclusion that the only solution to the so-called *Jewish problem* was an independent state for the Jews.

Does this really mean that the State of Israel came into being thanks to Captain Dreyfus' loss of rank and his broken sword?

Does this mean that if the Jews had been treated decently in the Diaspora the state would not have been restored? Would that have been acceptable?

Modern political Zionism came into being in order to solve *the Jewish problem* by establishing the State of the Jews. Zionism did not endeavor to create a state in which the mission and destiny of the Jewish people would be realized. One hundred years of a Zionism of physical and material survival and fifty years of the state whose purpose was to preserve that situation have come to a close.

The Jewish national identity that united the Israelis around their young reborn state rested upon the will to survive. The existential need, the threat to life, the objective dangers, anti-Semitism and persecution that demanded a political solution occupied a central role in explaining the need and justification for an independent Jewish state.

The Holocaust served as the ultimate justification of this approach. Holocaust survivors who arrived in the newborn state were treated with condescension by the native-born Sabras. The 'new' Jews, who stood upright in their homeland and held their destiny in their own two hands, despised those "who had gone meekly like sheep to the slaughter and shown no resistance". Had they, the new, proud Israelis lived through that period in Europe, they would have stood up to the tormentors and heroically vanquished the German army (the most efficient in history) and its many collaborators. The refugees found themselves experiencing shame over what had befallen them, and many tried to conceal their past. But when Zionism sought to justify its existence (and later demand reparations from the Germans), there was no hesitation over making wide use of the memory of the Holocaust atrocities.

As part of their education, Israeli children are taken to visit Yad VeShem (the Jerusalem Holocaust Memorial) where they learn how vital it is to have our own state (for otherwise it could happen again), and every visiting dignitary is taken on a tour of the horror scenes.

In a tone of apology: What's the alternative? We simply must have our own state.

"Look," says the State of Israel to the statesman conducted past the frightful photographs, "we have established a state but have never dared to honestly confront the question 'Why?' The truth is that we are wary of the answer, for it necessarily leads to all sorts of embarrassingly primitive matters of which we are ashamed and from which we try our best to distance ourselves, issues like the 'vision of the prophets', for example, or messianic expressions like 'a light unto the nations'. But just between us," the State continues its brief dialogue with the bewildered statesman, "why get bogged down in such questions? Just observe how miserable we have been; note carefully what your kind has done to us in the past. Would you dare to question our right to existence? In light of these authentic photographs, you must agree that we simply have no alternative. That is why we established our state. So please do not ask too many questions."[1]

But, in the face of changing reality, this existential argument no longer holds. The State of Israel, which, in accordance with classic political Zionism, should be the safest place in the world for Jews, has turned out to be the most dangerous. The

---

[1] Obviously, it is not the intention of the author to question the need to transmit to succeeding generations the memory of the Holocaust. Quite the contrary – every effort must be made to intensify this activity and broaden it beyond anything done to date. But this effort must be directed *inward*.

As for the nations of the world, it is preferable to simply produce the Bible – and also enable a look at the IDF....

number of Jews who pay with their lives for their Jewish identity is higher in Israel than anywhere else in the world, including the most hostile countries.

Zionism has therefore failed to provide security to Jews by the establishment of their own state, creating instead a zone carrying the highest degree of risk.

In total contrast to their fragile personal security, Israel's citizens do not view the State as destructible. A generation has passed since the Yom Kippur War and the fear of annihilation that accompanied it. The 'drums of peace' beating on all sides drown out the true intentions of neighboring states, so that national security no longer has top priority but is simply another component in the governmental concerns of an ordinary Western country. Thus the anxiety of having a 'Sword of Damocles' hanging above our heads has dissipated, and with it the understandable justification it had brought for an independent State. Post-Zionism entered our lives through this breach in our understanding of why we need a state, which became existence for its own sake rather than existence for a national purpose. The original values of Zionism have been replaced by emphasis upon individual achievement and self-fulfillment. Self-actualization has taken top priority over every national value.

Promoted by the example set by imported television series, a successful personal career has become the primary goal of the individual. A secondary school in Ra'anana has changed its name to 'Metro-West'. It would be interesting to know how they teach the history of Zionism and how they explain the need for our national existence in the 'Metro-West' secondary school.

National solidarity based on the Zionist ideal has vanished; Zionism has entered advanced stages of disintegration and decline, and in the absence of an external threat, will simply receive the kiss of death. At the same time, Arab nationalism is flourishing and expanding. Our reigning post-Zionism is incapable of coping with this growing nationalistic force, nor is it interested in doing so. The developing Arab nationalism simply justifies the basic doctrines of long-time post-Zionist thinking.

Matters have come to such a pass that the Deputy Minister of Education in the Rabin government, Micha Goldman, suggested replacing Israel's national anthem, which includes the words "the Jewish soul is stirred", with a new anthem that would be appropriate for all its citizens.

The national flag, which displays clearly Jewish motifs, has also been laid on the surgical table, and the Singapore of the Middle East, the state 'for all its citizens' envisioned by the architects of the 'New Middle East', has begun to take shape.

★ ★

The processes and dangers described above are obvious to anyone willing to see. Most Israelis have not internalized the message of post-Zionism, but an opposing trend has appeared. Ever-widening circles of *'chozrim beteshuva'*, persons returning to a religious way of life, have already become a recognizable phenomenon on a nationwide scale. The classic penitents of the seventies were stars of the cultural and entertainment world who, after achieving fame and recognition in their fields, changed their entire life-styles and became ultra-observant. Today's penitents do not rush to alter their attire and external life-style, but are becoming increasingly observant in a manner that is in conformity with a modern way of life.

This phenomenon is likely to increase in the coming years. It provides an answer for the individual's search for meaning in his life and for his identity as a Jew, but it does not solve the problem on a national level or fill the emptiness in Zionism. In these circles, the influence of the *haredim*, whose religious life is characterized by alienation from national life, is great, and one can understand people who undergo a complete transformation in their personal way of life but are unprepared to devote their energies to addressing national concerns.[1] In the eyes of these penitents, observance of the law as defined in the *Shulchan Aruch* [the Code of Jewish Law] by as many more individuals as possible is the ultimate goal of life, and everything else will fall in place. That is the way the *haredim* thought and lived before the Holocaust and in its wake. And that is the way that the settlers thought: that the primary *mitzvah* was settling the land, and all the rest would fall into place. The problem is that nothing comes in isolation. The temptation to see the lack of religious observance as the root of all the problems, and the process of penitence as restoring what has been lacking in the Return to Zion, is a very real one. It allows one to believe simplistically that this will solve all our national as well as personal problems. "We, the religious, have the truth; you, the non-religious, have only falsehood; all you need do is transfer to our side, and all will be well."

The arrogance of this approach is aggravated by its intellectual shallowness. The Torah of Israel is meant to be a vibrant, vital force for the Jewish nation in its sovereign state in the Land of Israel. This fundamental axiom ought to compel Orthodox leadership to wrestle with contemporary issues. Not just the observance of religious minutiae, not simply matters like the presence of worms in lettuce, but issues like policy regarding bank interest, security, and the drug problem. The world of *'Halacha'* [the whole legal system of Judaism] is not attempting to meet head-on the challenges posed by the realities of a modern Jewish state.

The *Halacha*, in its present form, was developed for a people in a protracted exile, and was designed to maintain its living spirit despite the loss of a physical state with all the responsibilities and obligations of sovereignty. The Jewish sages succeeded

---

[1] The penitent generally does his best to convince others to follow in his footsteps, but this is always limited to efforts of an interpersonal nature, never on the national level.

miraculously in preserving the uniqueness and unity of the Jewish people until their eventual return to the Land. However, thousands of years had elapsed since the days when an independent Jewish state functioned in practice according to the Torah. The nation returning in our time to their ancestral homeland did so with a religious code of conduct suited to the conditions of exile. The Torah of Eretz Yisrael, which applies eternal verities to a people renewing itself in a modern state – this Torah has remained obscure.[1]

Thus was created a mutually acceptable 'division of labor' between the two camps. The actual administration of the state was entrusted into the hands of the secular.

It was taken for granted by the religious public that the Torah was not relevant to a modern democratic state, and that the venerable Rabbinical establishment would not attempt to stand up and hew out of the Jewish sources the bricks that would enable the construction of a revived Jewish regime.

We, the religious, would therefore leave practical matters in secular hands, while we would tend to the preservation of the coals that warmed and preserved us over the past two thousand years.

While we, the secular, knowing that we are incapable of developing a true Jewish identity for the Jewish state, will forfeit this role, and leave our national roots to be tended by the faithful hands of the religious.

Both the secular and the religious political parties faithfully performed their roles according to this formula. The small groups on the extremes of the political spectrum, the anti-Zionist *haredim* on one side and the anti-religious secular on the other, profited politically from their mutual recriminations, but in the final analysis, they too played according to these rules. The average Israeli does not mind traveling a bit longer in order to allow the closure of Jerusalem's Bar Ilan Street on Shabbat, but Yehuda Meshi-Zahav of the extreme ultra-Orthodox Neturai Karta and Arnon Yekutiel of Meretz both thrive on the anger and hate generated by the argument about closure. The religious thus monopolized 'Judaism', without ensuring its relevance to present realities, and the secular reigned in the area of 'ordinary living conditions', deprived of any tint of Jewish identity, with the result that the state fell between two stools. It is in this vacuum that post-Zionism has made its great headway. The public domain completely lost its distinctly Jewish character. The Sabbath, considered a day of welcome rest in Israel's towns in the first years of the state, has now become the primary day for sundry public activities and business. The values of economic success and efficiency require that this day be exploited, and who finds the time to consider

---

[1] This is not to ignore, Heaven forbid, the extraordinary cultural and Torah edifice developed during the exile, but rather the expression of a desire to build upon these foundations and march ahead.

the Jewish future of the state when one's child wishes to go off with his pals to the mall?

And if anyone tries to halt this development, they are accused of religious coercion. "What's this – religious coercion?"

The secular have won.

After all, MacDonald's and Kentucky Fried Chicken are to be found at every corner – and the Sabbath is the national shopping day.

The ultra-Orthodox have won – Bar Ilan Street is closed.

But Israel has lost – its Jewishness.

The religious parties and institutions on the one hand, and the post-Zionist stream with its parties on the other, have sown dissension and animosity between 'religious' and 'secular'. Both camps 'have won' and have received their share of the national pie. This rift reached its climax during the term of the Rabin government. The Minister of Education in his cabinet, Shulamit Aloni, one of the archetypal leaders of the post-Zionist school, deliberately poured oil on the bonfire of hate.

A superficial glance at the media and the public domain gives the impression that the vast majority of the Jewish population in the country have adopted Aloni's world outlook. However, a comprehensive and thorough research conducted by the Gutman Institute[1] in 1993 produced results that astounded the investigators. It transpired that the Jews of Israel are more aware of and tied to their Jewish roots than it might appear to the uninvolved spectator. The research, which took months and covered a representative sample of thousands of interviewees (and this, following the great influx of immigration from the previous Soviet Union, a wave that was understood to have diminished the percentage of believers), revealed surprising findings, such as the following:

55 to 60 percent of Israelis (Israeli Jews) believe in a Creator who directs the universe, and that Moses received the Torah at Mt. Sinai. (!)

Over one-third of Israelis believe in an afterlife and in the coming of the Messiah.

---

[1] The research was funded by the Avichai Foundation and the results were presented at a study day held in the Van Leer Institute.
I am indebted to Chagai Ben-Artzi who called my attention to these figures.

Over 80% believe that the rites of passage (circumcision, bar mitzvah, marriage and burial) should have a Jewish religious character.

79% of Israeli males have 'tefillin', and about half don them either regularly or occasionally

56% of Israelis always light the Sabbath candles, and about half make the *kiddush* on the wine; 77% view the Sabbath as an important element in their lives and believe that the Sabbath evening should remain a tranquil, family-oriented evening.

65% keep a Kosher home, and 80% eat kosher 'normally'.

Almost 80% always participate in a Passover Seder, and 65% desist from eating '*chametz*' during the holiday.

71% always fast on Yom Kippur, and most of them participate in the synagogue services.

(This year [5758 - 1997/98]), surveys show that the percentage of those who fast has risen to 77%.)

The final conclusion of this research is that a mere 21% of Israeli Jews do not observe anything related to Jewish (religious) tradition. The remaining 79% fall into one of these categories: completely observant, observant to a considerable degree, or somewhat observant. The authors of the report even add that "a third indicated that they would prefer to be somewhat more or much more observant".

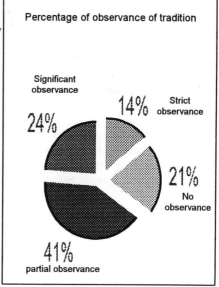

Percentage of observance of tradition

Significant observance
24%

Strict observance
14%

No observance
21%

partial observance
41%

There is, therefore, a very large gap between the real Israeli and the portrayal of the average Israeli as reflected by the media. The Israeli who resents 'religious coercion' – for that is the type constantly aired on Israeli Radio's Shelly Yachimovitch talk show – is the same Israeli who makes sure to light candles on Sabbath eve! The Israeli who feels 'choked' by the weekly closure of Bar Ilan Street in the ultra-Orthodox neighborhood in Jerusalem on Sabbath (although he has never driven there) is the same Israeli who fasts on Yom Kippur! And the Israeli who champions the right of homosexuals and lesbians to form a 'marriage' is one of the 80% who insist on maintaining the Jewish rites of passage.

It transpires, therefore, that the philosophy of 'integration into the Middle East' and changing Israel into a 'state of all its citizens', a modern state espousing western values of consumerism and individual success and severing itself from its burdensome legacy of Judaism, has been adopted only on a superficial level by the Jews of Israel. In their hearts, 80% of the Israelis have remained steadfastly loyal to their Jewish identity and feel committed to it to some degree or other. But the shapers of public opinion and those in key positions in the élites that control the country – in the courts and academia, education and culture, economics, industry, internal and external security, and, of course, the media – belong exclusively to the proponents of post-Zionism. A survey taken of the broadcasters, correspondents, editors and decision-makers in the Broadcasting Authority shows that over 90% of them do not fast on Yom Kippur. This figure alone should suffice to point out the huge gap between the masses living in Zion and the shapers of their cultural fare.

The fact that post-Zionism has taken control of all the agencies of power in the Jewish state means that the nation is marching in a direction which is diametrically opposed to the natural preferences and will of the population. The post-Zionists deluded themselves into thinking that the population had already acquiesced in acceptance of its philosophy and drew the conclusion that, after the Rabin assassination, there would be an easy victory for Peres and his camp. However, in the final analysis, the 56% of the Jewish population that gave Netanyahu his victory in 1996 voted neither for the Likud's 'Security and Peace' nor against Labor's 'Peace and Security'. Actually, they felt that their Jewish identity was being threatened by post-Zionism and voted for the contender.

Interestingly, 56% is approximately the percentage of those who believe in 'Torah from Sinai' according to the Gutman Institute research. In other words, Netanyahu could have saved the bother and cost required to conduct all the pre-election surveys; the real survey prophesying his election victory had been made three years earlier by Gutman![1]

One of the groups that came into being in an attempt to contend with post-Zionism was an organization called 'Chayil', composed of secular intellectuals, which publicly called for all Jews to vote for the National Religious Party (NRP). These people were

---

[1] It is of particular interest to note the mobilization of the *haredi* community in support of Netanyahu. Netanyahu the Zionist, the self-confessed adulterer, ostensibly represented all that was loathsome and reprehensible in the eyes of this public. But the *haredim* understood that post-Zionism and post-Judaism were one and the same. The *haredim* will never admit it, but Zionism, which 'has nothing to do with religion', is a natural outgrowth of Judaism, in that it represents a longing for Jewish redemption and meaning. It may indeed be a defective branch, but it grew from a healthy tree. It was not a hatchet aimed at cutting down the tree itself, as classic *haredi* thinking claimed.

very aware of the real danger to the survival of the state, a danger that has nothing to do with external threats. Chayil thought they could find in the NRP the potential for the creation of a new Israeli, an Israeli rooted in his authentic origins, which would lead to national cohesion, and integrating them with modern critical and cultural instruments for the development of the Jewish state.

But Chayil was to be deeply disappointed, for they did not realize that the NRP was unable to build a new structure upon the foundations of disintegrating Zionism. At best, the NRP could simply support the crumbling edifice. The Mizachi party had been a partner to the Herzlian approach to Jewish statehood, had supported Herzl's ill-fated Uganda Plan, had feared the consequences of the liberation of Jerusalem in 1967[1] and had not initiated the settlement movement in the seventies but had been drawn into supporting it almost against its will.

The NRP could neither offer a true alternative nor did it desire to do so. It refrained from including non-kippa-wearing supporters in its Knesset election list and missed a golden opportunity to initiate a move toward a new culture based on authentic Judaism.

Chayil had sought a new Jewish leadership in a flowerbed where they believed it would flourish. They had before them the model of the kibbutz movement. Although the kibbutz population had never been more than 3% of the general population, it had produced all the prominent leaders in all the major areas of life in the state. No one had been particularly perturbed by this phenomenon. Israelis felt that it was quite acceptable that national leadership should spring from this stratum, regardless of its proportion to the general population, since it was a movement dedicated to the common national goals, a movement leading the drive to settlement of the furthermost corners of the country, a movement whose sons were outstanding in select army units and on the battlefields, a movement which displayed ideological steadfastness and readiness for sacrifice.

All the above-listed functions are today fulfilled by the crocheted-kippa-wearing (modern Orthodox) Zionists, who are much more than 3% of the population.[2] One would therefore expect that national leadership would arise naturally from the Religious Zionist camp. But that is not happening. The traditional seclusion which called for influencing only externally – has come arm in arm with the kippa, whether black (ultra-Orthodox) or crocheted.

★★

---

[1] "If we enter Jerusalem, we will not be able to leave it" – Minister Moshe Chaim Shapiro, the Mafdal representative in the Unity Government, on the eve of the outbreak of the Six Day War.
[2] "Where can you be found in our military cemeteries?" was the question posed by Ben-Gurion of the religious in the early years of the state...
Even this terrible price has since been paid, doubled and tripled.

The sanitation crews apathetically cleaned up the tons of litter, the street posters and other paraphernalia produced for and by the elections. The photographs of the two candidates, Peres and Netanyahu, and their hollow slogans, finally ended up in the same garbage bins. Life returned to its normal course, as did the processes ingrained in Israeli society.

YOU and US
> You have in your hands control of the radio, television and newspapers;
> you have at your service all the leftist programs... the evil, the cynicism,
> the mockery and the superciliousness.
> What we have is the voting booth!

Ma'ariv, 17.04.97

The turbulence above the surface of the water had no effect at all on the permanent undercurrents that determine the flow's direction. As in the previous times when the Likud was running the government, the party had shown itself capable of winning an election – but the real power remained in the hands of the Left, which determines the reigning ideology and controls all the avenues of influence and power.

Roni Gabai of Ramat HaSharon wrote the following 'Letter to the Editor', which was printed in *Ma'ariv* on April 17, 1997:

Roni Gabai was mistaken – and it was a very big mistake. He never had even the voting booth.

Netanyahu, bereft of any alternative ideology, and as a result, unable to supplant the existing élites with other foci of influence, tried to hold on with all his might to the reins of government which apparently had fallen into his hands. At first, he did try to fend off the impending evil, and even 'dared' to enable tourists to tour the tunnels of the Western Wall, but as soon as he realized that a determination to hold fast to national principles would endanger his lofty position, he rushed to carry on the Oslo process, the dismantling of Zionism. The policy snowballed to the point where even a private developer (Dr Irwin Moskowitz), who had building permits for construction in privately owned property in Jerusalem, was denied permission to go ahead. Paradoxically, then, Netanyahu was the one to carry out his election warning that – "Peres will divide Jerusalem".

Netanyahu, who thought that the post-Zionist élites would think highly of him if he abandoned those whose votes brought him to power, soon found himself without support in either camp.

When Israeli soldiers were murdered by Palestinian 'policemen' armed with rifles supplied by the Rabin government, Netanyahu was blamed. When he subsequently met with Arafat and embraced him warmly, the same élites loudly voiced their anger at the "heavy price that we paid so that that 'fool' will wake up". Unable to forgive him for winning the election, the Left did everything possible to make his life miserable. He became the target of criminal investigations, legal actions and media accusations for incidents and actions that were standard practice in the days of the leftist governments. Netanyahu found himself under continuous crossfire from all the élite circles that shape the national agenda. No sooner was one affair resolved than another one appeared to plague him, severely damaging his public image. The media recovered from the shock of the election defeat and returned with renewed energies to furthering the post-Zionist goals.

When Israeli soldiers withdrew from Hebron, city of our ancestors, I and others who had been prominent in our opposition to the policies of the previous government were provocatively challenged with the question: "Where are you folks? Why are you now not out in force in the streets, not demonstrating, not blocking roads?"

It was very difficult to reply to that question, since it was clear that this government was continuing the very same policies against which we had protested. We had been beaten for our opposition to these steps, arrested, humiliated, and had gone on hunger strikes, and now it seemed that nothing had changed. Why were we resigning ourselves to this? With the exception of a very small core of protesters, the bulk of the public that had taken to the streets now remained closeted at home.
This question, so popular with the media, in effect expressed the following accusation: You really are not such sincere ideologues. Your struggle was not over principles, and all your ranting about the sanctity of your ancestral homeland, Zionism, and security, was a mere pretense. What really bothered you is that the Left was in power, and you used all those nice slogans for simple political ends. All the traffic stoppages and demonstrations were simply designed to get someone elected from your own camp. That...and nothing more! And you did that without any concern for the damage you were creating.

The answer was, unfortunately, quite simple. The public was no longer prepared to engage in protests in the same way that it had been previously. 'Bibi' should have experienced the same degree of public resentment as Rabin had, if not more, but there was no point in attempting protests that were doomed to failure for lack of participation.

So perhaps the journalists are right, and the only thing that had disturbed the faith-keeping public was Rabin's visage?

No, they are not right. But we cannot provide them with a satisfactory explanation, since they can absorb only tidy, short soundbytes; they are not attuned to accepting responses that are deeper than the level of sidewalks and messages which cannot be compressed into four words.

The masses had not demonstrated out of personal antipathy towards Rabin; after all, he was for a long time a most likable character. The sabra ruggedness, the shy smile, the (unjustified) aura of military hero, all served to make him an endearing figure. I have to admit that I too liked him, until I learned, the hard way, who and what he really was.

The people had demonstrated because post-Zionism had become the official religion of the Jewish state. The state had been transformed into an agency for the furtherance of this religion. It was not specific episodes that prompted the demonstrations – not Hebron or Shechem, nor the security danger. Even terrorist bombings could be downplayed in such a way – after all, the country cannot be sealed hermetically, etc.– as to keep potential demonstrators at home. All of these were merely symptoms of a much more acute threat that aroused the masses to leave their homes and go out to demonstrate: the threat to their Jewish identity. The people felt that the Jewish State was actively battling against their basic essence. It was not without cause that the religious elements were so much more prominent in the protest movements than their secular compatriots.

Can anyone believe that the religious do not want peace? Do they not have families and children for whose welfare they are constantly concerned?

Do the religious want war?

Nonsense. It is simply that in the religious camp the concept of Jewish identity is more highly crystallized – and the secular elements who joined them in demonstrating or supported them on the sidelines were those fellow-countrymen whose Jewish identity was dear to them.

'Bibi' was not perceived as the prototype of the post-Zionist and a threat to Jewish identity as were his predecessors, Rabin and Peres, but as someone who was dragged against his will in that direction. For this reason, the masses would not go out in protest. We gritted out teeth and allowed him to continue on his path.

Try explaining this on media talk shows like 'Popolitika'.

'Zo Artzeinu' had now become irrelevant. It had come into being in a storm of mass public disaffection, and established itself almost overnight as an activist, dynamic, militant force. It had acquired the trust of the Faithful to the Land, and thousands of people awaited its every word. I could have transformed its public support into political or establishment assets. I could have turned it into an established political organization, a right-wing body like the leftist 'Peace Now' or 'Dor Shaleim'. The public looked forward to such a development. But it was not to be. Had I taken this step, I would have been untrue to myself. The instrument would thus have become the objective.

I felt that the solution that the Israeli public really seeks for its present dilemma couldn't come from a movement perceived only as a protest movement, a movement of demonstrations of opposition. It could only come from a movement built upon positive upbuilding and presentation of an alternative.

'Zo Artzeinu' did not close up shop. It remains in the consciousness of the thousands who rallied to its flag and took to the streets. Whenever I encounter a veteran rank-and-file supporter who naturally recalls the highlights of 'Zo Artzeinu's' activities, I am again aroused by the realization of the deep and lasting mark we had made in Israeli consciousness within such a brief period. Maybe it will someday indeed be needed again, and maybe it will once again be possible to raise the flag of 'Zo Artzeinu', but I did not think that any objective would be served by institutionalizing it. There are enough organizations that raise money and build power only for the aggrandizement of its leadership and retention of special privileges for its members.

I decided to join Motti Karpel and several intellectuals and professors, religious and secular, who were forming a national movement to further the development of authentic Jewish leadership.

We believe that the State of Israel will only be able to face the coming challenges if its focal point is concentrated on its Jewish identity, not on security issues, peace and economics *per se*. In these areas, the need and desire for progress is ever present, but they are not at the heart of our existence as a nation in this land. The state must strive to weave together the various strands of Jewishness in the general population, in order to nourish and build a genuine, vibrant culture and society. We are not simply advocating old, worn-out concepts, whether religious or secular.

We are appealing to those whose Jewish identity, as individuals and as a nation, is the primary factor that guides their lives, to join with us. We are not concerned with the level of personal observance. That is immaterial. The national answer to the Jewish significance of the state lies with all those who identify with their Jewishness and wish to strengthen and develop this identity – definitely not only among the religious.

We have labeled this public, which is the majority of the Jewish population, the 'faith-keeping public'.[1] Each individual carries within his heart a piece of the mosaic, the 'jigsaw puzzle', of the total picture of the modern Jewish state being finally rejuvenated in its ancient homeland. We must begin the processes of putting together these disparate pieces. We believe that these processes must be led by a national leadership that must first of all be committed to the Jewish identity of the state.

Our immediate goal will be to submit a candidate to run against those of the post-Zionist streams (of the Right or of the Left – what's the difference?) for the position of prime minister, a candidate with truly Jewish credentials, posing a new ideological challenge – a candidate of the faith-keeping public. We have begun publishing a regular newsletter called *Lechatchila,* in which ideas are discussed and developed, including the nature of such a state, how it can preserve its democratic character, how it will function within a modern reality. The periodical has proved to be very popular, with over 50,000 copies of each edition being distributed throughout the land. It transpires that the public is avid for new thought-provoking messages. The original ideas propounded have impressed the subscribers.

If we are indeed a Jewish State, why shouldn't *all* Jews have the right to participate in our national elections, whether resident in Israel or abroad? If we are a Jewish State – why don't we uniformly employ the dates of the Jewish calendar on all documents and correspondence, as envisioned by the founders of Zionism?

If we are a Jewish State, why doesn't the national insurance system collect a uniform tax which would enable every interested citizen to enjoy a sabbatical year every seventh year? This year would be devoted to study and furtherance of learning and advancement in any Jewish subject appealing to him or her, from Jewish history to Talmudic studies. The Yeshivot and universities should be accessible to all, such an interactively mutual flowering leading to the hoped-for identity.

If we are a Jewish State, why are we constantly apologetic before the outside world for our commitment to the roots and culture of the world's oldest nation? Why do our prime ministers like to serve concurrently as minister of defense instead of opting for minister of education, by which step they would signal a reversal in national priorities? And what of family values? How can we accept the fact that the heads of government, on both sides of the political divide, betray their spouses, and yet continue to function with full public legitimacy? Are we not entitled to model behavior on the part of our national leaders in this basic area?

---

[1] Even the minority have an important role to play. Post-Zionism can be like the leaven that makes the dough rise. It will act as a watchdog to ensure that the mainstream remains true to its declared aims. Without it, the process will be unattainable, so we must be sure to strictly maintain its democratic rights. It too has its part to play in the 'jigsaw puzzle'.

The reaction in the circles of secular intellectuals to this message has been particularly surprising. At first, many of them were apprehensive about 'missionary preaching' for religious penitence, but when they perceived that our agenda was quite different, the enthusiasm with which our message was received by them exceeded even that accorded it in the settlements. Once, for example, I returned home at three in the morning from a parlor meeting attended by a few score Haifa intellectuals, which had begun at eight in the evening amid great skepticism, and was brought to a close at half past one in the morning to great applause and enthusiasm.

By the way, none of them knew that I refueled my car for the trip home with my last pennies.

My public activity brought great suffering upon my family. 'The Doubling Operation', followed by the second resurgence of 'Zo Artzeinu' and further public activity, the arrests and the trials, all took their toll. Our family's livelihood was undermined. It became impossible to maintain a normal family life; there was neither the time nor the patience that children merited. Go explain to a child in the first grade why the nice policeman was searching among his toys.

After the elections, I lowered my media profile and tried to limit my television appearances. Gradually I began the return to precious anonymity. Finally I was able to take a leisurely evening stroll with Tzippy, or view a film in a cinema, without all heads turning towards us as soon as the lights went on.

Tzippy took on two jobs in order to earn the necessary income and I –

I was sentenced to 18 months' imprisonment, of which six were to be imposed immediately – a light sentence in view of the attorney-general's demands. This was then commuted to six months' public service.

At times I feel the urge to shut an iron gate behind me, and begin a totally new chapter in my life, a completely private one.

But then I hear a low, disbelieving snicker from somewhere in the recesses of my subconscious.

"There is one people..."
(thus did the wicked Haman try to persuade
Ahasuerus to exterminate the Jews)

Megillat Esther 3, 8

Haman said to Ahasuerus: Come, let us
destroy them. Ahasuerus replied: I am afraid
of their G-d, lest He do to me as He did to
my predecessors. Haman replied: They are
negligent of the precepts (and their G-d will
no longer protect them).
Ahasuerus said: There are Rabbis among
them [who keep the precepts, and for whose
sake they will be protected]. Haman replied:
They are 'one people' [and all hang
together].

Babylonian Talmud, Tractate Megillah, 13:

Yaron

Chapter 13

The Paris airport has known better days. The modern-optimistic architecture of the seventies is muted by layers of soot which cover the elliptical ceilings, the carpeting is worn and shabby, and a never-ending sea of humanity flows by, all types and races, ages and sizes, but not one individual face; a flow from somewhere to anywhere through this nowhere.

Yaron authoritatively inspected the store windows and his wristwatch over and over again. There were still two hours remaining until his El-Al flight back to Israel and he gave the appearance of a person who was in total control of his time. He was not the type of person to sprawl out on one of the couches in the waiting room, to thumb through some tasteless magazine and to surrender to the norms of this passenger factory.

He was accustomed to taking charge of things – or at least gave that impression. Even when he was inducted into the army as 'fresh meat', which is how new conscripts were labeled, he managed to maintain this image. When the other rookies saw his husky figure, square-jawed face and authoritative stride, they did their utmost to avoid bumping into him. After all, who needed trouble from some 'general' prowling around the recruits' tents in search of victims.

His comrades did not particularly care for him. He was not a typical inductee. While others like myself exploited every free moment to write a note to their girlfriends, he would undertake impossible challenges, like cleaning the gas regulator on the company machine gun, and .accomplish what he had set out to do.

While we were trying to snatch a few moments' shut-eye, he would be engaged in making improvements in his personal weapon. And whenever a discussion or argument developed over a topical issue that bothered the fellows (and as the religious fellow of the company, I always found myself dragged into these polemics), he simply was not to be seen.

To tell the truth, I sort of enjoyed observing him. The touch of haughtiness he displayed never bothered me. And, watching him, I grew to like him.

The army's training setup propelled us from one course to the next, until we found ourselves enrolled in an officers' training course. From my place in one of the back rows of the mustering out parade, I enjoyed seeing Yaron receive a citation as the most outstanding graduate.

From that point on, we did not meet again. He stayed in the army and advanced rapidly. But when the army no longer met his standards, he left, completed his studies, and became a successful businessman. He had just completed a business deal in France and was returning to Israel.

I was traveling on an inexpensive ticket that required a stopover in Paris to change planes. Thus I found myself wandering the hallways of the airport when I caught sight of the profile of the 'general'. He was wearing a civilian suit, but it was his unmistakable profile. He saw me. His wide grin indicated that he had softened somewhat in the fifteen years since we had last met.

We were both genuinely glad to see each other and, perhaps, our feelings of isolation increased our pleasure at the meeting. We sat down at a coffee shop and we both tried to fill in the gaps in our lives over the last fifteen years.

He knew something about me, thanks to what he had seen in the media, and he had an idea of what I was up to in those days, but I knew nothing about him. We chatted amiably. A few minutes before our meeting we were each just trying to kill time till our flight, but now we did not seem to have enough time. We arranged to sit together on the flight and continued our talk, oblivious to our surroundings.

Yaron was upset with me for not entering politics. "Do you want to really change things? Then there are ways!"

His direct manner of speaking suited my image of him. Our conversation traversed the whole gamut of the reality of Israel – security, religion, and state – until we touched upon the topic of army service for yeshiva students. I did not think that there was much to discuss, because I am of the opinion that every citizen is obligated to serve. I was therefore surprised at the position taken by Yaron, a declared secularist. He made a remark that I cannot forget.

"You know," he said, "I do *not* think that the *haredim* should serve."

??

I'll tell you why. Look, I know some history and I find that it generally repeats itself.

"I know that this so-called peace process is going to break down. Like you, I also know the real strength of our army.

"No one can guarantee that we will always be victorious. It is logical to assume that at one point we will fail."

Yaron paused. For a few moments he remained silent, deep in contemplation.

Passengers sitting nearby who had been listening strained to hear his comments.

Yaron suddenly interposed another time frame.

"Look, if I were living in the time of the Crusades and I was given the choice of death or conversion to Christianity, I would convert immediately. But if they gave *haredim* the same choice, they would prefer to be burned at the stake. So," he concluded, "it is better that they do not serve."

This statement was followed by a heavy silence. All the neighboring antennas were left in confusion. It seemed that he and all the listeners were awaiting my response.

I remained deep in thought.

"Forget who I am for a moment," I said suddenly.

"What do you mean by that?" he asked in surprise.

"Just for a moment, assume that we have never met, that we were not in the army together. Pretend that I am dressed in black from head to toe – a genuine *haredi*."

"Okay, now what?"

"Now listen very carefully to what I am going to tell you."

??

I continued: "You know what – I too would accept conversion rather than death!"

Now it was Yaron's turn to be shocked. "What are you saying? You are a *haredi*..."

"What do you take me for? Your sucker?" I interrupted him with feigned anger. "You should go on enjoying life while I am burned alive on the stake? Forget it! I will make the same choice as you!"

Yaron was struck dumb.

"Look," I continued, myself once again, "you want me to be responsible for the problem of the Jewish identity of the state.

"You do not want to struggle with this issue yourself and you think it is easier if I handle it for you. You are even willing to allow me not to serve in the army in order to perform this other service for you. Forget it! I don't want to play according to those rules. This state belongs to me just as it belongs to you, and I am not content to function as part of a museum piece that preserves some half-forgotten folklore.

"Do you want this state to have a Jewish identity? Is it important to you? Okay, let's work on it together. We have to realize that we have a common interest in this – an existential interest, a matter of national survival – not a conflict!

"I don't care for religious political parties. The Jewishness of the state is too serious a matter to subordinate it to narrow political interests. I want the issue of Jewishness to lie on your head, too, since it is your problem just as much as it is mine.

"That's it," I concluded. "We have been saddled with a very difficult mission. Until now, each side renounced its responsibility, and held on to what it found convenient. That is how the whole wagon got bogged down and is falling apart, is breaking up. We now have to work together to rebuild it all from scratch – or we will all be left with nothing!"

Yaron was rather taken aback by the assignment which I had now suddenly placed on his shoulders.

In the distance, the shoreline of Eretz Israel came into view.

This is a sight that never fails to bring tears to my eyes – which I somehow manage to conceal somewhere back between my nose and throat.

"Sorry," retreated Yaron, "but I surely am not the man for such matters."

"Try," I answered, hypnotized by the sight of the approaching shoreline. "Just try."

"What do you mean by 'just try'?"

"To be a man...Try to be a man..."

SEQUENCE OF MAIN EVENTS

BACKGROUND DEVELOPMENTS

- MADRID CONFERENCE (1991)
- LABOR PARTY WINS THE ELECTIONS (1992)
- OSLO ACCORDS SIGNED (1993)
- CONSTRUCTION IN YESHA FROZEN (1993)
- 'DON'T GIVE THEM RIFLES' PROTESTS (1993)

'ZO ARTZEINU' MOVEMENT LAUNCHED IN ARIEL (Winter, 1993)

- FAILURE OF NEGOTIATIONS WITH THE YESHA COUNCIL

THE 'DOUBLING OPERATION' (January 1994)

- NEW ENCAMPMENTS ERECTED

A massacre in Hebron   (Febuary 1994)

SECOND CONVENTION IN ARIEL (July, 1995)
'THIS IS OUR LAND' OPERATION

- BLOCKING OF 80 INTERSECTIONS THROUGHOUT THE LAND
- ESTABLISHING OUTPOSTS THROUGHOUT YESHA

'RABIN, GO TO THE PRESIDENT' CAMPAIGN (August 1995)

- A MARCH FROM ALL OVER THE COUNTRY TO JERUSALEM AND A DEMONSTRATION BEFORE THE PRESIDENT'S RESIDENCE

PARIS SQUARE EVENT (September 1995)

- ALIYAH TO JERUSALEM AND A DEMONSTRATION OPPOSITE THE PRIME MINISTER'S HOME

'PROTESTING BY LIGHTS' OPERATION (September 1995)

- DEMONSTRATING BY MEANS OF ELECTRIC CURRENT

'LIKE SHEEP TO THE SLAUGHTER' OPERATION (October 1995)

- A FLOCK OF SHEEP DEMONSTRATE

BOYCOTTING THE CENSUS (October 1995)

HECKLING RABIN AT BINYANEI HA'OOMA CONVENTION (October 1995)
- CHAINED ACTIVISTS DISRUPT RABIN'S ADDESS

Rabin assassinated (November 1995)

HEBRON PROTEST (December 1995):
- "YOU GAVE AWAY HEBRON -- YOU TOOK AWAY MY HOME"

TRIAL FOR SEDITION (January 1996)

Hasmonean Tunnel opened -- the PA soldiers fire (September 1996)

ISRAEL AND DEMOCRACY
An appendix to *Where There Are No Men* (by Moshe Feiglin)
by
Dr Re'aya (Ra'issa) Epstein
Lecturer in Political Science

In academic research literature one finds repeated emphasis on the fact that the concept of 'democracy' has multiple definitions. Thus, for example, the work by A. Naess, *Democracy, Ideology and Objectivity* (Oslo University Press, 1956), has amassed a list of 422 definitions of 'democracy', suggesting different and contrasting perceptions of the essence and significance of the socio-political phenomenon which this term connotes. Naess even goes so far as to state that the meaning of 'democracy' is the one which the individual wishes to assign it through the application of his particular definition (p. 21).

Such a claim is not devoid of basis. The United States of America sees itself as a democracy, but the Soviet regime in its day also viewed itself as such. The Athenian democracy condemned its eminent citizen Socrates to death because his activity was considered as being in violation of its laws. The democracy of Lenin, Stalin and Khruschev butchered, exiled and incarcerated in concentration camps millions of people classified as 'enemies of the state'. Between these extreme poles, there are intermediate levels. There are regimes that label themselves democracies, in which people are not exterminated nor exiled to concentration camps, yet whose democratic character becomes open to question upon closer acquaintance.

Democracy is sometimes called 'the dictatorship of the proletariat', and, at the opposite pole, 'the rule of law'. It is commonly accepted (and this may indeed by the case) that between the first pole, the totalitarian one, and the second pole, the liberal, lies an unbridgeable chasm. However, Israeli reality clearly proves that even a liberal rule-of-law system of government can transform a democratic state into one bearing full dictatorial attributes. The importance of emphasizing the existence of a multiplicity of definitions of the concept of 'democracy' lies in the danger of absolutization, that is, assigning this concept one definitive meaning.

It is this dangerous tendency that researchers ascribe to the 'totalitarian democracy' school of thought, arguing that in its underlying principles lies the assumption that in the political arena there exists only a single truth, and any dissenter is an absolute enemy, condemned to neutralization in a more or less violent manner.

This process of neutralization at the hands of the ideocracy of 'the peace process' is described in Moshe Feiglin's book. In its conduct towards its opponents generally, and

'Zo Artzeinu' in particular, the 'peace' regime in Israel (1992-1996) acted as an outright totalitarian regime. Israeli democracy had been far from ideal from the very start, but in this period it adopted one definitive truth, and quickly degenerated into the depths of violence, intolerance and cruelty.

The extreme shift in the policy of the regime was the result of a drastic conversion in ideology regarding the direction to be taken in the development of the state and the purpose of its existence.

A crisis and the psychological need to flee from reality and its challenges can surface from a variety of causes in any country throughout the world, and at any time.

The record of the State of Israel during the 'peace' period can serve as a universally meaningful 'laboratory case' revealing the possibility of a democracy's decline into totalitarianism.

There is a universal aspect to this degeneration of Israeli democracy, an aspect that reminds one of the American trauma of the '50s (the period of McCarthyism). Fear of the totalitarian power of the American communists almost converted the challenged democracy into a dictatorship. Similarly, in Israel, the Left's fear (real or imagined) of their opponents, who are always considered 'fascists', changed the 'democracy on-the-defensive' into an aggressive dictatorship.

The American and Israeli examples differ in that the communists in America did indeed signal a danger to democracy (as is the case with communists in every place and time), while in Israel the communist approach to the essence of democracy (a totalitarian democracy) was embraced by the Left. Those sectors labeled by the Israeli Left as 'fascists' were actually liberal in their world outlook and in their political behavior, much more than their uncompromising and antagonistic opponents. The story that unfolds in this book by Moshe Feiglin leads inexorably to this conclusion.

The Israeli case is indeed a unique one. In it, intertwined, are various sorts of dictatorships, their fusion creating an overall almost-unbeatable power. When this force identifies ideologically with the elected government, it merges with it and together creates delegitimization of any political opposition and competing ideologies. On the other hand, if and when this power bloc is antagonistic to the ideology of the elected government, it neutralizes such an administration politically and ideologically, and compels it to run the country in keeping with the path determined by these dominant dictatorships. These dictatorships include the following: the judicial dictatorship, the media dictatorship, the cultural and intellectual dictatorship, and perhaps a few other dictatorships. In any case, the will of the people, which found expression in free elections, does not materialize as a decisive factor in this reality; what is more, this will is effectively neutralized. It is not only the will of the majority that is marginalized, but also the will of minority groups (apart from the minority which has the real governing power), such as the religious-haredi minority, the national-religious minority, the Yesha settlers minority, and other minorities – if they do not toe the line, the only politically correct line, set in this state with its liberal-totalitarian regime.

This regime does indeed comprise both liberal and totalitarian elements. Its liberal element is the liberal ideology proclaimed by the ruling oligarchy. Chief Justice of the Supreme Court of *Justice*, Aaron Barak, repeatedly emphasizes that the rulings of the judiciary generally and of the Supreme Court in particular are in conformity with the liberal world outlook of 'the enlightened public'. Hence it follows that those elements of the public that not subscribe to the views of the 'enlightened public', as defined by Mr Barak, fall outside the realm of judicial legitimacy and of democracy itself, since these, according to the school of thought represented by the 'enlightened' Justice Barak and his associates, are the exclusive possession of the 'enlightened public'. One of the supporters of Justice Barak, who had recently served as Minister of Justice in the State of Israel, while addressing the Israeli Knesset vehemently denounced religious-haredi citizens, arguing that they had no right *to speak* of democracy since "they have nothing at all in common with democracy". Others of his fellow-travelers lecture and write almost unceasingly that the anti-democratic forces (meaning, the ultra-Orthodox, the settlers, and other 'dangerous' groups that immigrated to Israel fairly recently from undeveloped countries "where there never was any democracy" – depending on the context) endanger 'our democracy' and undermine its stability. Some (not at all merely a few) even draw a parallel with Hitler and the usurpation of power by the Nazis in Germany by democratic means, again having in mind the 'non-democratic' and 'anti-democratic' forces, beginning with the haredim and ending with Benjamin Netanyahu and the Likud Party.

This is the 'liberal' viewpoint. If this (that is, the expression of opinions, formulations and declared principles on the part of 'free individuals in a free country', however problematic and anti-democratic they be) were the whole picture, we would not raise the specter of a real threat of totalitarianism. The problem is that these principles are enunciated and proclaimed by a ruling elite (governing not necessarily by virtue of democratic elections), which compels the entire state to function in line with their principles.

This paradoxical reality has its source in the inherent affinity (not just historical but also deeply-rooted emotional and tangible ties) between the de-facto governing elite, to wit, the Israeli Left, and its spiritual fathers, who emigrated from the Soviet Union. Democracy in the State of Israel during the unyielding rule of Mapai was definitely a totalitarian democracy (democracy of the party, a one-and-only ideology). This was due to the Israeli State's viewing itself openly (at least in the early days) as a loyal protégé of Soviet Russia, which found expression not only in the red flags and the singing of the Internationale.

From the Six Day War and until the collapse of the communist regime in Russia, Israel passed through a stage of liberalization. However, this liberalization actually was limited to a change in terminology alone. The people, their way of thinking, the political culture, and above all, the deeply-rooted conviction that the right and duty to hold the reins of power were vested exclusively in 'us' -- remained as firm as heretofore. Thus the previous totalitarian democracy assumed the guise of liberalism, appearing as a liberal-totalitarian or totalitarian-liberal dragon -- in other words, 'Israeli Bolshevism in the guise of Liberal Democracy' (See R. Epstein, Nativ periodical, 1997, no. 3, pp. 42-49).

After the fall of communism, this unusual regime had to adopt an appropriate alternative ideal. It was found in the ideal of 'peace', the Peres utopia of a 'New Middle East', which became, upon the takeover of power by the Left in 1992, an ideocracy, -- a 'reverse theocracy', a totalitarian messianic religion, which held disbelieving individuals to be 'ideological criminals', or, put more bluntly, enemies of the state. In this manner an intrinsic continuity was preserved between the innovative Israeli liberalism and those factors that begot and nourished it, namely, the late Russian totalitarianism.

The Kafkaesque reality defined above has a deeper and more fundamental root. This root is tied to the umbilical cord not merely of the Socialist-Marxist foundations upon which the fledgling state came into being, but of much wider foundations of secular-Zionism. We are referring to the most fundamental basis, the aspiration to achieve 'normality' and to become 'a nation like all other nations'. In this trend, which is nothing less than spiritual assimilation and universalization (while preserving 'materialistic' nationalism), one discerns from the start a renunciation of a basic Jewish world outlook that proclaims the uniqueness of the purpose of the Jewish nation's existence. Is it therefore just by chance that on the basis of such an alienation no other form of democracy could have arisen in the State of Israel except one providing some sort of alternative to Jewishness? Couldn't another form of democracy have been created?

"Actually, there was never any need for a frontal clash between Judaism and democracy. Had we been fortunate, an original, authentic Israeli democracy could have sprouted here, one nourishing from Jewish sources, and not seeing itself required to clash with them (Prof. Daniel Shalit, *Getting out of this Regrettable Situation*, 'Panim' periodical, 1997, no. 2, page 21)."

In its Declaration of Independence, the State of Israel was defined as a Jewish and democratic state. In this dual formulation we already find a contradiction in terms, because if it is necessary to add another word to 'democracy' -- the word 'Jewish'-- it tells us that 'democracy' in this context is not necessarily Jewish, and that 'Jewish' in this context does not sit well with 'democracy'. Such a definition not only contains an internal contradiction, but also raises the need to choose between an un-Jewish democracy and a Jewish non-democracy. It was only natural that at the end of the process, this unstable situation became transformed into current post-Zionism, which in essence is also post-Jewishness, insofar as the character of the present-day Israeli State is concerned. The 'choice of democracy' made by those circles who define themselves as the 'enlightened liberal public' really
means the choice of a non-Zionist and non-nationalist character for their state – 'the state of all its citizens'

The political process propelled by the Oslo Accords is simply a function of this non-Jewish choice, whether or not the supporters of the process are aware of this negative connection. It is no wonder that among the most fervent advocates of the democracy identified with 'the state of all its citizens' one finds the leaders of the Israeli Arab sector, who do not trouble to conceal their goal – de-Zionization and de-Judaization of the State of Israel (see journalist Ari Shavit's interview with Azmi Bashara in Ha'aretz on May 29, 1998). On the other hand, it is likewise no wonder that the main and firmest opponents of this political process are religious Jewish citizens of the state and those secular Jews who have maintained their connection to original Judaism.

During the period of the leftist government (1992-1996) a delegitimization of the opponents to the Oslo process was furthered in, of all things, the name of democracy. When eventually a rightist government came into being, it felt coerced to pursue the political process it inherited, in order to remain within the bounds of the unique Israeli democracy legitimized by the Left. Thus the government of the Right felt compelled to continue to bestow legitimacy on the persecution of the 'enemies of democracy', to wit, the 'settlers'.

It may be assumed that had a serious protest movement arisen against the policy of the Netanyahu government, which was pursuing the policy of its predecessor, we would have witnessed a repetition of those ugly and painful scenes described so vividly in this book, since the main doctrine of the 'peace' ideocracy remained as it had been despite the changeover in government: he who does not subscribe to the general line conforming to the one and only ideology is an enemy, and all means are acceptable and valid in order to neutralize him.

Prominent among those cognizant of the flaws of Israeli democracy are former citizens of the Soviet Union (one of whom is the writer) and former citizens of the United

States (one of whom is Moshe Feiglin's colleague, Shmuel Sackett). The former – because their life's experience has taught them precisely what real totalitarianism is; the latter – because their life's experience has taught them what true democracy really means. For these reasons, both groups clearly discern the lack of democracy in Israel and its totalitarian features.

These immigrants to Israel are conscious of how their conceptual world has been completely overturned. Totalitarian forces and processes are labeled 'democracy' and 'liberalism' in Israel, while phenomena which are essentially democratic and liberal are considered 'fascistic' and totalitarian.

Mrs Esther Wachsman, mother of the IDF soldier Nachshon Wachsman of blessed memory, who was kidnapped and murdered by Arab terrorists, once pointed out that, as an American, she was viewed, according to accepted criteria, as democratic, liberal and left-wing. But, oddly enough, after arriving in Israel she found herself, according to accepted local criteria, identified with the camp considered 'extreme right', 'nationalistic', and 'racist'. All this, despite her not having changed any of her basic views.

Moshe Feiglin writes in his book (page 61) about his friend Shmuel Sackett:
Shmuel arrived in Israel as a veteran of public struggles. Throughout his youth he was actively involved in the struggle for the release of the Jews of the Soviet Union. He was thoroughly familiar with all the techniques of civil campaigning in a democratic country, and we benefited greatly from his experience.

Further, describing the detention of 'Zo Artzeinu' members in jail:
Among the jailed sat a quiet, whimsically smiling person, the prominent former Russian Prisoner of Zion, Dr. Yosef Begun, who identified with our struggle, had joined the activists, and was arrested with all the others...... Shmuel, who as a student in the USA had been jailed a number of times for demonstrating on behalf of Begun's release from the Russian prisons, found the situation particularly amusing. "See here," he remarked to Begun, "you were imprisoned in Russia, I was imprisoned on your behalf in America, and now the two of us are jailed together in Eretz Israel..."

This is what Shmuel remarked long before the close of the trial of the 'Zo Artzeinu' leaders, long before they were indicted for 'sedition'. Exactly where does the Israel of the peace process fit in the range between the democratic-liberal regime in the United States and the totalitarian regime of the late USSR?

The upheaval in which the State of Israel finds itself today is manifest to all. It is evident in the fact that an entire people and an entire country (regardless which government rules) are incapable of putting a stop to a process leading inevitably to the suicide of the Zionist entity. There must be inexplicable metaphysical and transcendental factors accounting for this tragic reality.

Nonetheless, there is a dimension to this situation that lends itself to definition and understanding, making it possible to cope and deal with it in a rational and political way. This dimension, as is clear from all the above, is related to the definition of 'democracy' in Israel. Democracy in Israel is essentially totalitarian and anti-Jewish. On this plane, the situation is lamentable not only within the leftist oligarchy that created this democracy and utilizes it for its own benefit and political needs. The situation is lamentable also within the other components of Israeli society, the political Right and the religious Jewish sector inclusive, because all these, against the background of the general political culture, which conforms to the existing type of democracy, have internalized this distorted definition of democracy.

This internalization of the given interpretation of the concept of democracy leads to two dangerous outcomes. One, 'to appear democratic', that is, to totally renounce Zionism, Judaism, and, essentially, the existence of the Zionist state. The other, rejection of democracy, while contenting oneself with the Jewish religion per se. Both of these courses serve the interests of the aberrant, totalitarian, anti-Jewish democracy. Both play (unconsciously) on the same terrible playing field of national self-immolation. Even the bravest movements and organizations in the struggle for the preservation of the Land of Israel and retention of the Jewish character of the Israeli State completely distanced their struggle from the issue of democracy and the urgent need to cope with the problem of the true nature of the current regime. Perhaps herein lies one of the main causes for their indubitable failure, for the ideological and political retreat which is leading the State of Israel to an inevitable existential breakdown.

In light of all this, the extraordinary undertaking (in thought and in practice) by the author of this book is most impressive and stirring. The movement which he founded, a non-violent civil disobedience protest movement, is the ultimate manifestation of the living spirit of liberal democracy, and, what is no less important, is the embodiment of central ideas created in authentic Jewish thought. (Regarding the background and Jewish sources for civil non-compliance in particular and the approach of liberal democracy in general, see: Yoram Chazani, *Jewish Sources for the Tradition of Western Disobedience,* 'Techeilet' periodical, 1998, no. 4, pp. 14-58.)

However, what is most important is the fact that the protest of the 'Zo Artzeinu' movement was and will remain in the collective historical memory of the State of Israel an outstanding expression of the inherent feelings of the people and an appropriate materialization of the compelling need for a truly Jewish response to the anti-Jewish and anti-democratic coercion.

Actually, we are not referring to something that *was*. It is not buried in the past; it is with us in the present, in the State of Israel, and it will be so in the future.

This book by Moshe Feiglin, a rank-and-file Israeli Jew, will eventually find its way to its well-earned top position as one of the earliest intellectual sources instrumental in the creation of a liberal democracy in Israel "whose roots lie deep in Jewish foundations and which does not feel required to contest them".